The Everyday Investor

The Everyday Investor

A blueprint for salaried professionals to build wealth without high risk or complexity

Zayn Elric

Mindful Pages

Published in 2025

ISBN: 9789371346344 (PB)
ISBN: 9789371344838 (eBook)

Published by

Mindful Pages
Imprint of Alpha Editions LLC
312 W. 2nd St #1834
Casper, WY 82601, USA

This book was developed using advanced writing tools to support the drafting and ideation process. All content has been thoughtfully curated, refined, and reviewed to ensure quality and relevance.

Content

Introduction
The Myth of the Missing Millions

There's a quiet falsehood stitched into the way contemporary culture speaks about money. It rarely makes a scene—no shouting, no headlines—but it hums constantly in the background, shaping how countless people interpret their financial reality. The myth is simple, seductive, and corrosive: unless you've inherited wealth, possess freakish genius, or sacrifice your health in pursuit of entrepreneurial glory, genuine financial freedom isn't meant for you. For the average salaried professional, this message is rarely spoken aloud. It seeps in through images, lifestyles, assumptions. It's present in how wealth is glamorised—presented as the domain of extraordinary people living extraordinary lives. The quiet, consistent contributors—the nurse, the project manager, the civil engineer, the educator—rarely show up in these stories unless they've deviated from the very path they're walking.

This book exists to upend that illusion—not by peddling fantasy, but by anchoring you in strategy. *The Everyday Investor* isn't a guide to outsmarting the market, getting rich by Friday, or morphing into someone you're not. Rather, it's a map back to something far sturdier: the right to build durable wealth without losing your footing, gambling your future, or overcomplicating your life. It doesn't call out to the elite few. It reaches quietly—and insistently—towards the many.

You don't need to be wealthy to start building wealth. But you do need to dismantle the mindset that tells you you're not allowed to.

That mental permission—it won't come from your job title, your economic background, or some external authority. It must come from you. And once it does, it becomes your first and most irreplaceable asset. Because, if we're being honest, wealth has very little to do with raw numbers. It's about capacity—the capacity to choose your time, to weather storms without shattering, to provide for those you love without mortgaging your mental wellbeing. Money is merely the instrument. Wealth is the design.

Much of what passes for personal finance literature is obsessed with externals: rates of return, money-saving hacks, economic forecasts, comparison charts. Not that those are useless—they have their place—but they're often distractions masquerading as depth. They create the illusion of progress while quietly neglecting the basics. The financial services industry thrives on this kind of complexity. It translates simple principles into incomprehensible jargon, wraps common sense in layers of branding, and implies that unless you pay a professional to decipher it all, you're likely doomed to fail. The result? Smart, diligent people end up overwhelmed, uncertain, and stuck—resigned to a cautious inertia disguised as prudence.

The Everyday Investor refuses that premise outright. It starts from the belief that most financial complexity is a performance—often more about hiding insecurity than demonstrating intelligence. It insists that what you truly need is not another financial product, but a philosophy you can actually live by. That a successful investor isn't necessarily the most informed, but the most self-aligned. Someone who's built a cadence—a rhythm—in their money life, anchored by systems that respect who they are.

If you've ever looked at your payslip and wondered why it brings less peace than it should, you're not misreading the situation. If you've ever felt that despite your diligence, something essential remains elusive, you're not asking the wrong questions. If your financial behaviours feel like a mismatch for your deeper values, and mainstream advice has left you cold or conflicted, then yes—this book is for you.

It's written for the engineer burdened by responsibility but robbed of calm. For the schoolteacher generous to a fault, yet quietly unnerved by a dwindling savings account. For the up-and-coming professional who's excelling at earning but adrift when it comes to planning—and more than a little fatigued by the breathless tempo of hustle culture. And for the mid-career leader who has dutifully met every milestone but can't shake the sense that something vital has been missed along the way.

This book doesn't promise shortcuts. It offers a compass. You won't learn how to outwit the system—you'll learn how to grow roots within it.

Roots that are deep, not dramatic. Approaches that are graceful in their simplicity. Habits that are perhaps even a little mundane—but that's their strength. Because they work. More importantly, *The Everyday Investor* seeks to fundamentally shift your relationship with money: from a game to be won, to a foundation on which a fulfilling life can be built. You'll learn to cultivate momentum without sacrificing wellbeing, to embed discipline in your systems rather than willpower, and to track progress not only by what's in the bank, but by how your life feels.

At its heart, this book is a treatise on mindset, cleverly disguised as financial instruction. It recognises that the hardest part of building wealth isn't figuring out markets or loopholes—it's untangling the internal stories we carry, and the outdated identities we cling to. What does it mean to live as someone who assumes they will thrive? Who builds from understanding, not fear? Who knows what "enough" looks like—and honours it?

The journey begins by exposing the trap many fall into: what we'll call the Working-Class Wealth Trap. This first section dissects both the external systems and internalised beliefs that keep salaried professionals feeling financially stuck, even as promotions and pay raises roll in. It's about the subtle erosion—caused by lifestyle inflation, status competition, and the slow drip of complacency—that undermines progress without ever setting off alarm bells.

Next, we challenge the very definition of wealth. In *Rethink Wealth*, we step away from spreadsheets and toward something more human—freedom of choice, psychological safety, meaning. Here, you'll meet the concept of Emotional Return on Investment (eROI), a tool that prioritises how your money *feels* to use—not just how it performs. This single shift can liberate decades of financial angst.

From there, we focus on rhythm. *Rhythm Over Risk* dismisses the culture of hot tips and hero investing. Instead, you'll learn how to lean on time, automation, and consistency—tools that, when used properly, can transform even modest pay into long-term stability. This isn't a siren song of instant success—it's a steady drumbeat of reliability.

Later chapters dive into the theme of *Alignment Over Ambition.* This isn't about thinking smaller; it's about aiming true. You'll learn how to reject advice that conflicts with your values, and uncover your personal 'wealth type'—a compass for making decisions that feel as right internally as they are sound financially.

As we move toward the conclusion, we turn to systems. You'll learn how simplicity, automation, and protective routines can create not just efficiency, but resilience. We'll unpack how to spot and sidestep exploitative advice, how to structure your income with clarity, and how to prepare for the long-term without being driven by anxiety. The book ends not with a grand flourish, but with an invitation to pause—on freedom, on legacy, on what truly matters when the numbers fade.

What you're reading isn't a thought experiment. Everything here is forged in real-world trenches, tested with individuals who are competent, thoughtful, and simply tired of feeling excluded from a game they never asked to play.

You won't find hype here—just candour. No outlandish predictions—just tools with integrity. And perhaps above all, you'll find a steadying sense of control. Not the brittle kind born of micromanagement, but the kind that grows naturally from rhythm, structure, and self-knowledge. The sort that doesn't demand perfection—just presence.

Here's the truth: you've always had what it takes to build wealth. But you were taught to mistrust that truth. This book aims to change that—not through noise, but through form. Not through force, but through flow.

So then—shall we?

Chapter 1
The Working-Class Wealth Trap

At first glance, today's salaried professional appears to have arrived. Armed with degrees, respectable job titles, and earnings that surpass national averages, they embody what earlier generations might have pointed to as success. On paper, they've made it. Yet beneath the polished surface, something gnaws—something quieter, less obvious. A creeping dissonance between competence and control, between effort and the rewards one expected to follow. The paycheque lands on schedule, yet security remains just out of reach. Promotions arrive, but peace of mind lags behind. Work expands, always. But wealth—the kind that buys autonomy, not just more things—remains, somehow, deferred. This isn't failure in the conventional sense. It's something more insidious. A trap. And the worst part? It rarely looks like one.

This is the working-class wealth trap. Subtle, because it doesn't look like deprivation. It feels, instead, like chronic underachievement. You're not destitute—but neither are you at ease. You're not impoverished, but still find yourself lying awake at night, running mental budgets or dreading unplanned expenses. Your income keeps up appearances, but your financial life remains precarious, reactive—more governed by default than design. This paradox shapes the lives of millions: people who earn just enough to avoid immediate panic, but not enough to feel real power over their futures.

What follows is an unmasking. This chapter dissects the hidden architecture of that trap—a structure built not from cruelty, but from inheritance. Inherited assumptions, inherited norms, inherited stories about what work means, what it's worth, and where it's meant to take us. The systems that underpin professional life are rarely questioned, largely because they're presented as natural. One job flows into another, one title into the next. And all the while, the ladder we think we're climbing is often just a treadmill with better lighting.

Let's begin with a particular myth: the False Idol of Hustle. Few modern icons have commanded such reverence, or scrutiny, as the side hustle. What once served as a necessity for the underemployed has been rebranded as a moral imperative. If you're not monetising your evenings, cultivating a "brand," trading crypto before bed, or transforming hobbies into income streams, the cultural message is unmistakable—you're squandering your potential. Hustle has become a performance, a kind of virtue signalling disguised as self-discipline. But beneath its sleek veneer lies something else: a rejection of sufficiency, a compulsive need to prove productivity, and, more often than not, a deeply inefficient method for building actual wealth.

There's irony here. Many professionals, already working full time, now spend their spare hours chasing pennies through digital side gigs—effort that's disproportionate to the financial return. Meanwhile, the core salary—the largest source of income—goes underutilised as a tool for compounding wealth. Instead of optimising their savings rate or investing with long-term intent, people are lured into a flurry of fragmented effort. Hustle culture hijacks energy better spent on intentional design, diverting it into low-leverage labour. And in doing so, it ensures one thing: you're always the worker, never the architect. Never still. Never sovereign. Hustle, then, becomes not a path to freedom but a familiar cage, now dressed in entrepreneurial chic.

To be clear, this isn't a blanket dismissal of ambition or additional income streams. The critique here is more precise: distraction masquerading as progress. A financial life built on solid ground doesn't need endless complexity. It needs a handful of robust systems, executed consistently and with care. Yet simplicity has little market value in a culture that profits from your exhaustion.

And so we come to the next force at play: the Illusion of Complexity. If hustle culture consumes your time, the financial industry plays a more cerebral game—it sells confusion. Personal finance, in its worst form, has turned into a theatre of jargon: brimming with acronyms, layered strategies, and content that feels more like noise than insight. For every fear, there's a product. For every desire, a glossy new tool. And just behind this ecosystem lies a subtle, profitable logic: keep people uncertain, and they will forever depend on experts.

The truth is rarely sold, because it is so unremarkable: most financial success for the average professional comes down to a few actions, repeated calmly over time. It does not require heroic stock picking. It does not hinge on timing the market. It requires automation. Discipline. Long horizons. And it demands that we strip away the aesthetic of sophistication to return to something more enduring: simplicity. But simplicity, when it threatens profit margins, becomes taboo.

Which is why this book—this chapter—advocates for what we call radical simplicity. Radical not because it is new, but because it resists a billion-dollar myth. It tells you to stop chasing novelty and start honouring fundamentals. It argues, quite seriously, that the smartest money lives are often stunningly boring. And that this boredom isn't a weakness. It's a strength—a signal of design over drama.

Still, even if we discard hustle worship and see through the smoke of financial complexity, something remains—a quieter, more stubborn obstacle. One lodged not in the world around us, but in the self. It's the third layer of the trap: our internal programming.

We call it the Permission to Prosper.

Humans don't operate by logic alone. We live by stories—by identities shaped through upbringing, education, culture, class. And for many professionals, particularly those raised with modest means, wealth still feels like something that belongs to other people. Investment is something "rich people" do. Property, ownership, assets—these can feel presumptuous, even alien. Comfort may be acceptable, but actual abundance? That stirs unease. Guilt, even.

These beliefs run deep. Often invisible, they nonetheless guide behaviour: under-saving, over-spending, deferring financial decisions indefinitely. They show up in hesitations, in imposter syndrome when dealing with investments, in discomfort at the idea of accumulating "too much." Or they drive a constant, low-level deference to outside authority—never quite trusting oneself to make decisions, always waiting for someone else to validate the next step.

This, too, must be unlearned. Because no institution, no adviser, no book—not even this one—can give you permission. That must come from within. And claiming it is not arrogance. It is dignity. The decision to pursue financial wellbeing without apology is an act of self-respect. And it marks the true beginning of empowerment—not as a spreadsheet, but as a stance.

So consider this chapter your diagnostic. It's not here to hand out ten tips or listicle wisdom. It's here to ask better questions. To help you see how the daily rituals of your money life are shaped not just by logic or laziness, but by larger currents—cultural, systemic, psychological. It asks you to pause, not push harder. It asks whether, perhaps, the sense of stagnation you've felt is not a flaw in you, but a feature of the very system you've been told to trust.

And what if, instead of breaking that system entirely, you simply designed your way out?

The pages ahead won't hand you hype. What they will offer is provocation—the kind that shakes loose assumptions and invites something better. You'll confront the false sanctity of grind, the theatrical fog of complexity, and the quiet scripts that have, perhaps unknowingly, kept your ambitions in check. This is not self-help rhetoric. This is structural literacy. Because without it, tactics will always fail. But with it? Even modest, unglamorous moves can produce profound results.

You're not flawed. You're navigating a landscape that benefits from your confusion. That clarity you've been craving? It starts here.

Let's get to work—deliberately, honestly, and with just enough friction to make it last.

The Invisible Ladder

There's a peculiar frustration that afflicts many salaried professionals. It doesn't erupt all at once, but accumulates quietly over time—a growing unease that whispers: *Something isn't adding up*. You're earning more than you did five years ago. You've advanced in your career, acquired a better title, perhaps even upgraded your wardrobe, your postcode, or your dining preferences. On paper, this is upward mobility. Yet emotionally and financially, it often feels like you're standing still—or worse, slipping backwards. This is not a personal failing. It is the natural consequence of climbing a ladder that moves as you do. And, crucially, no one told you it was motorised.

This is the invisible ladder—an economic and psychological mechanism that ensures perceived progress without material freedom. At its core, it keeps professionals tethered to a script where more work leads to more income, which leads to more spending, which leads to...more work. Its genius lies in how it disguises inertia as momentum. The higher you climb, the further you seem from the kind of financial calm and autonomy that initially motivated you. The problem isn't that salaried professionals don't make enough. The problem is that the system ensures they never *feel* like it's enough.

The phenomenon begins with *lifestyle inflation*—the subtle, socially sanctioned process by which increased earnings are immediately absorbed by enhanced consumption. Each raise is not an opportunity for freedom, but a cue for upgrades: the nicer flat, the better car, the more exclusive holiday, the slightly more ambitious dinner reservations. None of these changes feel extravagant in isolation; they're small steps in a world where 'treat yourself' has become both moral imperative and economic strategy. But collectively, they absorb the financial surplus that could otherwise build long-term wealth. Lifestyle inflation is not about indulgence—it's about normalisation. What was once a luxury becomes expected, then necessary, then invisible.

This phenomenon is compounded by *social comparison*, a force far more potent than most financial advice ever acknowledges. Behavioural economists have long documented how relative status exerts a stronger pull on our choices than absolute gain. In a now-classic study, participants were asked whether they would prefer to earn £50,000 in a world where everyone else earned £25,000, or £75,000 in a world where everyone else earned £150,000. A significant number chose the first option—less money overall, but higher relative standing. Financial decisions are rarely made in isolation. They are filtered through a sense of how we *appear* to be doing.

Modern social life intensifies this impulse. Platforms like LinkedIn and Instagram compress personal and professional identity into public signals. Your peers' promotions, purchases, and milestones are not merely shared—they are algorithmically amplified. What might have been a private win now becomes an implied benchmark. And every benchmark raises the ladder. If someone your age just bought a second home, or posted from a Michelin-starred restaurant in Tokyo, what exactly are you doing wrong?

The result is a psychic treadmill disguised as a career path. And yet, rather than interrogate the structure, many internalise the dissonance as a personal inadequacy. "Maybe I need to work harder. Maybe I'm just bad with money. Maybe everyone else knows something I don't." What goes unacknowledged is that this feeling—of running fast and still feeling behind—is not a glitch. It's a feature of the system. A system that rewards productivity without promising freedom, and praises busyness while quietly eroding wealth.

But this trap is not only external. The more insidious mechanism is *system inertia*—the unspoken assumption that if you simply keep doing what you're doing, things will eventually get better. It's a comforting narrative, especially for professionals raised to believe that education and diligence are sufficient foundations for financial stability. Yet the economic architecture of the modern workplace does not reward passive loyalty in the way it once did. Real wage growth has stagnated for decades in many sectors. Pensions have eroded. Job security has become a euphemism for conditional expendability. The idea that a good job, held long enough, will produce financial independence is increasingly misaligned with economic reality.

And yet, most people don't course-correct—not because they're lazy or ignorant, but because the system is designed to *feel* stable even when it's not. Direct deposits, predictable schedules, small annual raises, and the occasional promotion all conspire to create the illusion of progress. The ladder keeps moving, so you assume you must be climbing.

What makes this particularly damaging is that it prevents intervention at precisely the moment it's most needed. Early-career professionals delay investing, assuming they'll "start properly" when they earn more. Mid-career professionals postpone re-evaluating their financial structures because their lifestyle has become enmeshed with their income. And late-career professionals may realise—too late—that their years of work were spent maintaining a lifestyle rather than building a legacy.

The invisible ladder thrives in this space between earned income and unexamined habit. It ensures that money flows in, but rarely accumulates. It rewards those who play along with symbols of success, while punishing those who ask uncomfortable questions. And perhaps most critically, it exploits the psychological bias toward inertia—our tendency to overvalue the status quo simply because it is familiar.

Breaking free from this pattern requires more than tactical advice. It demands a shift in consciousness. First, an honest audit: not just of numbers, but of assumptions. Are your financial decisions reflecting your values, or merely echoing your environment? Are you allocating money with intention, or defaulting to patterns inherited from peers, parents, or platform culture? Do you measure progress in autonomy—or appearances?

Second, it requires an appreciation of *the difference between income and wealth.* Income is a flow; wealth is a stock. Income allows you to live. Wealth allows you to *stop working.* Most professionals focus on increasing the former, often at the cost of the latter. But unless you convert a portion of your income into assets—investments, savings, equity—you are not building wealth. You are simply upgrading expenses.

This is not to suggest that comfort or lifestyle improvements are wrong. The point is not austerity. The point is *awareness.* Awareness that every financial decision is a trade-off. That every pound spent on upgrades is a pound not spent on autonomy. And that unless these trade-offs are made consciously, the system will make them for you—quietly, efficiently, and indefinitely.

Consider the case of Marcus, a software engineer earning well above the national average. Over a decade, his income doubled. But so did his housing costs, his travel habits, and his wardrobe. He owns no assets beyond his employer-matched pension. He feels more anxious about money today than when he was earning half as much. He doesn't understand why. But the answer is simple: Marcus climbed the ladder, but the ladder moved with him. He has changed jobs, but not frameworks. He has improved cash flow, but not financial structure.

To escape the invisible ladder, you must build an alternative system. One that prioritises *financial autonomy over lifestyle optics.* One that invests in *systems over willpower,* and *identity over impulse.* You must resist the gravitational pull of social proof and learn to orient your money around your values—not your feed. And you must recognise that real progress often feels *quieter* than performative success. It looks like automated savings, not spontaneous splurges. It feels like increasing options, not increasing expenses. And it functions like a rising floor beneath you—not a dangling carrot ahead.

The chapters that follow will equip you with tools to build this alternative system. But first, you must see the trap clearly.

Understand that the feeling of being stuck despite doing everything right is not irrational—it is diagnostic. It is the first sign that you are ready to stop climbing someone else's ladder and start building your own foundation.

Because the problem was never your income. The problem was mistaking motion for meaning. And once you see that, you can start investing in something far more powerful than salary or title: *agency*.

The False Idol of Hustle

There is a modern superstition that has taken root in professional culture: the belief that constant motion is synonymous with financial success. Wrapped in motivational slogans and aesthetic Instagram reels, it is the dogma of hustle—a belief system that elevates relentless productivity to a kind of moral imperative. We are told, almost religiously, that the key to wealth lies in waking up earlier, doing more, resting less, and squeezing income out of every waking hour. If you have a job, you should also have a side-hustle. If you have a side-hustle, you should be scaling it. If you're not exhausted, you're not ambitious enough. But beneath this surface energy lies a contradiction. For all the movement it demands, the hustle ideology rarely delivers genuine financial peace. In fact, it often does the opposite.

This chapter dissects the cultural glorification of hustle not as a harmless motivational trend, but as a deeply counterproductive narrative that undermines the financial and psychological wellbeing of salaried professionals. Far from being a gateway to wealth, the hustle mindset can entrench people further into reactive, unstable financial lives—especially when it distracts from systemic clarity, long-term planning, and identity-aligned decision-making. To understand why, we must first ask: *Who benefits from hustle culture?* And more provocatively: *Why has exhaustion been rebranded as ambition?*

To begin with, it's worth acknowledging that the side-hustle, as a concept, originated from necessity. In underpaid, underemployed segments of the population, taking on additional work outside of traditional employment was a matter of survival. This pragmatic hustle had no hashtags and no romanticism—it was simply a response to precarity. But over time, particularly through the rise of social media and digital gig platforms, hustle was rebranded. It became aspirational. No longer a fallback, it was marketed as a path to personal freedom. Entrepreneurship was glamourised, not just as an occupation but as an identity.

This transformation did not happen by accident. Platforms like Uber, Etsy, and Upwork, while providing flexible income opportunities, also relied on a workforce willing to work outside the bounds of traditional labour protections. The romantic language of "being your own boss" conveniently disguised the fact that many of these hustles still involved trading time for money—often at a lower effective hourly rate than full-time work. What had once been a contingency plan became a lifestyle. And as with all ideologies, the costs were moralised: if you're tired, it's because you care. If you're burned out, you're building something. If you're broke, you just haven't hustled hard enough.

Psychologically, this is seductive. The idea that success is purely a matter of effort gives people a sense of agency. It flatters the ego. But it also subtly shifts the blame for financial dissatisfaction away from structural inefficiencies and towards the individual. If you're not thriving, you must not be trying hard enough. This framing erodes financial sanity in two ways: it pathologises rest, and it devalues strategic thinking. It encourages people to chase money reactively, often in inefficient or unscalable ways, rather than build systems that compound quietly over time.

Consider Priya, a 35-year-old marketing professional working full-time in a mid-sized consultancy. Inspired by LinkedIn posts celebrating multi-hyphenate professionals, she starts a digital course on personal branding in the evenings. On weekends, she freelances for small businesses. Her calendar is full. Her income, marginally improved. But after two years, she is more anxious than ever. She has no clear investment plan. Her savings have plateaued. Her expenses have increased to reflect her more "entrepreneurial" lifestyle—coworking spaces, software subscriptions, outsourced tasks. Hustle, in this context, has become a trap: all activity, no consolidation.

From a financial standpoint, side-hustles rarely scale without significant time, energy, and strategic intent. Most salaried professionals do not have the surplus bandwidth to turn side-gigs into full-fledged businesses—and often, they were never meant to. The average hourly return on these hustles, once all hidden costs are accounted for, is frequently underwhelming. When you consider opportunity cost—the time not spent investing, reflecting, automating, or re-skilling—the math becomes even less favourable.

But the real danger lies not in the inefficiency, but in the displacement effect. Hustle culture encourages professionals to focus on earning more through sheer activity, rather than building wealth through structural leverage. It shifts attention away from *how money works*—compounding, tax efficiency, asset allocation—and toward *how to squeeze more money out of each day*. It is a fundamentally short-term orientation, dressed up as long-term ambition.

Wealth is rarely built through income alone. It is built through the intelligent conversion of income into assets, through the design of low-maintenance systems, and through the patient execution of consistent strategies. Hustle culture resists all three. It is obsessed with immediacy. And in doing so, it trains individuals to identify not as investors or builders, but as perpetual strivers—people who are always "on the grind," even when the grind leads nowhere.

This is not merely inefficient. It is psychologically corrosive. The constant pressure to be doing more, earning more, building more—on top of full-time work—leads to decision fatigue, chronic stress, and ultimately, financial avoidance. Research in behavioural psychology shows that humans do not make better decisions under pressure. They default to safety, routine, or impulse. Hustle culture, by keeping people perpetually overloaded, actually *reduces* the quality of financial decision-making. It creates noise, not clarity.

There is also a philosophical dimension worth exploring. What does it say about our society that rest must now be earned? That unless time is monetised, it is considered wasted? Hustle culture commodifies not just time, but identity. It demands that your hobbies be monetised, your weekends be productive, and your value be externally verified through constant visible output. This is not freedom—it is a colonisation of the self by market logic. And it leaves little room for the slow, quiet disciplines that actually underpin financial autonomy: reflection, consistency, patience, and intelligent risk management.

Contrary to popular belief, most high-net-worth individuals do not hustle in the way social media suggests. They design systems. They acquire assets. They build margin into their lives—not just financial margin, but cognitive and emotional margin. They understand that wealth is not about grinding harder, but about designing smarter. And perhaps most importantly, they are not addicted to *doing*. They are focused on *becoming*—the kind of person whose money works harder than they do.

The solution, then, is not to demonise all additional income streams. Side-projects, freelancing, and entrepreneurial ventures can be immensely rewarding when approached with clarity, alignment, and a long-term lens. The key distinction is between hustle as *identity performance* and strategic work as *value creation*. One is reactive, the other intentional. One is about proving worth, the other about building it.

To step out of the hustle mindset is not to abandon ambition—it is to upgrade it. To stop chasing dopamine through busyness and start cultivating agency through design. This requires redefining productivity away from output and towards impact. It requires trusting that wealth can be built slowly, without spectacle. And it requires giving yourself permission to be calm—even when everyone else is frantically sprinting on the spot.

The next time you feel the urge to start another hustle, ask: *Is this building leverage—or burning bandwidth? Is this moving me closer to autonomy—or just making me feel momentarily in control?* And above all: *Am I designing a financial life I want to live—or performing a financial identity I think I should project?*

The difference is subtle. But it is everything.

The Illusion of Complexity

There is a persistent myth embedded in modern financial culture: that to invest wisely, grow wealth, or attain long-term stability, you must first become fluent in a dense, ever-evolving language of economic abstraction. This myth, reinforced by decades of industry messaging, serves a specific purpose—it disempowers the average investor while enriching those who benefit from their dependency. Complexity, in personal finance, is rarely a natural feature of the system. More often, it is a product: engineered, packaged, and sold. And the result is a population of working professionals who are competent in their careers, but paralysed when it comes to money.

This paralysis is not irrational. It is the outcome of deliberate design. Much of the financial services industry thrives not on clarity, but on opacity. The more obscure the process, the easier it is to charge a premium for guidance. The more unpredictable the market appears, the more justification there is for aggressive management fees. And the more uncertain the individual feels, the more likely they are to outsource responsibility without developing comprehension. In this way, *complexity becomes a business model.* It creates an artificial barrier to entry—one that requires intermediaries, products, and subscriptions to cross.

To understand the mechanism at work here, consider the way investment products are often described. Terms like "actively managed growth equity fund with global diversification and alternative exposure" are not inherently meaningful to most people. Nor are acronyms like ETF, NAV, CAGR, or alpha. While these concepts have technical validity, their presentation is rarely instructional. It is performative. It signals expertise without conveying it. The aim is not to educate, but to dazzle—to imply that behind this complexity lies sophistication, and that sophistication is the key to success.

This phenomenon is not unique to finance. In fields from law to medicine to technology, jargon often functions as a gatekeeping device. But in finance, the stakes are more personal. The cost of misunderstanding a legal term may be inconvenience. The cost of misunderstanding financial structure can be decades of missed growth, illiquidity, or chronic stress. And unlike medicine or software development, personal finance is something every adult is required to engage with, whether they're prepared or not. *The illusion of complexity doesn't just intimidate—it disenfranchises.*

This is particularly damaging for salaried professionals. These individuals often possess high cognitive capacity and are accustomed to solving complex problems within their domains of expertise. But when faced with the labyrinthine language of investment brochures, fund performance reports, or even pension contribution statements, many retreat. They internalise a false narrative: "I'm good at what I do, but I'm just not a finance person." This belief is not only untrue—it's unnecessary. Because beneath the theatre of complexity, the fundamentals of wealth-building are astonishingly simple.

Spend less than you earn. Save consistently. Invest early and regularly. Diversify sensibly. Minimise costs. Leave it alone.

That is the radical simplicity principle this book defends—not as a reductionist platitude, but as a profound design philosophy. The principle asserts that financial success is not reserved for those who master the jargon, time the market, or follow the latest investment trends. It is accessible to those who commit to clear, replicable behaviours over long time horizons. The problem is not that people can't understand finance. The problem is that they've been conditioned to believe they shouldn't *trust* what seems too simple.

To illustrate this, consider the decades-long performance comparison between actively managed mutual funds and low-cost index funds. Numerous studies, including extensive analyses by Morningstar and S&P's SPIVA reports, have consistently shown that over a ten-year horizon, the majority of actively managed funds underperform their passive counterparts—often significantly so after fees. Yet active funds continue to dominate the retail landscape. Why? Because they sound more tailored. More tactical. More worth paying for. The reality—that a globally diversified index fund held over decades can outperform most expert predictions—is almost too simple to be satisfying.

This dissonance between what works and what feels impressive reveals a deeper human bias: *we tend to equate value with effort and complexity*. If a financial strategy requires no ongoing adjustment, no insider knowledge, and no dramatic risk-taking, we assume it must be inferior. Complexity, in this sense, acts as a psychological placebo. It gives the impression of control, even when it produces worse results. Financial firms understand this intuitively. Many offer multi-layered portfolios with exotic asset classes, variable hedging strategies, or market-responsive weighting algorithms—not because these add meaningful returns for the average investor, but because they *look* advanced enough to justify higher fees.

This isn't to suggest that all complexity is malicious or misguided. In certain scenarios—estate planning, high-net-worth tax optimisation, or business succession structures—detailed knowledge and nuanced tools are essential. But for the vast majority of working professionals seeking to build personal wealth, complexity does not improve outcomes. It obscures them.

What, then, is the antidote?

It begins with a shift in perception. Simplicity must be rebranded not as a lack of sophistication, but as a mark of mastery. A good financial system should not impress you—it should *free* you. It should reduce the cognitive load, not increase it. It should work while you sleep, not demand attention every time the market hiccups. In other words, a robust system is not one that reacts intelligently. It's one that doesn't *need* to react at all.

The radical simplicity principle, therefore, calls for a new approach to personal finance—one rooted in design, not performance. It invites you to automate core actions (like monthly investing), minimise variables (like too many accounts or asset types), and ignore noise (like market forecasts or economic commentary with no actionable value). It urges you to shift from optimisation to *sufficiency*—to focus less on squeezing every ounce of return, and more on building a strategy you can understand, commit to, and maintain.

This principle also holds ethical implications. A system that relies on obscurity to extract fees or justify expertise is not a neutral system. It is exploitative. Radical simplicity is, in this context, a form of resistance. It empowers individuals to make informed decisions, challenge unnecessary gatekeepers, and focus their energy on living—not deciphering.

From a psychological standpoint, simplicity fosters clarity. And clarity is a precondition for action. Research in behavioural finance, particularly from scholars like Daniel Kahneman and Richard Thaler, shows that when people are overwhelmed by choice or ambiguity, they tend to procrastinate, over-insure, or hoard cash unnecessarily. This is not irrational—it is protective. But it also leads to opportunity cost on a massive scale. Simplicity reduces friction. And reducing friction increases follow-through.

To illustrate this, consider the case of automation. Automating a monthly investment into a diversified index fund is one of the most effective financial decisions a person can make. It requires no forecasting, no frequent decision-making, and no emotional energy. Yet many people resist it—not because they doubt its efficacy, but because it feels too...hands-off. That discomfort is not a signal of inefficiency. It's a sign that our financial culture has mistaken complexity for competence.

As we move through this book, you will encounter repeated themes designed to reinforce the radical simplicity principle. Not because simplicity is easy, but because it is *hard to trust in a culture that equates value with noise.* You will learn how to build an investment portfolio that doesn't demand your attention. You'll construct budgeting systems that don't require granular micromanagement. You'll develop rituals and identity-based habits that anchor financial behaviour in personal values, not external pressure.

This is the core promise: you do not need more products, more predictions, or more pages of financial commentary. You need fewer distractions, fewer decisions, and fewer points of failure. Wealth is not built by those who know the most—it is built by those who act on a small set of principles with consistency and clarity.

The illusion of complexity is powerful. But once seen, it cannot be unseen. And once rejected, it becomes possible to build something far more enduring: a financial life designed not to impress others, but to *liberate yourself.*

Permission to Prosper

Wealth-building is often framed as a technical challenge: a matter of strategy, tools, and tactics. But for many salaried professionals—especially those from modest backgrounds or communities where financial abundance is rare—the greater obstacle is not ignorance, but *inhibition.* Despite having stable income, good intentions, and access to more information than any generation before them, they remain stuck in a pattern of passive financial behaviour. The budgets are loosely drafted, the investment accounts remain underfunded, and decisions are delayed until there's "more clarity." What's happening here is not laziness. It's not even indecision. It's *psychological constraint.* Before wealth can be built externally, permission must be granted internally.

Money, contrary to most financial literature, is not neutral. It is saturated with emotion, identity, and social meaning. From early childhood, we absorb beliefs about what is possible for *people like us*. These beliefs are often implicit—carried not in slogans but in silences, not in formal lessons but in everyday cues. For many professionals, especially first-generation earners or those raised in working-class families, prosperity has never been just about numbers. It has been about *permission.* Permission to save seriously. To invest confidently. To speak about money without shame. To believe that wealth can be both earned and *deserved.*

Consider the case of Ayesha, a 38-year-old mid-level executive in a multinational firm. On paper, her situation is strong: she earns well above the national average, lives well within her means, and has access to financial education through workplace resources. And yet, she finds herself hesitating every time she's about to make a financial move—whether that's increasing her investment allocation or switching to a more strategic tax structure. She reads extensively but rarely acts. In therapy, she eventually traces this hesitation to a childhood belief: that money is unpredictable, that enjoying it invites loss, and that too much financial confidence risks alienating the community she came from. These aren't statements she consciously believes. But they operate like background code—shaping her actions from beneath the surface.

What Ayesha experiences is not unusual. Psychologists call these *limiting money scripts*—unconscious beliefs about money that guide behaviour in ways that often contradict conscious goals. These scripts are formed early, typically before age ten, through family dynamics, social messaging, and lived experience. In one study published in the *Journal of Financial Therapy*, researchers found that common money scripts—such as "more money will make things better," "money is bad," or "I don't deserve wealth"—were significantly correlated with financial stress, avoidance, and suboptimal financial behaviours in adulthood.

These internal narratives are further reinforced by broader cultural messaging. In societies where financial modesty is equated with moral virtue, and ambition is treated with suspicion, aspiring to prosperity can feel like a betrayal. You are told to "be content with what you have," or warned not to "get above your station." For many, these admonitions become psychological handcuffs—discouraging not greed, but *growth.* The result is a kind of self-imposed ceiling, where even modest financial success feels precarious or undeserved.

This is not just a psychological phenomenon. It has material consequences. Passive earners often underutilise their financial capacity, defaulting to low-interest savings, ignoring employer-matched pensions, or avoiding long-term investment vehicles. They may give generously to others, but struggle to invest in themselves. They prioritise stability over strategy—not because strategy is inaccessible, but because it *feels* illegitimate. They wait for some external sign—validation, education, approval—before they begin to act like people who are allowed to build wealth.

This waiting can last decades.

To disrupt this cycle, we must separate two concepts that are often conflated: *having money* and *allowing yourself to build wealth.* They are not the same. You can have a good salary and still operate from scarcity. You can receive promotions and still feel unworthy of financial security. Prosperity begins when you stop negotiating with your own potential. When you decide that money is not something you must justify, but something you are allowed to master.

This is not about entitlement. It is about agency.

Granting yourself permission to prosper means consciously rewriting inherited scripts. It means recognising that financial competence is not a betrayal of your roots, but a contribution to your future. That thriving doesn't require abandoning humility—it requires updating your internal compass. It means replacing outdated beliefs like "wealth is for them, not me" with more accurate ones: *"Wealth is a function of behaviour, not background." "I can be loyal to my values and build assets." "Financial growth is not selfish—it's sustainable."*

This internal shift has profound external effects. When professionals make the psychological transition from *earner* to *owner*, their financial behaviour changes. They move from saving what's left over to paying themselves first. They stop treating investing as optional and begin seeing it as foundational. They stop asking for permission—from banks, from parents, from culture—and start giving it to themselves.

Crucially, this psychological work cannot be outsourced. No financial advisor, no app, no spreadsheet can grant you the permission you withhold from yourself. Tools matter—but only once the mental operating system has been upgraded. As behavioural economist Dr. Sarah Newcomb puts it, "Your financial plan is only as effective as the beliefs that support it."

This is why many high-income professionals still live in financial stress. They are not misinformed—they are misaligned. Their outer resources exceed their inner readiness. And until that inner readiness is addressed, no tactic will stick.

How, then, does one begin?

Start by naming the scripts. What did your family teach you about money—directly or indirectly? Were rich people admired, resented, or invisible? Was financial security modelled, or was money a source of anxiety? Did you learn to save out of fear, or invest out of confidence? These questions are not nostalgic—they are diagnostic.

The answers will reveal whether your current financial approach is rooted in strategy or in survival.

Next, articulate your *why*. Why do you want to build wealth? What kind of freedom, stability, or contribution does it enable? When prosperity is tied to a personal and moral framework—rather than vague status aspirations—it becomes easier to own. You are not just investing in mutual funds. You are investing in your capacity to care for aging parents without panic. To leave a toxic job without fear. To support causes you believe in. To rest without guilt. These are not luxuries. They are dignities. And you do not need to apologise for pursuing them.

Finally, act before you feel ready. Permission is not a feeling—it is a decision. Start investing with what you understand. Automate one small financial behaviour. Speak one honest sentence about money to a trusted friend or partner. Each action rewires the brain's expectation of what is normal. And each repetition builds an identity that says: *I am someone who builds wealth thoughtfully and confidently.*

The chapter you're reading now is not just theory—it's a quiet intervention. You do not need to hustle harder, read more books, or wait for the market to make sense before you start. You simply need to stop deferring to doubt. You are already enough. Your income, your intelligence, and your instincts—these are not liabilities to be overcome. They are assets to be deployed.

Prosperity is not something granted to the select few who figured out a secret. It is something accessible to those who stop waiting for permission and start building on what they already have.

So consider this your psychological green light.

You're allowed.

Chapter 2
Rethinking Wealth

Imagine someone hands you a detailed breakdown of your investment portfolio. It's done well—returned 9.6% over the past year. By most standards, that's commendable. On paper, at least, it's the kind of figure that deserves a nod of approval. But let's say that same portfolio also kept you tethered to your phone, nervously scanning the markets, second-guessing every fluctuation. Was it really a good investment? Now consider an alternative scenario: a more modest 5% return from an approach that asked little of you, sat comfortably within your ethical framework, and, perhaps most tellingly, let you sleep soundly. Which of the two would you look back on with greater satisfaction?

We begin here, not to romanticise lower returns, but to confront a quiet assumption embedded in most personal finance thinking: that numbers alone are the story. The dominant script tells us wealth is a formula—optimise inputs, maximise returns, reduce risk, rinse and repeat. And yes, the arithmetic matters. But numbers don't govern behaviour. Emotion does. People don't stick to what looks best in Excel—they stick to what feels right in life.

That's where the notion of *Emotional Return on Investment*—eROI—enters. Not a soft cousin to ROI, but a companion measure that fills in what the spreadsheets leave out. Traditional ROI measures what something grows into. eROI, on the other hand, asks what it costs you to stay the course. It's about sustainability. What toll—psychological, emotional, relational—does a financial decision exact? And does that toll compromise your ability to remain consistent? Often, the two diverge dramatically. ROI chases maximisation. eROI cares about alignment. Both are valid. But only one helps explain why people with enviable incomes and well-managed portfolios can still feel financially brittle.

So, if we're serious about rethinking wealth, we must also reframe its definition. More assets? Yes, perhaps. But also more sovereignty. Not just higher returns, but richer resonance. A financial life designed not merely to accumulate, but to afford freedom—freedom to choose work, relationships, priorities, pace. To live not by default, but with discernment. That kind of life doesn't start with a mutual fund. It starts with a mindset.

And here we come to a familiar, if under-discussed, pattern: *fear-based saving*. On the surface, it looks responsible—cautious, even prudent. Beneath, however, lies a dynamic that often masquerades as wisdom while quietly bleeding opportunity. This is the tendency to save reactively, compulsively, without a corresponding willingness to act. It manifests as hoarding cash, postponing investment, endlessly researching options but never committing. It's not irrational. Far from it. It's the legacy of uncertainty—often shaped by past instability, cultural caution, or a hyper-awareness of what can go wrong.

Take Rahul, for instance. Forty-two. Works in IT. Has squirrelled away over £120,000 in low-yield accounts—instant-access savings, premium bonds, that sort of thing. He follows the finance blogs, knows the podcasts, even opened an investing account some years ago. He's waiting, he says, to feel more "prepared." But it's been four years. In that time, inflation has quietly chewed through the real value of his money, and the compounding power he's forfeited outweighs the likely cost of any missteps he feared. This isn't a lack of knowledge—it's a lack of readiness. What Rahul needs isn't another article. It's psychological permission.

This pattern is common among the conscientious. These are not impulsive spenders. They're planners—serious ones. But their planning is defensive, not directional. Their mindset is governed by scarcity logic: that danger is always imminent, that money must be guarded, not engaged. And under that logic, systems that rely on trust—trust in time, in markets, in themselves—rarely take root.

Now, this is not an argument for bravado or speculative gambling. What's needed is a shift—not from fear to recklessness, but from fear to intention. A reorientation. When that happens—when you move from reactive to proactive, from conserving to creating—something fundamental changes. This is not about ignoring risk; it's about redefining it. Because for most professionals, the greater risk is not in beginning too soon, but in waiting too long. Markets wobble. But indecision accumulates. And over decades, hesitation can be ruinously expensive.

So then—what is money for? Without a compelling answer, the default becomes accumulation for its own sake. Bigger salaries, higher balances, more complicated strategies. But at its essence, money is not an endpoint. It's a tool. And like all tools, its utility depends on the clarity of its user. What do you intend to build?

This chapter invites you to define wealth not as a distant figure, but as something lived. Tangible. Grounded. What does *enough* feel like—not as a ceiling, but as a compass? Which financial behaviours energise you, and which quietly drain you? Which risks are legitimate, and which simply threaten the version of yourself you're used to? These questions aren't just for reflection. They're foundational. Because when clarity is missing, strategy becomes reactive. But when it's present, even modest moves carry weight.

To that end, rethinking wealth isn't about disruption. It's about refinement. Recognising that a resilient financial life rests less on tactical brilliance than on internal coherence. That no spreadsheet can save a strategy at war with your values. That a plan you can't emotionally sustain is already broken—no matter how elegant it looks on paper.

So we'll dig into the cost of delay. Not just in returns missed, but in identity deferred. What happens when well-meaning professionals try to do everything "right," and end up paralysed by perfectionism? We'll examine how the firehose of financial media can overwhelm rather than enlighten. And we'll explore frameworks for decision-making rooted in personal integrity, not market noise or trend-chasing. Because this isn't about outperforming others. It's about aligning your resources with a life you actually want—not one you're rehearsing, rescheduling, or pretending to enjoy.

Ultimately, this chapter is an invitation to step into financial authorship. Not simply by owning assets—but by owning the relationship you have with money itself. The permission to prosper, to build, to move forward—that's meaningless unless you're willing to claim it. Earning potential is only part of the equation. The courage to deploy it—that's where transformation begins.

You don't need to become someone else to thrive financially. You don't need secret knowledge, lucky timing, or endless hustle. What you need is a reshaped definition of wealth. One that reflects your reality, your rhythm, your values—not just the performance you think the world wants.

There are no shortcuts here. But there is something far more valuable: clarity. The kind that cuts through fear, sharpens intent, and allows your financial life to grow—not in spectacle, but in substance. Because the most enduring wealth isn't just measured in what you hold—it's reflected in how you live.

Beyond the Balance Sheet

If wealth were only about numbers, the richest people would always be the freest. But they're not. Some high-net-worth individuals spend their days tethered to schedules they resent, projects they can't exit, or lifestyles they no longer control. Conversely, others with modest incomes live with a palpable sense of freedom—clear boundaries, purposeful days, and space to think without financial anxiety breathing down their necks. What separates these two realities isn't income or asset class. It's *autonomy*.

This subchapter invites a radical reframing of what wealth means. Not as a static sum on a spreadsheet, but as a dynamic condition of *personal agency*. This shift matters deeply—especially for salaried professionals—because the conventional financial metrics they are conditioned to chase often mask the very absence of what they most crave: time, flexibility, energy, and the power to choose. *Wealth is not only what you accumulate. It is what you're able to opt out of.*

Mainstream financial culture often reduces wealth to net worth: assets minus liabilities. This framework is mathematically sound, but spiritually inert. It fails to capture how you *experience* your financial life. You can have a rising net worth and a collapsing sense of control. You can reach a six-figure salary and feel more trapped than ever. In such cases, the tools of personal finance—saving, investing, paying down debt—may still be present, but the *why* has evaporated. You're earning, but not steering. The balance sheet looks impressive, but your life feels outsourced.

To move beyond the balance sheet, we must foreground autonomy as the true currency of wealth. Autonomy is your ability to make decisions that reflect your values rather than your financial constraints. It is the space to say no to toxic jobs, yes to unplanned opportunities, and maybe to paths still forming. It is, as philosopher Isaiah Berlin described it, *freedom from coercion*—not just political, but financial coercion, which is arguably more pervasive in everyday life.

When autonomy becomes the central metric, wealth no longer looks like an external scoreboard. It becomes a framework for design. And like any design, it involves trade-offs. You may choose a smaller house to reduce mortgage pressure, giving you the option to work fewer hours. You might structure your work around school hours, not market hours. You might pass on a promotion that adds status but subtracts sovereignty. These decisions may reduce your *apparent* wealth. But they increase your *experienced* wealth—and for those paying attention, that distinction is everything.

This reframing also reorients us to time. Time is not just the backdrop of your financial life—it is the terrain. Every financial decision is a time decision. Buying a car on credit is not just a purchase—it is a contract on your future hours. Accepting a pay rise with additional responsibilities may improve your income, but at what cost to your flexibility? Investing aggressively for a retirement 30 years away is only rational if your present life remains livable. One of the most overlooked questions in personal finance is not "What will this earn?" but "*What will this cost me in energy, time, and optionality?*"

To ground this, consider two professionals with identical salaries and savings. Amir works 60 hours a week in a demanding corporate role. His income is high, but his evenings are consumed with decompressing from the day, and his weekends are for recovery. Lena, meanwhile, consults three days a week, earns slightly less, but has structured her life around predictable hours, deep work, and family time. On a spreadsheet, Amir might look more "successful." But if wealth includes *control over your time and energy*, Lena is far ahead. Her wealth may be less visible—but it is more *available.*

Economist John Maynard Keynes, writing in the 1930s, famously predicted that by now, technological advancement would allow us to work as little as 15 hours a week. What he didn't anticipate was our cultural attachment to productivity and accumulation. Despite gains in efficiency, we've used our time dividends to work more, consume more, and defer freedom until some theoretical later date. The deferred life plan—work now, live later—still shapes most professionals' relationship to money. And it often postpones autonomy until it's too late to use meaningfully.

This is where the balance sheet most powerfully fails. It cannot measure *when* your wealth will be available. A portfolio that grows impressively but cannot support any lifestyle shift for 30 years is functionally a locked box. If you're too stressed or exhausted to enjoy your life along the way, that wealth is abstract—not useful. And if your financial life is so optimised that it requires you to work at the edge of burnout, then by any rational metric, your net worth is inflated and your autonomy discounted.

But what about responsibility? What about children, ageing parents, housing costs? Isn't it naïve to prioritise autonomy when obligations are real and pressing? This is a valid tension—and one that underscores, rather than undermines, the case for this reframing. Because autonomy is not about abandoning responsibility. It is about *designing within it.* Strategic decisions made with autonomy in mind often lead to better long-term resilience. When your life isn't stretched to its financial limit, you can absorb shocks—layoffs, illness, family needs—without falling into crisis. The very same buffer that grants you freedom also grants you *stability*. That is why autonomy is not a luxury good. It is a core feature of financial intelligence.

The good news is that autonomy, unlike wealth in the conventional sense, is not entirely income-dependent. It can be built by reducing fixed costs, setting boundaries around work hours, investing in skills that create flexibility, or removing unnecessary complexity from your financial systems. In this sense, *the pursuit of autonomy can begin immediately, regardless of your current salary*. You don't need to be debt-free or retired to reclaim part of your day. You just need to decide that time, energy, and choice are worth something—and then begin re-allocating your resources accordingly.

This concept also changes how we evaluate progress. When wealth is defined by autonomy, then success is not just about numbers increasing—it's about *options expanding*. If you now have the ability to take a sabbatical, start a business, decline a client, or move cities without financial panic, then you are wealthier than someone with twice your net worth but none of those options. When people reflect on what wealth really means to them, they rarely mention yachts or luxury watches. They talk about being able to take care of family. To say no. To disappear for a week without consequence. These are *freedoms*, not figures.

As you continue through this chapter—and this book—you'll encounter tools and strategies designed to support the building of financial systems. But never forget the purpose of those systems. They are not there to maximise numbers for their own sake. They are there to *liberate your attention from money*, so you can deploy it elsewhere. They are there to support autonomy.

Because in the end, the richest life is not necessarily the one with the most assets. It's the one with the *fewest constraints*. And once you start measuring wealth in those terms, you begin to see a different financial landscape. One where the ultimate benchmark is not your balance sheet, but your ability to *act on your values in real time*. That is the definition of wealth that lasts. And it is the only one worth designing for.

The Emotional Return on Investment (eROI)

It is entirely possible to do everything "right" with money and still feel deeply unsettled by it. You may have a well-optimised portfolio, a robust pension plan, and a steadily growing net worth—yet still live in a persistent state of anxiety, guilt, or confusion around your financial life. This disconnect is not irrational. It is a signal that traditional financial metrics, however necessary, are incomplete. They tell us what our money is doing. They do not tell us how our financial choices *feel*—and feeling, as behavioural science continues to confirm, is what ultimately drives consistency, satisfaction, and long-term success.

That gap between numeric outcomes and emotional experience is the space where a new concept is needed. Enter *Emotional Return on Investment*, or eROI. This is not a rejection of traditional return on investment (ROI), but a necessary expansion of it. Where ROI measures monetary gain, eROI measures *the quality of the experience that accompanies the decision.* It asks: "Did this financial choice make my life feel more secure, more energised, more aligned with my values—or did it introduce friction, fatigue, and doubt?" In a field dominated by spreadsheets and performance graphs, eROI restores the human dimension to money.

The core idea is deceptively simple: *the sustainability of a financial strategy depends on how it feels, not just how it performs.* And yet, this insight remains largely absent from financial education. Most advice is delivered as if the investor were a rational actor in a vacuum: immune to stress, indifferent to complexity, and operating with infinite willpower. In practice, human beings are none of these things. We are emotional creatures, making financial decisions in real time, under real pressure, surrounded by conflicting signals, incomplete information, and deeply embedded scripts from our upbringing.

Under these conditions, *what feels manageable will often outperform what looks optimal.*

Let's ground this with an example. Suppose Priya has two investment options. Option A is a low-cost global index fund. It is diversified, simple, and recommended by most financial experts. Option B is a mix of actively managed funds suggested by her bank's advisor—more expensive, slightly more volatile, but presented in a sleek dashboard with personal updates and a sense of ongoing involvement. On paper, Option A is superior. But Priya chooses Option B because she feels reassured by the human contact, the interface, and the narrative of "professional guidance." From a strict ROI perspective, she's made a suboptimal choice. But from an eROI perspective, it may be the only choice she could have *stuck with.* And that matters more than perfection.

This does not mean we abandon rigour. The point is not to indulge emotional whim. Rather, it's to acknowledge that *any system which cannot be sustained emotionally will collapse behaviourally.* The most effective financial strategy is the one that aligns *well enough* with external performance standards *and* internal psychological dynamics. eROI helps us calibrate for both.

Importantly, eROI is not about indulgence or short-term gratification. It is about emotional *resonance.* That includes peace of mind, yes, but also a deeper sense of alignment between one's values and one's actions. For example, an individual may choose to invest in ESG (Environmental, Social, and Governance) funds not because they outperform the market (they may or may not), but because doing so reflects their ethical commitments. Or a parent may choose to allocate more funds to a child's education than to their own retirement—not because it is the most "efficient" use of capital, but because it expresses a non-financial priority. These decisions are not irrational. They are *contextually coherent.* eROI captures that coherence.

The power of this framework is that it surfaces otherwise invisible trade-offs. Traditional ROI tends to flatten financial decisions into abstract units of return. eROI reintroduces the full cost profile—including stress, time, cognitive load, and relational strain. A buy-to-let property might yield a solid ROI, but if it also consumes your weekends with repairs, disputes, or tax paperwork, the eROI may be negative. A side-hustle may increase your income, but if it leaves you perpetually tired and disconnected from your family, the real return is questionable.

Psychologically, eROI acts as a bridge between intention and implementation. Many salaried professionals already *know* what they should do: automate savings, reduce debt, invest consistently. But they struggle to act because they've internalised financial behaviours that are high-friction, misaligned, or intimidating. These behaviours generate anxiety, which in turn fuels avoidance. Over time, a pattern of postponement sets in—reading more articles, downloading more budgeting tools, but never quite changing course. eROI offers an alternative path: design financial actions that *feel low-resistance, emotionally affirmative, and congruent with identity*. These are the actions that stick.

The science supports this view. Studies in behavioural finance—especially those by Daniel Kahneman, Richard Thaler, and Meir Statman—demonstrate that people rarely make decisions based on strict economic utility. Instead, they rely on heuristics: mental shortcuts shaped by emotion, memory, and social context. If a financial action is associated with stress, uncertainty, or self-doubt, it is more likely to be delayed or avoided. But if it is associated with clarity, confidence, or alignment with personal values, it is more likely to become habitual. This is where eROI becomes not just a diagnostic tool, but a *design principle.*

Financial advisors, too, are beginning to integrate this thinking. The best advisors no longer push products—they co-create systems with clients that reflect their lived realities. They ask not just, "What are your goals?" but "How do you want to feel when you look at your finances?" This may sound soft, but it has hard implications.

Portfolios built around emotional clarity tend to have higher adherence rates, lower stress levels, and fewer reactionary withdrawals during market volatility. In other words, they are more durable.

There are, of course, limits to eROI. If taken to extremes, it can justify decisions that feel good but have dire long-term consequences—overspending, under-insuring, avoiding necessary risk. This is where the concept requires *balance*. Think of eROI not as a replacement for ROI, but as a lens that helps you interpret traditional financial advice through the filter of personal relevance. The goal is *not* maximum comfort. The goal is sustainable confidence.

One of the most practical applications of eROI is in decision triage. When faced with competing options—buying vs. renting, saving vs. investing, staying in a job vs. taking a sabbatical—you can ask not only "Which one performs better on paper?" but also, "Which one feels more congruent with how I want to live?" That second question is not sentimental. It is strategic. It can reveal hidden costs, neglected values, or deferred needs that would otherwise be left unexamined.

Ultimately, introducing eROI into your financial thinking invites a richer question: *What kind of life is this money helping me build?* That question reframes money not as a scoreboard, but as a medium for living. It helps you replace comparison with coherence. Instead of asking, "Am I doing as well as others?" you begin to ask, "Is this working for me, right now, in this season of life?"

Because if your financial plan delivers strong returns but constant anxiety, it's not a plan—it's a burden. And if your system looks impressive but feels unliveable, you won't follow it. Wealth is not just the accumulation of assets. It is the reduction of financial friction in daily life, the expansion of psychological space, and the alignment of your money with your most enduring values.

That is the real return that matters. And once you learn to measure it, you will stop chasing someone else's ideal and start building your own. Quietly. Clearly. On purpose.

The Hidden Cost of Fear-Based Saving

At first glance, hoarding cash appears prudent. In a world increasingly defined by volatility—layoffs, market crashes, recessions, medical emergencies—having a healthy savings buffer feels rational, even responsible. And to an extent, it is. An emergency fund, typically three to six months of living expenses, is a foundational layer of financial security. But beyond that baseline, the decision to stockpile large sums of uninvested cash is rarely strategic. It is psychological. It is less about financial literacy and more about emotional control. And while it often masquerades as caution, *fear-based saving is frequently a form of self-sabotage*—quiet, socially acceptable, and ultimately costly.

This chapter challenges the myth that "waiting until you know more" is a risk-free approach to investing. In reality, delaying financial action—especially for professionals in their prime earning years—has measurable, compounding consequences. The cost of hesitation is not merely forgone gains. It is lost *momentum*. And over time, that loss is more damaging than most short-term mistakes. To understand this, we must examine what drives the impulse to save defensively, why it persists, and what it really costs over the course of a working life.

Start with the psychology. Fear-based savers are not illogical. They are usually cautious, conscientious, and risk-aware—qualities often mistaken for financial acumen. But the behaviour is rarely rooted in strategy. More often, it stems from *ambiguity aversion*—a cognitive bias that causes people to avoid choices when outcomes are unclear, even if those choices offer better long-term prospects. Ambiguity aversion explains why a cash account, with its fixed and visible balance, feels safer than an investment account subject to daily fluctuation—even when the latter consistently outpaces inflation and builds real wealth.

But what fear-based savers gain in emotional comfort, they forfeit in economic potential. Inflation quietly erodes the purchasing power of static savings year after year. This is not theoretical. In the UK, for instance, inflation has averaged around 2.5% annually over the last few decades, and significantly more in recent years. If your cash savings return less than that—say 1% in a high-interest account—the real value of your money is shrinking. Saving, in this context, is not safety. It is *regression.*

And yet, even with this knowledge, many professionals continue to wait. They postpone investing until they've read more books, finished a course, watched another documentary, or "feel ready." This phenomenon—what we might call *financial procrastination dressed as preparation*—is deeply human. It gives the illusion of movement while preserving the comfort of inaction. But learning, if not paired with implementation, becomes a loop: consuming more information to avoid taking the very action that would make the learning real.

Consider Raj, a 40-year-old software consultant who has earned well for over a decade. He saves aggressively—close to 35% of his income—but keeps nearly all of it in a savings account. His reasoning? "The markets are unpredictable. I want to understand everything before I commit." Over the last ten years, that hesitation has cost him hundreds of thousands in potential compounding. Not through poor decisions, but through *no decision at all.* His net worth is stagnant in real terms. His sense of control is brittle. And despite his discipline, his financial life is no closer to providing true autonomy.

This is the central irony of fear-based saving: it seeks control and security, but often results in fragility. Cash reserves feel safe because they're visible and liquid. But they're not productive. They do not generate passive income. They do not grow with the economy. They do not benefit from compounding. Over time, the saver who avoids all risk often ends up taking the greatest one—the risk of falling permanently behind.

But the deeper issue is not numerical. It is existential. Fear-based savers often carry internal scripts that tie money to safety, self-worth, and identity in rigid ways. For some, money represents survival—a legacy of upbringing, past trauma, or cultural conditioning. For others, money is a measure of control in an otherwise uncertain world. In both cases, the hoarding of cash becomes a proxy for *stability of self*. Letting go of that cash—even to invest in sensible, diversified funds—feels threatening not because the strategy is flawed, but because the identity it protects might be disrupted.

Breaking out of this pattern requires more than education. It requires *emotional permission*. To shift from saving as defence to investing as design. To stop treating cash as a security blanket and start using it as a launch pad. This pivot is not reckless. It's deliberate. It means acknowledging that building wealth involves uncertainty—but not chaos. That time in the market, not timing the market, is what matters. And that hesitation is not a hedge against risk—it is a form of risk.

This is where the numbers become unforgiving. Suppose you invest £5,000 annually for 20 years. If you begin at age 30 with an average return of 7%, you'll have over £200,000 by age 50. Wait just five years to start, and your total drops by nearly 30%. Delay a full decade, and you cut your outcome nearly in half. These are not abstract differences. They represent entire decades of reduced options, delayed freedom, and diminished legacy. The greatest cost of fear-based saving is *time not invested.*

The antidote is not blind optimism or aggressive risk-taking. It is structure. A simple, intentional financial system that reduces cognitive load and builds confidence through action. For many professionals, the first breakthrough comes not through a perfect plan, but through a *small, imperfect start.* Automating a modest monthly investment. Setting up a pension contribution. Choosing a diversified index fund and leaving it alone. These are not dramatic moves. But they are decisive. And they begin to reverse the passivity that keeps so many earners from becoming builders.

Moreover, investing—done properly—is not gambling. It is not impulsive or speculative. It is the disciplined allocation of resources toward long-term growth. The financial services industry may confuse this fact with jargon and product proliferation, but the underlying principle is elegant in its simplicity: *Own things that grow. Leave them alone. Let time do the work.* What's required is not mastery, but trust—in the system, in the strategy, and in oneself.

To make this shift sustainable, professionals must also revise their internal scripts. Instead of "I can't afford to make a mistake," try "I can't afford to do nothing." Instead of "I need to understand everything," try "I need to start with what I know." Instead of "Markets are too volatile," try "Volatility is the price of admission for long-term growth." These reframes are not motivational slogans. They are recalibrations—ways of aligning financial action with actual values rather than inherited anxieties.

Finally, it's worth reflecting on what wealth is *for*. Fear-based savers often conflate money with preparedness. But money that sits idle does not prepare you for life—it merely delays your engagement with it. Real preparedness includes the ability to adapt, to generate income from multiple sources, and to use resources as a tool for *freedom*, not just for fortification. That freedom doesn't come from hoarding—it comes from building.

So if you find yourself saving and saving, but never quite starting, pause and ask: *What am I really protecting?* Is it your money—or your sense of certainty? Is it your plan—or your self-image? And what would change if you acted not from fear, but from intention?

The truth is, a few mistakes early on will cost far less than chronic inaction. The goal is not perfection. The goal is momentum. And momentum requires movement. Not after you've read the next book. Not when the market calms down. Not someday.

Now. Even in small steps. Especially in small steps.

Because the biggest risk is not that you'll invest and get it wrong. It's that you'll wait so long trying to get it right, you'll never begin at all.

From Scarcity to Strategy

There is a fundamental shift that separates reactive earners from intentional builders. It's not their income bracket, their job title, or even their financial literacy. It's their *default orientation to money*. Most people, even those with steady paycheques and professional credentials, manage money defensively. They monitor expenses, avoid big financial decisions, and hope stability will reward their caution. Their focus is on preservation—making sure nothing goes wrong. This scarcity-driven mindset, though often masked as pragmatism, is not neutral. It shapes behaviour, narrows options, and limits the compounding effect of confident, forward-looking choices.

Scarcity is not defined solely by income. It is a mindset—a framework that interprets money through the lens of fear, caution, and control. In this view, money is always one bad month away from vanishing. Opportunities are risky. Simplicity feels naïve. And success, if it comes, is assumed to be temporary. Professionals operating from this stance may have surplus income but still experience a chronic sense of financial fragility. They over-rely on saving, under-leverage their assets, and hesitate to make moves that would materially improve their long-term autonomy. This is not irrational. It is *overfitted risk aversion*—a behaviour pattern shaped by uncertainty, historical instability, and cultural conditioning.

But scarcity management is not the same as wealth creation. One protects. The other *builds*. And to build intentionally, a new framework is needed—one that treats money as a tool for *agency*, not just security. This is where strategy begins. Not as a product, or plan, or spreadsheet—but as a *mental shift from reacting to designing.* From using money to minimise loss, to using it to expand optionality. From asking, "How can I avoid going backward?" to asking, "What structure would move me forward with integrity?"

To illustrate the difference, consider two professionals with identical incomes. Anita focuses on budgeting, checks her account balances daily, and worries about whether she's spending too much. She saves diligently, keeps her money in cash and low-yield accounts, and avoids investing—convinced she doesn't yet "know enough." By contrast, Leena allocates a portion of her income to long-term investments, tracks only key metrics, and spends time designing a system that will run without her daily input. She automates contributions to her pension, sets annual financial reviews, and builds buffers rather than obsessing over every transaction. Leena isn't fearless—she's strategic. Her approach creates space, while Anita's tight control reinforces anxiety.

The irony is that many professionals believe they are being "responsible" by staying in control of every financial detail. But hyper-control is not the same as clarity. In fact, it often reflects *uncertainty masquerading as diligence.* When the scarcity mindset dominates, decisions are deferred. People wait for the perfect time to invest, the ideal conditions to switch jobs, the certainty that they won't regret a purchase. This chronic postponement is dressed up as caution, but its long-term result is stagnation. *Strategy, by contrast, accepts uncertainty as a given—but plans anyway.*

A core distinction here is between *tactical reaction* and *systemic intention.* Scarcity thinking is tactical. It focuses on what to cut, how to economise, or where to stash cash. Strategy focuses on what to *enable.* It sets principles: automation over improvisation, rhythm over urgency, structure over willpower. It asks not just "What can I afford today?" but "What would make this financial life more *resilient*, more aligned, and more freeing in the long term?"

This is not to dismiss risk. Strategy isn't about blind optimism. It's about *calibrated action.* It understands that there's no such thing as a risk-free financial decision—only risks you understand and risks you ignore. Scarcity thrives on avoidance. Strategy thrives on design. And design is a function of values. Strategic money management begins when you define what you want your money to *do for you*, beyond simply preventing disaster.

From a psychological standpoint, this shift is supported by a wealth of behavioural research. Scarcity, as studied by Sendhil Mullainathan and Eldar Shafir, impairs decision-making by narrowing attention and increasing mental bandwidth consumption. When individuals operate under financial strain—or even the perception of it—they become more myopic, less innovative, and more prone to short-term thinking. This isn't a moral failure. It's cognitive economics. Scarcity makes it harder to think long-term because survival overrides strategy. What's sobering is that this effect can be present *even when money isn't objectively scarce*—so long as the mindset of scarcity persists.

The transition to strategic thinking, then, is not about having more money. It's about changing the internal architecture from which decisions are made. That architecture includes identity ("Am I someone who builds wealth or someone who just gets by?"), agency ("Do I believe I can shape my financial outcomes?"), and purpose ("What matters enough to structure my life around?"). Without these anchors, even sophisticated financial plans become fragile. They collapse under stress or change. With them, even basic strategies can generate momentum and confidence.

One of the most transformative realisations for working professionals is this: *you can earn a high salary and still be financially passive.* Many high-income earners outsource all planning, avoid engagement with their finances, or overconsume out of fatigue and compensation. Scarcity mindset can look like excess too—it's the quiet fear that this level of income won't last, so it must be converted into visible comfort now. Strategy offers an alternative: build systems that reflect your current capacity *and* prepare you to operate from strength when conditions shift.

To operationalise this, consider the power of *default settings*. In a scarcity framework, every financial decision feels discretionary—"Should I save this month? Can I afford to invest now?" These questions drain energy and invite delay. In a strategic framework, the key decisions are made *once*, then automated. Contributions go out monthly. Categories are pre-allocated. Adjustments are periodic, not perpetual. This isn't rigidity—it's *designed consistency*. The bandwidth saved becomes a dividend you reinvest into thinking, learning, or simply living.

Strategic money management also recognises that *freedom is built incrementally*. It doesn't require quitting your job, reaching FIRE, or selling a company. It might mean reducing your fixed expenses so that your income buys you margin, not more pressure. It might mean choosing to prioritise time over money in key moments—because the value of one good hour with your child, your health, or your ideas often outweighs the price of postponing a financial milestone. Strategy is where finance meets *philosophy*: how do you want to live, and what does your money need to do to support that?

Ultimately, the shift from scarcity to strategy is the shift from reacting to shaping. From treating money as a constraint to using it as a lever. From hoarding it to deploying it. This mindset doesn't guarantee immediate transformation. But it does change the quality of every financial decision—from budgeting to investing to spending—because it is rooted in *forward motion*, not in fear.

And that shift, once made, is irreversible. You begin to look at each pound not just as currency, but as a signal: of what you value, what you believe about the future, and how much agency you're willing to claim in shaping both. That is strategy. That is wealth-building. And that is where real financial peace begins—not when you finally feel "safe," but when you start acting like someone who already knows they're capable of more.

Chapter 3
Rhythm Over Risk

When most people picture wealth, they tend to see it as the reward for a singular, shrewd decision: catching the right stock before it soars, flipping property at the perfect moment, getting in early on a booming market. It's a narrative built for headlines—high stakes, quick moves, dramatic results. And yet, when you peer beneath the surface of most enduring fortunes, you won't find flashes of brilliance. You'll find rhythm. Steady, patient, deliberate rhythm.

This chapter invites a shift—not just in how we think about money, but in how we orient ourselves to it. Rather than chasing the elusive high of financial events, we consider wealth as something built in cadence. Not an outcome, but a pattern. Not a windfall, but a habit. This change in lens is no minor tweak; it rewires the entire framework. You begin to move from the anxious question of "What should I do right now?" to the sturdier, more transformative "What should I do every time?" The answer, as this chapter will show, is simple but powerful: consistency trumps brilliance. And not by a sliver—by a mile. Not just in your net worth, but in your sense of agency.

Let's begin with the notion of *financial gravity*. We often hear compounding described as magic, a kind of alchemical force. But that's a romantic distortion. Compounding is not magical—it's mechanical. Predictable, even. Like gravity, it operates according to a known formula: time and direction. Yet culture has trained us to treat investing as the realm of outliers. We're taught to believe that real success lies with those who know more, move faster, or sit closer to the levers of the market. The reality? For the everyday professional, the greatest wealth-building tool is not stock-picking savvy. It's sustained, rhythmic exposure to productive assets.

Stick with it long enough, and the system begins to turn in your favour. Market swings, rather than threatening your position, start to improve your average entry point through pound-cost averaging. The volatility that once seemed alarming becomes background noise.

Your emotional muscle—resilience—builds through repetition. And crucially, you shed the need to get it right every time. Rhythm absorbs the margin for error. It turns imperfection into progress.

This is not conjecture. It's repeatedly confirmed by decades of research. Data from Vanguard, Morningstar, and the behavioural finance world tells a consistent story: investors who automate contributions, keep their hands off the wheel, and let the process run—those are the ones who outperform not only the average individual but often the so-called experts managing funds full-time. The differentiator? It's not intellect. It's structure. Rhythm, baked into system.

So, if the evidence is so clear, why do so many people still chase complexity over consistency? The answer is, in part, psychological. We have a cultural allergy to stillness. We've conflated motion with mastery. To do nothing feels unsophisticated. Surely, a "smart" investor is adjusting allocations, rebalancing every quarter, scanning the news, tweaking strategy. And of course, the financial industry does little to challenge this bias—after all, every tweak is a transaction, and every transaction is a fee. Stillness doesn't sell.

But stillness—when deliberate and well-designed—isn't laziness. It's identity. And that's where we must go next: the idea of *automating identity*. On the surface, automation sounds like a concession—a crutch for the time-poor or undisciplined. But looked at properly, automation is something far richer. It's a codification of intent. You are, in effect, formalising your values. Turning decision into default. And defaults, sustained over time, shape outcomes far more reliably than willpower ever could.

Consider identity not as a label you wear, but as a sequence of behaviours you repeat. If every month, without fail, you invest 15% of your income before spending a pound, that's not just discipline. It's declaration. It says: I build before I consume. I prioritise future over impulse. Over time, that rhythm sculpts self-image. It turns financial action into personal architecture.

Importantly, automation is not rigidity. You retain flexibility—but you're no longer starting from zero. You begin from a place of design. And when life throws the inevitable wrenches—job shifts, economic dips, unexpected expenses—you aren't left scrambling. You fall back on a pre-committed version of yourself, one who made decisions calmly, with clarity. This is what maturity in finance looks like—not constant optimisation, but prepared steadiness.

And now, to a dimension too often left out of financial conversations: *ritual.* Rhythm isn't just mechanical. It can also be deeply human. Think of it like journalling or meditation or prayer—not mystical, but grounding. A monthly ritual that ties your life to your money—not in panic, not in pursuit, but in presence. You set aside a particular day—perhaps the last Friday, or the first Sunday—and you engage. Not obsessively, but with intention. Four things: check your accounts, review your automations, confirm your contributions, and reflect—briefly—on whether your financial system still reflects who you are.

This is not micromanagement. It's rhythm in action. Over time, this small monthly act becomes a kind of stabiliser. A gentle, regular nudge that says: you're paying attention. You're not drifting. Even if the progress is quiet—even if the numbers aren't dramatic—you're engaged. And crucially, you're engaged on your terms, not because of market panic or media noise.

Most people only look at their money when something's on fire. That's no way to build. If your financial engagement is only reactive, your system will never move beyond survival mode. But rhythm creates a counterpoint to chaos. A signal stronger than the noise. A pulse that reminds you, again and again, who's really in control.

That's the core of this chapter. Wealth does not require theatrics. Nor brilliance. Nor clairvoyance. It requires rhythm. A preference for structure over spontaneity. A habit of returning to what works, even when it's unglamorous. Especially when it's unglamorous.

So we'll challenge the myths—the heroics of market timing, the seduction of constant change. We'll look at how compounding actually behaves, not as metaphor but as mechanism. We'll explore what it looks like to become someone whose financial growth is not personality-dependent, but system-driven. And we'll close with a vision of a financial life anchored by ritual—not fear.

Because rhythm is not a lesser ambition. It is its scaffolding. Once you anchor your financial life in rhythm, you'll come to see that freedom is rarely explosive. It is, more often, a slow accrual of quiet decisions, repeated with care. Again and again. With purpose.

The Myth of the Magic Stock Pick

Every financial media cycle has its darlings. One day it's the explosive rise of a tech unicorn. The next, a biotech disruptor, a crypto coin, or a startup riding the wave of hype and volatility. The headlines are arresting, the price charts seductive, and the language urgent: "Don't miss the next big thing." For many professionals trying to invest wisely, this drumbeat creates a dangerous expectation—that building wealth hinges on discovering *that* one breakthrough stock, before everyone else does. This mindset isn't just misleading; it's corrosive. It distorts time horizons, hijacks decision-making, and undermines the quiet, disciplined approach that actually grows wealth over decades.

The myth of the magic stock pick persists because it promises asymmetry. The idea that a single, clever choice could compress decades of effort into a few years of returns is incredibly appealing—especially to time-poor professionals who feel behind. But in practice, this obsession with the exceptional distracts from the achievable. The paradox is stark: the more you chase outperformance, the more likely you are to underperform.

To understand why, we must interrogate the structure of the market itself. Publicly traded equities, especially in developed markets, are priced by millions of participants operating with vast pools of information. When a stock price moves dramatically, it usually reflects something already known—or anticipated—by those with deeper access and faster reactions. Unless you have a specific informational edge (which is rare and increasingly regulated), your "insight" is likely a recycled version of yesterday's news. By the time a stock becomes a household name, its most outsized gains have already been captured—often by institutional investors who bought in long before it appeared in mainstream conversation.

Moreover, the psychological profile of someone hunting for the magic pick is rarely compatible with long-term wealth creation. It promotes impulsive behaviour: checking prices obsessively, reacting to media noise, and reallocating capital based on short-term narratives. These actions might feel productive, but they are fundamentally reactive. They create churn, not clarity. The illusion of activity masks the absence of structure.

There's also the survivorship bias baked into our cultural memory of investing. We remember Apple, Amazon, and Tesla. We do not remember the hundreds of companies launched with similar fanfare that vanished or stagnated. For every celebrated winner, there are dozens of quiet failures. And statistically speaking, your odds of selecting the next Amazon in its infancy—without deep sector knowledge, insider access, or a willingness to endure years of underperformance—are vanishingly small. *Luck can be profitable, but it is not repeatable. Strategy must be.*

This is not a call to abandon equities. Far from it. Equities remain one of the most powerful tools for wealth-building over the long term. But the value lies not in isolated picks—it lies in *systematic exposure to productive, diversified assets over time.* The disciplined investor doesn't chase opportunities; they build a mechanism to *own progress* broadly and repeatedly. They understand that the market is a mechanism for transferring money from the impatient to the patient.

This brings us to rhythm—a concept too often overlooked in discussions of investing. Rhythm is not timing the market. It's choosing to engage with it regularly, regardless of timing. Pound-cost averaging, for instance, is a practical application of this principle. By investing fixed amounts on a set schedule—monthly, quarterly—you decouple your contributions from market volatility.

Sometimes you'll buy high. Sometimes you'll buy low. But over time, you reduce the risk of buying at a single bad moment and instead smooth your entry across cycles.

Rhythm also mitigates the emotional volatility that destroys wealth. It acts as a behavioural anchor, allowing you to step back from the noise and trust your process. This is no small feat. Studies in behavioural finance, from Daniel Kahneman to Meir Statman, have shown how emotional decision-making erodes returns. The average investor earns far less than the market average—not because the market is inaccessible, but because people sabotage themselves through overreaction. Rhythm immunises you against this. It gives you a pre-committed structure that outperforms your instincts.

This is particularly relevant for salaried professionals. You are not paid to be a full-time investor. Your comparative advantage lies in earning steadily and deploying capital efficiently, not in analysing balance sheets or reading market signals. In fact, the most powerful edge you have is *consistency of income*—a predictable inflow that allows you to invest rhythmically. This is not a limitation. It's a superpower—if used well.

Consider the results of real-world portfolios. The most successful long-term investors—those who retire comfortably, fund their children's education, or achieve financial independence—rarely cite a single investment that "made" their wealth. Instead, they describe a rhythm: a contribution schedule, a few low-cost index funds, and an unshakeable commitment to ignore panic. Their wealth is not a product of brilliance. It is a consequence of *systems*.

By contrast, those who treat the market as a casino often end up with scars. The 2021 retail investor boom in meme stocks like GameStop and AMC is a cautionary tale. Fueled by social media excitement and a desire to outsmart Wall Street, thousands of individuals poured money into stocks based on momentum, not fundamentals. A few exited early with profits. Many more were left holding plummeting shares. The psychological cost was high: anxiety, regret, and a diminished appetite for future investing. The lesson is clear—*when your strategy depends on being right, your margin for error collapses.*

Instead, imagine an investor who puts aside £500 every month into a diversified portfolio: global equities, some fixed income, perhaps a small allocation to real assets. They rebalance annually, not reactively. They increase contributions as income grows. They don't chase returns—they build towards them. Over time, market cycles become irrelevant. Volatility becomes background noise. The investor doesn't "beat" the market, nor do they need to. Their goal isn't excitement. It's sufficiency. Their power lies in the quiet compounding of consistent decisions.

There is also a deeper philosophical shift here. Chasing the magic stock pick treats investing as a game of *extraction.* Rhythm reframes it as a practice of *participation.* You don't need to know which company will dominate next decade's economy. You need to own enough of the economy, over enough time, for its progress to enrich you. This approach is not passive in the psychological sense—it's *deliberately restrained.* It reflects confidence in systems over speculation.

And rhythm scales. It allows you to optimise other parts of your life—career development, family, creativity—without being consumed by market vigilance. This isn't just an investing strategy. It's a quality of life strategy. It asks: *how much of your attention do you want to spend on markets, and how much on what markets allow you to do?*

Ultimately, the myth of the magic stock pick is not just bad investing—it's bad philosophy. It reinforces the idea that wealth is for the clever, the plugged-in, the privileged. Rhythm rebuts this. It says wealth is available to those who are patient, structured, and humble enough to admit they won't outsmart a trillion-dollar system. That insight alone frees you to focus on what *you* can control: your inputs, your pace, your systems.

Because in the end, successful investing is not about prediction. It's about *participation with consistency*. And the most powerful asset class of all may not be equities, bonds, or real estate—it's *your ability to act repeatedly on a plan, even when it's boring*. That is the beating heart of rhythm. That is how ordinary investors achieve extraordinary results.

Financial Gravity: Why Slow Wins

There's a persistent misconception in the modern imagination that wealth is made through speed—through agility, reactivity, timing, and bold bets. We've inherited this belief from a culture that venerates instant success: IPO windfalls, viral cryptocurrencies, overnight trading gains. But financial reality is rarely built on velocity. It is built on *duration*. And it doesn't reward the fastest thinker in the room—it rewards the one who can stay in the room the longest, doing the same small things well, over and over again. In this chapter, we reframe compounding not as magic, but as physics. Because that's what it is. It's not mythical. It's mechanical. It behaves with the reliability of gravity—and just like gravity, it is only visible to those who are still around long enough for it to take effect.

Compounding is often explained as exponential growth—a snowball rolling down a hill, growing larger as it accumulates. But this metaphor, while technically correct, is emotionally misleading. It suggests momentum starts immediately. In practice, compounding begins as *painfully slow*. The initial gains are modest—almost insultingly so. A few pounds of interest, barely worth noticing. For the impatient, this phase feels like stagnation. But what's actually happening beneath the surface is alignment: the system is beginning to turn in your favour, like gravity pulling a mass that's barely started moving. The longer you hold your position, the stronger that gravitational force becomes.

Consider this with a concrete example. Suppose two investors each invest £10,000 at a steady 7% annual return. One holds for 10 years, the other for 30. After 10 years, the first investor ends up with approximately £19,671. Respectable. But the second, who merely stayed put for three times longer, ends with over £76,000—nearly *four times* the result, with no additional input, no cleverness, and no market timing. Just presence. What changed wasn't the return—it was the *duration of exposure to financial gravity.*

This is the quiet superpower of compounding: its benefits don't increase linearly—they *accelerate* over time. It is a nonlinear phenomenon, governed more by time than talent. This makes it fundamentally different from most things in adult life, where effort and results are proportionate. If you work twice as hard, you usually get twice as much done. But in investing, doing more often yields less. Because the system doesn't reward busyness—it rewards *staying put.*

Why, then, do so few people experience this compounding effect in full? The answer lies not in intelligence but in behaviour. Most individuals interrupt the process before it gains strength. They exit the market during downturns, switch strategies when they feel behind, or delay starting altogether until "the time is right." Each of these actions weakens financial gravity. They introduce friction and disrupt momentum. And unlike a physical system, financial gravity isn't inevitable. It requires participation. You have to stay tethered to the force for it to pull you.

The finance industry does not help. In fact, much of its structure is designed to encourage motion, not stillness. Turnover drives transaction fees. Activity creates the illusion of control. If clients are doing something—buying, selling, reallocating—they feel engaged. But engagement is not synonymous with effectiveness. In truth, the best financial moves often feel *boring.* There is no daily drama to rebalancing a diversified portfolio annually. There is no rush of adrenaline in auto-investing into low-cost index funds. But these are the very behaviours that financial gravity rewards most consistently.

This is where behavioural psychology becomes critical. Our brains are poorly wired to appreciate compounding. We are short-term evaluators. We discount the future too heavily. We prefer immediacy over patience—even when we know, rationally, that patience pays more. Daniel Kahneman, in *Thinking, Fast and Slow*, explained this cognitive flaw as "present bias"—a hardwired tendency to favour smaller, immediate rewards over larger, delayed ones. In the context of investing, this bias causes us to overvalue short-term performance metrics and undervalue structural discipline.

But there is a counterforce: *systems.* Systems are behavioural scaffolds—structures that protect us from our worst instincts. By designing investing habits that function independently of mood, news, or market noise, we create a stable environment for financial gravity to operate. A standing order to invest a portion of your salary each month. A portfolio allocation that balances risk and return without frequent intervention. A scheduled review ritual, not driven by panic but by routine. These aren't advanced techniques. They're low-friction, high-fidelity behaviours that, once set in motion, resist disruption. *They keep you tethered to compounding's gravitational pull.*

There's also a moral dimension worth noting. Fast finance encourages individualism, secrecy, and zero-sum thinking. If you believe wealth comes from finding the next winner before anyone else, you naturally hoard information and view others as competitors. But compounding—true compounding—has no scarcity. Your success does not require someone else's failure. Everyone can participate in the market's long-term growth. The engine is collective, not competitive. This makes the philosophy of slow finance not only smarter, but *kinder.* It encourages cooperation, humility, and generosity—values strangely absent from most investment discourse.

From a historical perspective, some of the most enduring fortunes were not built on single breakthroughs but on multi-decade compounding. Warren Buffett's wealth famously illustrates this. Despite beginning his investing career as a teenager, over 90% of his net worth accumulated *after* his 60th birthday. The mathematical reason is simple: he's been investing for over 70 years. Buffett is often described as a genius stock picker—but his real edge is *time.* He understood financial gravity, trusted its pull, and resisted the urge to interfere with it.

So what does all of this mean for the everyday investor—especially the salaried professional who feels behind, busy, or uninformed? It means you don't need to be brilliant. You don't need to guess the next trend. You don't even need to be perfect. You just need to *be there.* Start. Automate. Stay. Let time do what it does best. Resist the temptation to outthink a system that rewards staying power. Understand that in this domain, *the reward doesn't go to the fastest, but to the most consistent.*

Slow doesn't mean passive. It means deliberate. And financial gravity doesn't require heroics—it requires patience. The irony is that the more you internalise this, the more effortless wealth-building becomes. Not because it's easy, but because you stop interrupting your own progress. You stop trying to bend the rules of physics and instead align with them. You stop sprinting and start orbiting.

That's what this chapter is about. Replacing noise with structure. Speed with duration. Impulse with rhythm. The real challenge is not understanding compounding. The challenge is *waiting for it to matter.* Financial gravity is slow to start, but once it accelerates, it becomes unstoppable—*as long as you stay tethered to the force pulling you forward.*

Automating Your Identity

The modern professional often views personal finance as a task list—budgets to draft, investments to review, subscriptions to cancel. These are seen as chores, maintenance items, always threatening to slide into neglect. The dominant metaphor is one of labour: something you must *do.* But the most effective approach to wealth-building is not based on activity, but on *architecture.* It doesn't rely on willpower, perfect timing, or bursts of discipline. It's built into the structure of your life. And this chapter begins with a radical premise: *automation isn't about laziness—it's about identity.* It's not merely a financial tactic; it's an act of self-definition. You don't automate your money so you can avoid responsibility—you automate so that *responsibility becomes automatic.*

Let's begin by considering how people typically try to improve their financial lives. They make resolutions. They download budgeting apps. They vow to "be better" with spending. But none of these interventions endure unless they're built on a behavioural infrastructure. If every good decision relies on you being in the right mood, having the time, or remembering what to do next, it's destined to fail. *This is not a personal weakness—it's a structural flaw.* Behavioural science has made this clear: the human brain is a poor executor of long-term plans when it operates on short-term energy. Habits, not intentions, run the show. And automation is the only reliable bridge between who you are today and the financially stable version of yourself you hope to become.

To understand the transformative power of automation, consider the idea of *defaults.* In behavioural economics, defaults are the settings people stick with in the absence of active choices. One of the most studied examples is retirement savings. In countries where employees are automatically enrolled in pension plans—with the option to opt out—participation rates skyrocket. Where the reverse is true—requiring workers to opt in—savings rates plummet. The implication is profound: people don't always choose what's best for them. They choose what's *easiest.* Or rather, they default to what has been made easiest. Therefore, *if you want better outcomes, you must design better defaults.*

Translating this insight to personal finance means constructing a life in which the default behaviour is wealth-building. That means your salary gets split the moment it hits your account—some to essentials, some to long-term investments, some to guilt-free spending. It means your bills get paid on time without intervention. It means your investments grow in the background, without demanding constant attention. Most crucially, it means that *who you are financially is not a function of how motivated you feel in any given month*. You've set the system; now the system sustains you.

This is not about surrendering agency. In fact, it's the opposite. Automation gives you more control—not by making more decisions, but by making *fewer better ones up front.* You decide once how much to invest. You decide once where your savings go. And then you let time and consistency do their work. What emerges is not a hands-off investor in the passive sense, but a highly strategic one. A person who has moved beyond reactive money management and into a mode of *quiet command.*

But automation goes deeper than mechanics. It begins to shape *how you see yourself.* Each automated decision signals something about your identity. If your investments happen automatically each month, you are no longer someone who "tries to invest"—you are *an investor.* If you've systematised debt repayment, you are not struggling to be responsible—you are someone who honours commitments. Over time, these actions compound not just financially, but psychologically. They create a feedback loop of self-trust. You begin to believe you are the kind of person who follows through, who makes intelligent decisions, who protects their future self without needing constant supervision.

This internal identity shift matters far more than any financial tactic. Because people act in accordance with who they believe they are. If you see yourself as financially erratic, you'll second-guess every investment. If you believe you're "not good with money," you'll delay decisions until you feel more prepared—which often means never. But if your systems are structured to reflect competence, clarity, and consistency, your self-perception will catch up to the reality you've engineered.

Let's be clear: automation is not a universal panacea. It won't make you immune to market downturns or protect you from every financial misstep. But it *does* provide a psychological buffer. When the market dips, you're less likely to panic-sell if your contributions are automated. When unexpected expenses arise, your emergency fund—automatically stocked—catches you. Automation doesn't eliminate uncertainty, but it gives you the resilience to respond instead of react.

There's also a philosophical dimension worth surfacing here. In a world that celebrates hyper-productivity and relentless optimisation, the idea of doing less—but doing it better—is quietly subversive. It challenges the cultural belief that success must be effortful at all times. Automation is a rejection of this myth. It says: *I don't need to be in constant motion to move forward.* It embodies a more elegant principle—*non-interventionist discipline.* You show discipline once, in how you design your systems. And then you let those systems express that discipline indefinitely.

This approach also has ethical implications. When your financial systems are strong, you make fewer decisions in a fog of stress. You avoid desperate moves. You reduce the cognitive load required to act in alignment with your values. For example, if charitable giving is automated, generosity becomes a steady presence in your life—not an afterthought when you feel guilty or flush. If investing is automatic, you're less susceptible to gambling on the latest meme stock because you feel behind. Automation, in this way, reinforces *integrity*—the alignment between your values and your actions, even when no one is watching.

Of course, automation must be designed thoughtfully. Systems that are poorly calibrated can ossify bad habits. If your auto-payments leave you in overdraft each month, you've automated stress, not stability. If your "set and forget" investments are in high-fee funds you never revisited, you've built inertia, not intelligence. The point is not to eliminate engagement altogether—it's to *elevate it.* You engage *once* at a higher level, then let the system carry the weight. Periodic reviews—not daily tinkering—become your role. You are no longer the labourer. You are the architect.

For the everyday investor, especially salaried professionals with limited time and energy, this model offers more than convenience. It offers peace. The kind of peace that doesn't come from knowing every detail, but from knowing the fundamentals are handled. It allows you to get on with your life—your relationships, your work, your leisure—without money becoming a constant psychological background noise. And that, arguably, is the highest return of all.

So, ask yourself: What are your current financial systems signalling about your identity? Are they designed by intention or by inertia? Do they reflect who you are—or who you were before you knew better?

The beauty of automation is that it doesn't require perfection. You don't need to optimise every variable or predict the future. You simply need to commit to a path that, if repeated consistently, will lead somewhere good. You don't have to be right all the time. You just have to stay in the game long enough for your identity and outcomes to align. And the best way to stay in the game? *Set it up so that even your default behaviour moves you forward.*

Because in the end, success is not about what you do occasionally when you're highly motivated. It's about what happens by default when you're not thinking about it at all. Automation, done right, ensures that *even your autopilot is moving you in the right direction.* That's not laziness. That's wisdom.

The Monthly Ritual

There's a quiet dignity in routine. In a world that worships spontaneity and disruption, routine is often misunderstood as dull or lifeless. But to those who understand systems thinking, ritual is a mark of mastery. It is structure with meaning. Repetition with intention. The most successful investors—those who build not just portfolios but financial peace—are rarely the loudest or the boldest. They are the ones who show up consistently, precisely because they've turned wealth-building into something sacred: a recurring, deliberate act of self-alignment. This subchapter introduces a concept at the heart of this book's philosophy: *the monthly ritual.* Not a spreadsheet sprint. Not a budgeting emergency. But a standing appointment with your financial self—where presence replaces pressure, and consistency outperforms brilliance.

Modern personal finance tends to oscillate between two extremes: frantic over-management and total neglect. On one end, the obsessive micro-manager tracks every penny, tweaks their allocations weekly, and compulsively watches the markets. On the other, the avoidant procrastinator touches their finances only when forced—typically under duress. Both styles are unsustainable. They burn out the individual or leave them vulnerable to chaos. The monthly ritual is an alternative to both: a stabilising force that requires only an hour, once a month, yet compounds in value over a lifetime. Not because it changes everything at once, but because it ensures nothing important is ever left unattended.

The concept draws from disciplines outside finance. In behavioural psychology, *ritual* is recognised not merely as habit, but as habit with symbolic intent. Rituals are repeated actions that reinforce identity. They invite reflection, structure, and emotional engagement. In religious or cultural contexts, rituals are used to mark transitions, honour commitments, and create meaning from repetition. Applied to money, this framing shifts our mindset. A monthly financial check-in is no longer a chore. It becomes a conversation between your present self and the future you're building. It is a space to measure alignment—not just metrics.

The monthly ritual can take many forms, but its structure is deceptively simple. First, it is calendared—fixed, not reactive. Second, it is limited in scope—focused only on key indicators and course corrections, not wholesale overhauls. Third, it is reflective, not purely transactional. You are not just checking numbers. You are checking *narrative.* Is your current financial trajectory congruent with your stated values? Are you still investing in what matters—both literally and metaphorically?

Consider what such a ritual might entail. A salaried professional sets aside the first Saturday of each month. They review their automated savings and investments. They scan their spending for anomalies, not obsessively, but curiously. They assess their discretionary budget: not with guilt, but with gratitude. Did their money reflect their values this month? Did they prioritise health, learning, connection? Or did their spending drift towards impulse and distraction? This isn't an exercise in punishment. It's a recalibration of intentionality. Over time, this ritual becomes not just a habit but a grounding practice—akin to a meditation, only with spreadsheets instead of silence.

Critically, this monthly check-in is also where *adjustments are made without panic*. Markets fluctuate. Expenses spike. Plans evolve. But because the ritual is frequent and steady, no single disruption becomes catastrophic. A rough month does not require heroic intervention. It simply requires showing up. Think of it as a form of *emotional amortisation*—spreading your financial attention evenly across time so it never becomes overwhelming. The cost of inaction is highest when problems accumulate unnoticed. The monthly ritual ensures nothing festers.

There's also a psychological elegance to anchoring money habits to the calendar. Humans thrive on rhythm. Circadian rhythms govern our sleep. Seasons shape our mood. Rituals like the monthly financial check-in provide a meta-rhythm—a cadence of clarity within the often-chaotic tempo of adult life. By linking financial awareness to a specific day each month, we reduce mental clutter. You no longer have to carry financial questions in your head all the time: *Can I afford this? Should I invest now? Am I saving enough?* The ritual holds those questions for you—and answers them, quietly and consistently, in due time.

Furthermore, there is deep power in *making your finances visible*. Too often, we outsource our financial reality to apps and dashboards, thinking the data alone will keep us engaged. But observation does not equal ownership. The monthly ritual invites you to *see yourself in your money*. Not through vanity metrics or net-worth comparisons, but through the lens of alignment: does this life reflect what you say you want? If it doesn't, you now have a structure for adjustment—not a crisis, not a revolution, just a series of modest corrections.

This idea of rhythm over risk, which anchors the entire chapter, is beautifully embodied in the ritual. While much of investing culture is addicted to the thrill of prediction—trying to guess the next hot stock, time the next dip, or beat the market—the ritualist investor plays a different game. One that doesn't rely on superior intelligence, but superior *reliability*. The monthly ritual acts like a compounding behaviour. It's the financial equivalent of brushing your teeth—not glamorous, not intellectually demanding, but transformative over time. You don't need to be a genius to succeed. You just need to *not disappear* from your financial life for months at a time.

It's important to say this clearly: *rituals are not rigid*. A good monthly ritual evolves with your life stage. Early in your career, it may focus on debt management and habit formation. Later, it may centre around investment rebalancing, tax efficiency, or legacy planning. The structure stays, but the content shifts. This flexibility is what makes it sustainable. You are not locked into a script. You are engaging in a living dialogue with your goals, your values, and your resources.

To those who find this overly reflective or abstract, consider this: the biggest financial regrets people carry into later life are not mistakes of analysis, but mistakes of alignment. They worked too long in a role that drained them. They postponed joy because it didn't feel "responsible." They chased returns but sacrificed time. The monthly ritual is an antidote to that drift. It slows you down just long enough to ask: *Is this path leading somewhere I'll be proud to arrive?*

Finally, we must acknowledge the emotional architecture of wealth. Financial wellbeing is not just about numbers. It's about coherence—between your money, your mind, and your meaning. The monthly ritual is where that coherence is built. Quietly.

Repetitively. With reverence for the fact that money, when managed with awareness, becomes a tool not just for survival, but for sovereignty.

So the question is not whether you have the time to check in with your finances. The question is whether you can afford not to. In a system that profits from your distraction, presence is a radical act. And ritual is how presence becomes practice. One month at a time.

Chapter 4
Alignment Over Ambition

There's a moment—quiet, almost imperceptible—in every professional's financial life when the question begins to shift. Not loudly, not with fanfare. But unmistakably. It moves from "How much can I earn?" to something subtler, and far more consequential: "What am I building toward—and why?" This turning point rarely announces itself. And yet, it changes everything. For it is here that wealth ceases to be a numbers game and begins to take shape as a vehicle for meaning. Chapter 4 is about that turning. The slow but critical transition from raw ambition to deliberate alignment. From relentless more to intentional enough.

For decades, the dominant blueprint for personal finance has been built on accumulation. More salary. More assets. More returns. More revenue streams. More leverage. And while there's no denying the role of growth, unexamined ambition can harden into a kind of trap. It becomes less a plan and more a reflex. Success, in this model, isn't chosen—it's chased. No surprise, then, that many high-achieving professionals report feeling anxious, adrift, or curiously empty, even as their financial portfolios swell. Because without a sense of internal direction, external gain simply extends the treadmill. Not the finish line.

This chapter makes a case—one that runs counter to much of the noise out there—that sustainable wealth isn't born from doing more. It comes from doing what matters, and doing it well. Repeatedly. Letting go of the distractions masquerading as progress. It's not intensity that builds lasting prosperity. It's integrity. Of choices. Of systems. Of identity.

Let's begin with a straightforward, if slightly uncomfortable truth: most people don't actually possess a clear financial vision. What they have instead are hand-me-down aspirations. Scripts, really—cobbled together from family expectations, media portrayals, peer benchmarks. These inherited narratives solidify over time into what look like goals: own a home by 35, beat the market, retire early, crack a seven-figure net worth. But ask why those markers matter, and the answers often falter. Not because people are thoughtless. But because many of those ambitions aren't truly theirs. They're ambient. Unquestioned. And when your financial strategy is built on ambient goals, you're not charting a course—you're floating.

What's needed is not more hustle, but alignment. Not as a pursuit of flawlessness, but as a commitment to coherence. Alignment means your financial behaviours—how you spend, save, invest, and earn—are consistent with your personal understanding of what a good life entails. It asks not only if you're winning, but whether what you're winning at actually matters. In that congruence, anxiety begins to loosen its grip, and money starts to become not just a resource, but a mirror.

To bring this into practice, the chapter offers three keystone ideas—tools, really—for building a financial life around purpose, rather than performance.

First: *The Life Timeline Exercise*. Much of the financial advice that floods the internet assumes a strangely narrow profile: the reader is 35, upwardly mobile, single, probably childless, likely in tech. This isn't just reductive—it's useless for anyone living outside that frame. The Life Timeline asks you to sketch the next 20 to 40 years of your life, not in financial terms, but in life terms. Milestones. Transitions. Responsibilities. Aspirations. Children. Career pivots. Sabbaticals. Illness. Ageing parents. Grief. Joy. These are not side notes to your financial planning—they are the theatre in which your financial decisions play out.

Once you create that map, financial decisions stop floating in the abstract. They land. You stop asking whether an investment looks good in isolation and begin asking whether it supports the phase of life you're actually entering. That high-interest account becomes less important than ensuring you've built enough runway for unpaid caregiving. That idea of a second property might give way to the need for creative autonomy or flexibility. Suddenly, your idea of security morphs—because now it's being defined not by market metrics, but by real life.

Second: *Saying No to 'More'.* We live in an economy—and a culture—that glorifies expansion. Every swipe reveals a new investing platform, each podcast promises a trick you're not yet using, and your colleagues' LinkedIn updates suggest there's always another income stream you've not pursued. The implication is subtle, but relentless: if you're not doing everything, you're falling behind.

But complexity is not synonymous with competence. More often than not, it's the enemy of clarity. This chapter invites you to practise financial subtraction—not as an aesthetic gesture, but as a strategic act. Strip away the redundant accounts. The contradictory goals. The financial products you barely understand but felt pressured to own. This is not minimalism for the sake of neatness. It's minimalism for the sake of precision.

There's a deeper layer here too—an emotional one. Many people overbuild their financial architecture in an attempt to soothe anxiety. They equate volume with security: the more spreadsheets, apps, and backups, the safer they'll feel. But that's a mirage. Because true security doesn't arise from busyness—it comes from coherence. A simplified system, if it's truly aligned, will outperform a tangled one—both in return and in emotional sustainability.

Third: *The Identity Filter.* Perhaps the boldest claim in this chapter is this: every financial choice you make is a quiet act of self-definition. Not merely a transaction, but a vote for the kind of person you're becoming. Buy impulsively, and you reinforce the story that money is a salve for discomfort. Automate your savings, and you reinforce the identity of someone who protects their future freedom. Decline an opportunity misaligned with your values, and you teach yourself—deeply—that your wealth is anchored in integrity, not performance.

This chapter proposes that we approach money identity-first, rather than tactic-first. Before adopting any new tool, budget, or investment strategy, ask: "Does this reflect who I'm becoming?" That question, deceptively simple, has the power to change the tone of your entire financial life. Because in the end, money is not just a tool—it's a mirror. It reflects what you delay, what you justify, what you pursue, and what you're willing to protect.

Your portfolio, then, is not just a collection of assets. It's a portrait. Your calendar, a record of priorities. Your spending—a diary of belief. The more each of these aligns with your chosen identity, the less resistance you face. Friction fades. Flow emerges.

Throughout the chapter, you'll be guided through exercises, prompts, and frameworks that turn these ideas into practical action. But the first step is conceptual: you are not here to build the largest financial empire you can muster. You're here to build the right life. One that is funded by a smart, resilient, value-aligned financial system.

To do that, you'll need to trust your clarity over the crowd. Your inner compass over the algorithm. And to value internal coherence over external applause.

This chapter is not a rallying cry for playing the existing game more aggressively. It's an invitation to step outside it. To play a different game entirely—one where your wealth system is not a monument to comparison, but a reflection of your actual life. Lived more freely. With more texture. And, dare one say it, more soul.

Welcome to alignment. It may not dazzle like ambition, but it endures. And in the long arc of a meaningful life, that is what matters most.

The Wealth Type Compass

One of the most underexamined elements in personal finance is *temperament.* Not risk tolerance, which is often reduced to a questionnaire, but the deeper psychological framework that governs what people actually want from money—and how they behave when they have it. For all the advice about optimal asset allocation and compound interest, few professionals are ever asked the foundational question: *What kind of wealth are you really trying to build?*

Most assume the answer is obvious—"financial independence" or "more security." But beneath those catch-all phrases lie distinct orientations toward money, each shaped by experience, fear, aspiration, and identity. Ignoring these orientations is not harmless. It leads to the adoption of financial strategies that contradict personality, values, or life goals. The result is cognitive dissonance: someone saving aggressively but resenting every dollar deferred, or someone investing in high-growth assets while losing sleep over volatility. The mismatch doesn't just cause discomfort—it sabotages outcomes.

This subchapter introduces *The Wealth Type Compass*, a practical framework for understanding and aligning your financial decisions with your dominant wealth style. It proposes that most professionals fall broadly into one of three archetypes: the **Security-Seeker**, the **Freedom-Chaser**, or the **Legacy-Builder**. Each type has valid motivations, distinct anxieties, and different tolerances for uncertainty and trade-offs. Identifying your type isn't a gimmick—it's a form of strategic clarity. Once you understand the psychological posture from which you make financial decisions, you can stop copying other people's strategies and start refining your own.

The Security-Seeker views money as insulation. The primary goal is protection—against emergencies, instability, loss of income, or the unpredictable demands of life. For this type, a high savings rate isn't just smart; it's emotionally essential. Security-Seekers often favour low-volatility investments, emergency funds, insurance policies, and redundancy in their financial systems. They are often risk-averse not out of ignorance but from lived experience: job loss, family instability, or generational financial trauma.

The advantage of this orientation is resilience. Security-Seeking investors are often better prepared for economic shocks and less likely to be rattled by market fluctuations. But the downside can be stagnation. An excessive focus on safety can result in under-investing, over-saving, or hoarding cash out of fear—leading to slow capital growth and a creeping sense of missed opportunity. For the Security-Seeker, the challenge is learning to *trust time and strategy*, not just buffers and contingency plans.

The Freedom-Chaser sees money as a vehicle for autonomy. Their metric is not net worth, but optionality—how many choices they can buy back from the world. This orientation thrives on flexibility: geographic mobility, career shifts, sabbaticals, early retirement. For the Freedom-Chaser, wealth is meaningful to the extent that it enables independence from structures that feel confining.

This type often embraces more aggressive investment strategies: equity-heavy portfolios, side businesses, non-traditional assets. Their biggest risk is not volatility, but *boredom*. They are allergic to systems that feel too rigid or slow-moving. While this energy can drive creative risk-taking and rapid growth, it can also cause churn: over-optimisation, frequent strategy changes, and burnout from perpetual goalpost-shifting. For the Freedom-Chaser, alignment requires learning to distinguish between freedom and *avoidance*—and to recognise that long-term systems often produce the freedom they seek more reliably than constant improvisation.

The Legacy-Builder is guided by a multi-generational lens. They are less concerned with immediate returns and more invested in creating lasting impact—whether through family wealth, philanthropy, mentorship, or societal contribution. Legacy-Builders often think in decades, not quarters. They prioritise investments in property, trusts, businesses, or education that can outlast them. Their financial decisions are marked by deliberation, structure, and stewardship.

The strength of this type is long-term orientation. Legacy-Builders are often the most disciplined investors, less swayed by short-term trends or cultural FOMO. But their challenge is sometimes emotional detachment: focusing so intently on the future that they underprioritise the present. In some cases, they overextend themselves financially to "leave something behind," without first ensuring that what they're building is sustainable or aligned with those they hope to benefit. For Legacy-Builders, the task is to *balance impact with presence*—to build something enduring without deferring their entire life in the process.

These archetypes are not fixed categories; they are tendencies. Most people contain aspects of all three, and their dominant wealth type can shift over time—particularly through life transitions such as parenthood, health changes, career pivots, or ageing. What matters is not fitting into a label, but using the compass as a lens: *Are your current financial strategies consistent with your core orientation? Or are you unconsciously adopting tactics that belong to someone else's map?*

To illustrate this, consider three professionals earning the same salary. One puts 40% into fixed deposits and feels calm, even if the returns are modest. Another invests aggressively in global ETFs and spends freely on travel, citing a plan to work only ten more years. The third lives frugally, channels surplus income into a family trust, and volunteers every weekend at a literacy foundation. Technically, all three are "saving and investing." But functionally, they are building radically different lives—because they are driven by radically different wealth types.

The finance industry rarely accounts for this. Its default is to flatten everyone into the same model—maximise returns, minimise tax, automate contributions. But financial advice that ignores temperament is like fitness advice that ignores body type: it may work in theory, but it won't be sustainable. Behavioural finance, in fact, shows that alignment between financial strategy and personal values is one of the most predictive indicators of long-term success—not just in net worth, but in mental health, confidence, and resilience during downturns.

There is also a moral dimension to this compass. It nudges us to move beyond comparative metrics—outperforming benchmarks or peers—and toward intentionality. The question is no longer *Am I doing well compared to others?* but *Am I living in accordance with what matters most to me?* Wealth, when reframed this way, becomes a practice of congruence, not conquest.

As this chapter unfolds, readers will be invited to map their own wealth type—not through rigid classification, but through reflective prompts that clarify what they are optimising for. They'll be encouraged to audit their current strategies and identify misalignments. Does your budgeting method support your need for freedom—or does it penalise spontaneity? Does your investment plan reflect a long-term horizon—or is it driven by short-term fear?

More importantly, this section reinforces the book's central philosophy: *wealth is not just a numerical outcome, but a behavioural pattern rooted in personal truth.* When that truth is obscured—by noise, by mimicry, by insecurity—financial progress becomes erratic. But when that truth is clarified, strategy becomes effortless. You no longer need to be convinced to act—you are compelled, because the strategy makes emotional and logical sense.

The Wealth Type Compass does not tell you where to go. It helps you see where you are—and where you would travel most honestly and sustainably from there.

Because ultimately, the goal is not to build *the perfect portfolio*—but to build *the right life*, with money as a mirror, not a master.

Let that be your compass.

The Life Timeline Exercise

Most people plan their finances as if life were a straight road—linear, predictable, and governed by a single metric: accumulation. More is better, sooner is ideal, and faster is admired. But real life, unlike the spreadsheets and retirement calculators that presume constancy, unfolds in phases. It expands and contracts. It speeds up unexpectedly and stalls without notice. Your needs, values, obligations, and opportunities change not just over decades, but often within a matter of years. And yet, the vast majority of financial advice treats a 29-year-old in the early stages of her career the same as a 39-year-old juggling childcare and ageing parents, or a 59-year-old executive contemplating an exit not for money, but meaning.

This dissonance is not just impractical—it's dangerous. When financial decisions are made in abstraction from *life stages*, they often lead to either overreaching or underliving. That's why this subchapter introduces what may be one of the most important tools in modern personal finance: *The Life Timeline Exercise.*

This isn't a budgeting trick or retirement projection. It's a practical and philosophical mapping exercise that invites you to align your financial strategy with the actual arc of your life. Not the generic arc that models assume, but your real, textured, evolving reality—with its transitions, aspirations, and thresholds. This tool is about *contextual intelligence*—the ability to match decisions not to the market's cycles, but to your own.

At its core, the Life Timeline is a visual framework. You draw a horizontal line, divided into years or five-year blocks, stretching from your current age to around 90 or 100—depending on how long you expect (or hope) to live. Then, onto this timeline, you begin to plot key life phases and anticipated transitions. Not just the financial ones like "pay off mortgage" or "retire at 60," but the emotional and personal ones as well: when you expect to have children, switch careers, relocate, care for parents, downsize, or pursue a dream that may not pay for itself—like writing a book or starting a charity.

You might label sections: **Foundation Years (20–35)**, **Expansion Years (35–50)**, **Recalibration Years (50–65)**, and **Harvest Years (65+)**. These aren't fixed categories, but prompts. They help you shift from asking *"How much should I save or invest this year?"* to *"What is this phase of life asking of me—and what is money's role in helping me meet it?"*

Let's take a concrete example. Priya is 42. She has two children in school, a demanding but well-paid job in healthcare, and a mortgage that stretches her budget just enough to prevent breathing room, but not enough to provoke action. Like many professionals, she is defaulting to the conventional strategy: maximise retirement contributions, pay down the mortgage, hold off on any big shifts until "things calm down."

But when she maps her Life Timeline, she sees something new. Her parents are entering a phase of increased dependency. Her children will likely need the most time and money in the next 8 to 10 years—tuition, extracurriculars, mentoring. Meanwhile, her job, while financially rewarding, leaves her drained and absent from the very years that matter most to her family. The question the timeline raises is not just *can I afford to make a career shift?*, but *can I afford not to?* Suddenly, she begins to consider not how to maximise wealth indefinitely, but how to *reconfigure wealth for this season.*

That's the power of visualising life as a timeline rather than a target. It puts pressure on *prioritisation*—and relieves pressure from arbitrary norms.

This model also helps correct one of the most harmful biases in financial behaviour: *hyper-accumulation syndrome.* Many professionals believe the safest path is to hoard aggressively in their 30s and 40s, with the hope that "later" will be more flexible. But life doesn't always comply. Deferred dreams can calcify into regrets. Health, relationships, and creative aspirations don't always survive postponement. The Life Timeline Exercise reintroduces a long-lost idea in modern financial thinking: *sequencing.* That is, aligning capital deployment with the tempo of living—using money at the *right time*, not just the right amount.

It also adds granularity to risk tolerance. Instead of asking, "Am I a risk-averse or risk-tolerant investor?", the question becomes, "*In this life phase, where am I willing to stretch—and where do I need certainty?*" A 45-year-old preparing for a sabbatical might accept lower returns for liquidity. A 28-year-old with no dependents might prioritise long-horizon equities over buying property. Context drives clarity.

Psychologically, the exercise reduces the anxiety of "doing it all at once." When you see the decades stretched out before you, you realise you don't need to optimise for everything in the same year. You can pace yourself. You can say, *"This is my decade for growth."* Or, *"This is my decade for restoration."* The market may favour acceleration, but your life may require restraint. Knowing the difference is liberation.

It's also a diagnostic tool for overcommitment. If you find yourself stacking too many ambitious goals into one narrow band of years—start a company, buy a house, raise children, travel extensively, retire early—it becomes clear that the issue isn't motivation, but stacking. That visual dissonance helps you course-correct *before* burnout sets in. It invites you to subtract goals not because you've failed, but because you've become strategic.

What makes this exercise especially powerful is its invitation to revisit it annually. Each year, you don't just update your net worth—you update your *narrative.* Are your assumptions still valid? Has your sense of priority shifted? Has a new opportunity emerged? As your life evolves, your timeline becomes a living document—part journal, part strategy map.

Importantly, the Life Timeline Exercise is not an argument against ambition. It's an argument for *aligned ambition.* It doesn't tell you to downscale your dreams. It asks you to place them where they belong—so that your pursuit of financial independence doesn't rob you of emotional presence, and your desire for future comfort doesn't strip meaning from the present.

It also reinforces the book's central thesis: *money is not just an external tool, but an internal operating system.* The decisions you make about investing, saving, and spending are always in conversation with your identity, your timing, and your relationships. The more consciously you locate yourself in time, the more wisely you allocate your resources.

To that end, the Life Timeline is not merely a personal planning tool. It's a lens for justice, empathy, and community. When used in families, couples, or teams, it prompts shared understanding. Partners can see why one person is focused on stability while the other is itching for change. Children can see why financial choices shift across seasons. Colleagues can plan sabbaticals and transitions with greater foresight and less resentment. When we stop treating life stages as private struggles and start mapping them collectively, we create environments where financial decisions are not judged, but contextualised.

In a world saturated with advice about "beating the market," this exercise offers a more enduring imperative: *learn to listen to your life.* That doesn't mean abandoning metrics or forsaking growth. It means letting your numbers serve your seasons—not the other way around.

And perhaps the most radical insight the Life Timeline gives us is this: financial wisdom is less about foresight, and more about *fit.* The best financial decision is not the one with the highest yield, but the one that best fits the rhythm of your life *right now.*

Draw your line. Map your seasons. Decide accordingly. Not because you're settling—but because you're aligning. And alignment, not ambition alone, is what sustains prosperity across decades.

Saying No to 'More'

Exploring the power of subtraction in personal finance

The default impulse in most modern financial thinking is expansion. Earn more. Invest more. Optimise more. Learn more tactics, acquire more tools, chase more returns. From self-help literature to fintech platforms, the message is clear: success is additive. If you're not where you want to be financially, it's because you haven't done enough—yet.

But what if that premise is fundamentally flawed? What if the greatest financial breakthroughs come not from doing more, but from *doing less—but better*? What if the real leverage lies not in accumulation, but in subtraction?

This subchapter introduces a contrarian yet deeply liberating idea: the financial equivalent of *strategic quitting*. Saying no to behaviours, systems, and beliefs that no longer serve your life's direction can often produce more clarity, consistency, and compounding benefit than any new tactic. It's the logic of subtraction as strategy. And for professionals caught in the spiral of ambition, complexity, and optimisation fatigue, it may be the most important mindset shift they'll make.

The economic worldview we inherit—particularly in high-performance cultures—is built on escalation. More is not just preferred; it's moralised. To step off the treadmill, even briefly, feels like regression. We mistake activity for progress. The result is a finance culture obsessed with *inputs*—new stocks, new funds, new products, new platforms—while ignoring the inefficiencies introduced by mental clutter, time fragmentation, and behavioural drag.

Consider this: most professionals already have the *technical* means to build wealth. They know how to invest in a basic index fund. They understand, at least abstractly, the benefits of diversification and compounding. But knowledge doesn't translate into behaviour. Instead, they are paralysed by too many options, distracted by media noise, and exhausted by the emotional toll of decision fatigue. The problem is not ignorance—it's overload.

This is where the discipline of subtraction reveals its edge. By deliberately pruning habits, tools, and even goals, the Everyday Investor can regain traction. Wealth building ceases to be a chaotic sprint and becomes something quieter: rhythm, direction, and a renewed sense of mental spaciousness.

Let's ground this with a few concrete examples.

Take *portfolio sprawl.* Many middle-income investors, in the hope of diversification, accumulate a messy mix of assets: legacy mutual funds, employer-sponsored pensions, ETFs from a robo-adviser, a few speculative crypto bets, and halfhearted real estate ambitions. What they've really built is a *museum of strategies*—a timeline of experiments, rather than a coherent architecture. Every additional account or asset class creates new maintenance overhead: more logins, more tax implications, more micro-decisions. The drag is invisible but real. Streamlining down to a well-balanced, low-cost portfolio—executed with consistency—often outperforms both financially and emotionally. But it requires *the courage to simplify*.

Or consider the professional who says yes to every income opportunity: side gigs, freelancing, weekend consulting, and endless upskilling courses. From the outside, they appear "motivated." But inside, they feel scattered, burnt out, and unable to focus on the high-leverage moves that would actually transform their financial trajectory—like building a single, automated investment system or negotiating a better full-time salary. The paradox of hustle is this: *more motion can lead to less movement.* By saying no to unnecessary exertion, they open space for deliberate design.

The principle also applies to consumer behaviour. Financial freedom is not just a function of how much you earn or save, but of *how many dependencies you create.* Each recurring subscription, debt obligation, or lifestyle upgrade reduces your future optionality. The accumulation of fixed costs becomes a psychological prison—one disguised as modern convenience. Saying no to "just one more" recurring expense is not about denial; it's about protecting your future agency.

Philosophically, subtraction connects to an ancient idea across Stoic, Buddhist, and minimalist traditions: that discipline is freedom, and that restraint is not the enemy of abundance, but its source. Modern behavioural science echoes this in the concept of *addition bias.* Studies show that when confronted with problems, people tend to default to additive solutions, even when subtraction is more efficient. Whether redesigning a Lego model or adjusting a financial plan, we instinctively reach for more—because it feels productive. Yet real mastery often begins with asking, *What can I remove?*

Saying no also forces identity clarity. Every financial choice contains an embedded story about who you believe you are and what future you're preparing for. When you stop mimicking the financial behaviours of peers or influencers, and instead strip back your actions to what is *essentially you*, your financial system becomes an extension of your values, not a performance for someone else's metrics.

This has enormous emotional payoff. Subtraction lowers cognitive load. It enhances focus. It reduces the background stress that comes from managing a constantly expanding complexity stack. And crucially, it protects consistency. One of the most underrated virtues in investing isn't intelligence—it's endurance. A simplified system is easier to stick with across life's inevitable volatility. If more complexity increases the risk of abandonment, then subtraction is not just aesthetic—it's survival.

In fact, many of history's most successful investors practised this principle. Warren Buffett has famously said that his success is due more to saying *no* than to saying *yes*. Charlie Munger calls the ability to *avoid stupidity* more valuable than the ability to chase brilliance. Legendary hedge fund manager Ray Dalio built one of the most profitable portfolios in history using a surprisingly lean mix of asset classes—not by layering endlessly, but by balancing intelligently.

At a personal level, subtraction can also restore financial intimacy. In a culture obsessed with spreadsheets and projections, it's easy to lose touch with the *felt experience* of money—how it moves through your life, shapes your moods, or determines your sense of safety. When you strip away the excess, you create room to feel again. To notice when a certain expense brings joy versus when it numbs. To observe when an investment aligns with your season of life versus when it simply follows the trend.

In practical terms, here are a few questions that help initiate the subtraction process:

What recurring financial decisions drain your energy but add little value?

Which accounts, tools, or platforms could be consolidated without loss?

What behaviours or purchases have become automatic but no longer serve a purpose?

Which financial goals are inherited from someone else's blueprint?

What complexity are you tolerating because simplicity feels too unfamiliar?

This is not a call for austerity. It's a call for clarity. Saying no to "more" does not mean settling for less—it means *choosing better.* It means recognising that *enough* is not a compromise, but a strategy. That every yes carries a hidden cost. That silence, whitespace, and uncommitted capital are not wasted—they are reserves of future opportunity.

When we stop compulsively adding, we begin to design. Not just portfolios, but lives. Lives that are responsive, resilient, and rooted. Financial subtraction is not the opposite of growth. It's what allows growth to be sustainable.

Let the next chapter be built not by what you acquire—but by what you abandon.

The Identity Filter

Why clarity about who you're becoming matters more than what you're chasing

Financial advice is often backward-facing. It looks at spreadsheets, historical returns, and current net worth as if these artefacts are sufficient to tell you what to do next. Goals, when discussed, are typically external and measurable: buy a house, retire early, hit a round number in your portfolio. Yet these targets, however motivating on the surface, often yield diminishing returns in clarity over time. Why? Because they're rooted in *achievement*, not *alignment.*

This chapter explores a foundational reframing: *the most reliable compass in personal finance is not your goals—it's your identity.* Not what you want to accumulate, but who you want to become.

That distinction is more than philosophical. It is strategic. Decisions made through the lens of identity tend to be more consistent, coherent, and sustainable. Goals can shift, markets can surprise, and tactics can age. But if you know who you are becoming, your financial decisions begin to harmonise—even when external conditions don't.

Most professionals don't suffer from lack of ambition. They suffer from *misaligned ambition.* They optimise for the loudest metric, not the truest one. They chase strategies that work *in theory*, but that quietly undermine the person they are trying to be.

This is where the **Identity Filter** becomes essential—not as a concept, but as a practice. It's the discipline of holding each decision against a single question: *Does this align with the person I'm actively becoming?*

Let's explore why this is so powerful—and so rare.

The tyranny of disjointed tactics

Modern finance culture encourages fragmentation. You might be told to invest like Warren Buffett, hustle like a startup founder, consume like an influencer, save like a minimalist, and plan like a retiree—all in the same week. These scripts are not wrong in isolation. But together, they often produce incoherence. You're left with a life that feels overleveraged in some places and underfed in others.

What's missing is integration.

The Identity Filter restores integration by *forcing coherence between your actions and your narrative.* It asks not just, *'What are you doing?'*, but *'Why are you doing it that way?'*, *'What kind of person does this behaviour reinforce?'* and *'Will this version of you be proud of that path ten years from now?'*

These are not abstract reflections. They are concrete design tools. Used correctly, they reveal hidden incompatibilities between your values and your portfolio. And in the long run, *alignment is a better hedge against regret than performance ever will be.*

Identity as a decision framework

Let's take a real-world example. Suppose you're considering whether to invest in a friend's high-risk startup. Traditional financial questions might include:

What's the expected ROI?

How liquid is the investment?

How does this fit into your overall asset allocation?

All valid. But now add an identity-based question:

Would the person I want to become say yes to this?

That one question often reframes the decision entirely.

Maybe you're someone cultivating a calmer, more spacious relationship with money. Maybe your next chapter is about stability, not excitement. If so, then even a "smart" investment may be *wrong for you.* Not because it's a bad opportunity—but because it contradicts your intended identity.

Inversely, someone else may say yes to the same investment, not because they're chasing wealth, but because they're consciously stepping into an identity of *builder*, *risk-taker*, or *patron of innovation.* The same tactic can be self-betrayal or self-expression—depending entirely on whose story it's part of.

This is the underappreciated genius of identity-driven finance: it is self-protective and self-reinforcing at the same time.

The fallacy of achievement without selfhood

Too often, goal-setting in finance begins with external benchmarking. People ask what's "normal" for their income bracket, age, or peer group. The result is a blueprint stitched together from borrowed values. Over time, this creates a subtle drift: wealth grows, but meaning fades.

This is why so many mid-career professionals feel financially competent but existentially anaemic. They've achieved, but not aligned.

The solution is not to abandon goals—but to root them in identity. Instead of asking *'What do I want?"*, ask:

'What kind of person am I becoming?"

'What financial choices reinforce that identity on a regular basis?"

'What behaviours erode it, even if they appear rational on paper?"

These questions do not guarantee immediate clarity. But they reliably strip away the noise. Over time, they build what psychology calls *identity-congruent habits*—behaviours that reinforce your sense of self and are therefore far easier to sustain.

Identity filtering and decision friction

Every financial system introduces a certain kind of friction: decision friction (too many choices), moral friction (doing things you feel ethically uneasy about), or emotional friction (decisions that drain you). The Identity Filter acts as a friction minimiser. It reduces the need for deliberation by pre-aligning your rules with your deeper self.

In effect, identity becomes a form of *pre-committed design*. You don't have to decide whether to overspend during a salary spike if you've already decided that your identity is "a person who invests steadily, regardless of income fluctuation." You don't have to debate whether to optimise taxes to the extreme if your identity is "someone who values simplicity over maximum extraction."

This doesn't mean you become rigid or blind to opportunity. It means your starting point is internal coherence—not external noise.

What kind of investor are you becoming?

Let's bring this to the Everyday Investor. Many readers of this book are salaried professionals who want to build wealth without turning investing into a second job. For them, the Identity Filter might look like:

"I am the kind of person who builds wealth quietly and sustainably."

"I value freedom over prestige."

"I don't chase financial fads; I design financial systems."

"I don't sacrifice today's mental health for tomorrow's imagined wealth."

Each of these identities suggests not only certain behaviours (automated investing, long-term thinking, minimal account complexity) but also certain *omissions*—like ignoring media hype, avoiding unnecessary leverage, and saying no to overly complex financial products.

What's more, identity-based decision making resists self-sabotage. People don't fail to invest because they lack knowledge. They fail because they forget *who they're doing it for*. Identity keeps the vision alive—even when the numbers fluctuate.

Identity is not fixed—it's forged

One final note: identity is not a static label. It's a narrative you evolve through practice. You *become* someone who values discipline by taking disciplined actions. You *become* a strategic investor by making clear, repeated financial choices that align with that archetype.

And the beauty is, you don't need anyone's permission to start. Identity-based design begins wherever you are. It doesn't ask what degrees you have, what mistakes you've made, or how late you're starting. It simply asks: *What kind of person are you becoming now?*

Once that answer is clear, every financial decision becomes a lever—either moving you closer to that person or pulling you further away.

Choose accordingly.

Chapter 5
Simplicity as a Superpower

Complexity, for most people, doesn't signal sophistication. More often, it's what remains after decisions have been postponed, advice swallowed without scrutiny, and systems stacked one atop another with no real cohesion. What starts off as initiative—ambition, even—tends to calcify into clutter. A web of apps, spreadsheets, habits, half-formed plans. And slowly, that clutter turns corrosive. It weighs on attention, muddies judgement, and chips away at confidence. What felt like momentum morphs into mental noise.

This chapter invites a different lens: that simplicity is not a compromise but a design choice—and more than that, a quiet act of rebellion. In a financial culture obsessed with scale, with options and dashboards and marginal gains, choosing simplicity becomes not just a strategy but a stance. A refusal to mistake complication for competence.

We've been subtly trained to admire complexity. To see it as evidence of intellect. The more tabs you keep open—literally and metaphorically—the more serious you must be. But in practice, complexity is often a mask. A cover for uncertainty. An elaborate ritual disguising the absence of conviction. The sprawling budget template, the ten overlapping accounts, the relentless tracking—all of it can leave you further from clarity, not closer. Complexity, it turns out, does not reward insight. It buries it.

Simplicity, on the other hand, is not a dilution. It's a distillation. A stripping away of the non-essential so the essential can actually breathe. And there's a kind of power in that. Simplicity accelerates decisions. It reduces the friction of re-entry—because let's be honest, financial plans are rarely executed in perfect sequence. We drift, we pause, life interrupts. A simple system doesn't punish you for that. It welcomes you back without drama.

There's something else simplicity does, too. It fosters a kind of self-trust. The fewer levers you need to pull, the more confident you become in pulling them. The more often you act from clarity, the less tempted you are by novelty for novelty's sake. And when setbacks come—as they inevitably do—you recover faster. You know where to look. You know what matters. There's no fog of contingency to wade through.

It's important to say here: this isn't a plea for dumbing things down. Quite the opposite. It's a call to elevate—to raise the bar for what your financial life should feel like. Simplicity doesn't mean naivety. It means discernment. You're not rejecting tools. You're rejecting tool worship. You're not against strategy. You're against noise masquerading as insight.

Because the truth is, many of us are not suffering from a lack of financial knowledge. We're drowning in it. We've read the blogs, followed the experts, experimented with the apps. What we need isn't more input—it's subtraction. Thoughtful, honest subtraction. The courage to let go of what no longer serves. The grace to return to what works without apology.

So we begin here, with a simple but potent idea: Simplicity isn't the default that remains once you've exhausted all your options. It's what you'd have built had you started from a place of genuine clarity. The goal isn't to make your financial life smaller. It's to make it saner. More elegant. More yours.

Financial elegance: complexity respected, not indulged

It's important to say up front: simplicity is not the same as naivety. The goal here is not to pretend that personal finance is always straightforward. The world is complex. Markets are volatile. Lives are nuanced. A minimalist approach that pretends otherwise is neither sustainable nor honest.

But there's a difference between respecting complexity and surrendering to it.

Simplicity is about working with complexity—but refusing to be consumed by it. Like a great engineer, the financially grounded person seeks *elegance*: the fewest moving parts required to accomplish the most essential outcomes.

And often, that means designing systems that do not ask for constant attention. Systems that run quietly, reliably, in the background—freeing your energy for higher-order thinking, not forcing it into daily vigilance.

This is not laziness. It's strategy.

The Three-Account System: Clarity with zero micromanagement

We introduce in this chapter a minimalist architecture for everyday money management: the *Three-Account System*. Not a gimmick, not a budgeting fad—but a design response to the question: *What's the simplest structure that preserves control, supports growth, and doesn't require an MBA to run?*

At its core, the system divides your finances into just three buckets: one for spending, one for saving, one for investing. Each serves a discrete function. Each has clear inflows and outflows. Together, they reduce the need for granular tracking while preserving *full visibility*. More importantly, they reinforce behavioural discipline without requiring constant willpower.

The elegance of the system lies not just in how it allocates money—but in how it reinforces identity. You begin to think of yourself as someone who spends intentionally, saves automatically, and invests consistently—not because you remember to, but because your system *defaults* to it.

This is the heartbeat of simplicity: *when structure replaces struggle.*

Portfolio minimalism: enough, not everything

We'll then turn to one of the most neglected conversations in personal investing: how much is enough in terms of diversification, holdings, and strategies?

For too many, investing has become a performative exercise in optionality. Dozens of tickers, asset classes, rebalancing tools, accounts, dashboards—each promising a sliver of added performance or sophistication. Yet this abundance often dilutes attention and distorts behaviour.

Portfolio minimalism flips the script. It asks: *What's the minimum you need to own to capture the maximum benefit of markets, without outsourcing your peace of mind?*

Evidence suggests the answer is less than you think. A globally diversified index portfolio, rebalanced a few times per year—or even once—is enough to outperform the vast majority of active investors over the long run. But this approach is rarely marketed, because it's not profitable to sell. Simplicity doesn't require subscriptions, seminars, or complex software. It requires discernment.

Portfolio minimalism is not anti-risk. It's *anti-frenzy*. It favours resilience over cleverness. It doesn't pretend to outsmart the market—it respects the market, but more importantly, it respects the investor's finite attention and emotional bandwidth.

This isn't a compromise. It's a competitive advantage.

Financial decluttering: what you subtract is strategy

Finally, we'll address a task that few financial authors dare to spotlight because it isn't glamorous: *cleaning up*. Old brokerage accounts. Defunct savings goals. Credit cards kept "just in case". Subscriptions you haven't used in six months. Complex budgeting apps you abandoned by February.

These are not merely administrative annoyances. They are *ambient liabilities*—each one siphoning a tiny unit of attention, trust, or bandwidth. Over time, they create decision fatigue. They dilute the signal of your intentions. They make your financial life feel heavier than it needs to be.

Decluttering is not an afterthought. It is central to reclaiming financial coherence. And coherence is more than aesthetics—it is the psychological infrastructure of progress. *You move faster when nothing is pulling sideways.*

This chapter offers concrete prompts, workflows, and strategies to help you eliminate financial noise. Not because simplicity is tidy, but because *simplicity is sovereign.* It gives you back your time. Your clarity. Your sense of control.

And, ultimately, your ability to *act without hesitation.*

Why this matters now

Simplicity is no longer just a personal virtue. It is a survival skill in a world of infinite financial information and zero filters. As automation, AI, and real-time data reshape the investment landscape, the edge will not go to those who know the most—but to those who can *decide the fastest with the clearest mind.*

Simplicity isn't about knowing less. It's about *needing less in order to know what to do.*

If you've ever felt like personal finance is too tangled, too time-consuming, or too mentally taxing—this chapter is your reset button. Not because it makes money effortless. But because it makes *you more effective.*

The superpower, in the end, isn't simplicity itself.

It's what simplicity frees you to focus on.

The Paradox of Less

The modern financial system promises empowerment through options. Investment platforms offer hundreds of account types. Budgeting tools multiply categories like bacteria in a petri dish. Portfolios balloon with funds that mirror each other. The logic—often implicit—is simple: *more options mean more control.*

But this is a myth dressed in the robes of modernity. In truth, more options frequently produce the opposite of control: indecision, fatigue, and fragmentation. When every decision feels like a fork in a thousand-path maze, the most common reaction isn't mastery—it's paralysis. *This is the paradox of less: reducing your financial complexity often increases your financial effectiveness.*

Simplicity, properly understood, is not the absence of sophistication—it is the expression of *functional elegance.* And that elegance comes not from the number of variables you juggle, but from your capacity to direct attention to what matters most, with as few distractions as possible.

The Tyranny of Choice: How More Becomes Less

Psychologist Barry Schwartz coined the term *the paradox of choice* to describe a counterintuitive truth: while choice is essential to freedom, an abundance of it can create anxiety, regret, and dissatisfaction. The same dynamic applies to financial management.

Consider the typical professional with five current accounts, three investment platforms, two pension providers, four budgeting apps, and a rotating cast of fintech tools promising financial clarity. The result? A shallow sense of engagement with any of them. A low-grade sense of overwhelm, even if unspoken. Decision fatigue before a single decision is made.

This clutter fragments focus. And focus is not just a cognitive asset—it is a financial one. *Your attention is your real currency.* When it is scattered, so too is your agency.

Fewer Accounts, Better Behaviour

One of the most powerful interventions in personal finance is also one of the least glamorous: *closing accounts.* Not consolidating for simplicity's sake, but to strengthen behavioural coherence.

Every additional account introduces friction. It adds another login, another dashboard, another layer of decision-making. More importantly, it weakens *the feedback loop.* With your financial picture fragmented across platforms, you are less likely to spot trends, detect inconsistencies, or course-correct.

In contrast, when your financial life is centralised—or at least intentionally structured into a *small number of distinct purposes*—you gain what complexity obscures: pattern recognition. And with pattern recognition comes clarity. And from clarity, discipline.

The real benefit of fewer accounts is not just operational. It is psychological. You begin to *trust yourself more*, not because your knowledge has expanded, but because your system no longer betrays your attention.

The Myth of the 'Optimal' Decision

There is a popular assumption that the key to financial progress is simply making the "best" decisions—buying the right fund, switching to the highest yield, jumping into the perfect asset at the right time. But this approach misunderstands human nature.

Decision quality matters. But *decision frequency matters more.*

Why? Because for most people, their long-term outcomes are not defined by a few brilliant choices. They are defined by thousands of routine ones. If those routine decisions require substantial effort, friction, or re-evaluation, they will be delayed, skipped, or avoided. Eventually, the system breaks—not from incompetence, but from exhaustion.

This is why *defaults matter.* Simplifying your decision architecture doesn't just reduce stress. It increases consistency. And consistency—especially in investing—is *what actually compounds.*

Automation is often framed as a convenience. But viewed properly, it is a *behavioural safeguard.* A simplified, automated system—whether for contributions, allocations, or savings—does not rely on your motivation, mood, or market prediction. It relies on design.

Design wins where willpower fails.

Case Study: The Investment 'Clean Slate'

In 2021, a behavioural finance experiment conducted by Morningstar tested what happened when investors were asked to select funds from a menu of over 400 options. Most participants reported high stress, low confidence, and ultimately made no decision at all. A control group, given just 10 funds that were pre-filtered for quality and balance, had a 4x higher completion rate—and reported higher satisfaction six months later, regardless of performance.

The takeaway is critical: *better outcomes follow better architecture, not better theory*. People thrive with clear constraints.

A practical implication? The fewer holdings you track, the more likely you are to review them regularly, rebalance them intelligently, and sleep through volatility. Portfolio minimalism—discussed elsewhere in this book—is not just aesthetic. It is behavioural leverage.

The Cost of Cognitive Load

Every account, app, and decision point introduces *cognitive load*. And cognitive load, once exceeded, doesn't just slow you down—it makes you worse at the task itself.

Consider the research from Stanford psychologist Roy Baumeister, who showed that *decision fatigue reduces willpower*. In financial terms, this means that after too many small money-related choices—subscriptions, bill adjustments, card management—you are less likely to make optimal choices when it truly matters: deciding how much to invest, when to pause spending, or whether to adjust your financial strategy.

Simplifying your financial life is therefore not just efficient. It is protective. It preserves your energy for *the moments that count most.*

Redundancy Is Not Security

There is a defensive mindset that resists simplification: the idea that "spreading out" accounts and funds somehow offers protection. But this is often a misapplication of diversification.

True diversification protects against correlated loss across asset classes. *Redundant accounts, platforms, or tools do not provide meaningful security*—they provide complexity theatre. You appear prudent, but the system is harder to manage, more likely to suffer from neglect, and easier to breach through outdated logins or overlooked alerts.

Real resilience comes from *knowing exactly where everything is, how it works, and how it connects.* Simplicity supports this. Sprawl undermines it.

Subtraction as a Competitive Edge

In design thinking, the principle of *elegant subtraction* refers to removing anything that does not serve the user's purpose. Apple famously adopted this approach in its early product philosophy. So did Japanese architecture. So does every effective financial system.

Your personal finance infrastructure should not reflect how much you know—it should reflect *how well you can act.* In that sense, reducing friction, noise, and clutter is not an act of minimalism. It is an act of strategic refinement.

Ask any top-performing investor or disciplined saver their secret, and few will say it's about knowing more than others. Most will tell you: *they simplified their life until the right behaviours became automatic.*

Simplicity Requires Courage

Simplifying your financial life will require you to say no—to platforms, services, products, and narratives that insist you need one more tool, one more option, one more account.

It may feel uncomfortable. Complexity often flatters the ego. Simplicity threatens it.

But the reward is more than order. It is *alignment.* Between your values and your systems. Between your goals and your attention. Between your intentions and your outcomes.

This is the paradox of less. You don't get less. *You get more of what actually matters.*

The Three-Account System

Introducing a minimalist framework for budgeting that respects complexity without being consumed by it.

It is not complexity but clarity that builds lasting financial stability. Yet modern budgeting culture has become so saturated with tools, categories, notifications, and apps that many professionals end up spending more time tracking money than making meaningful decisions with it. We confuse sophistication with progress. But sophistication without structure quickly becomes noise.

This is the subtle tyranny of over-designed personal finance. Too many moving parts. Too much friction. Too little insight.

What follows is a framework that restores budgeting to its rightful function—not as an exercise in control, but as a scaffold for decision-making, values alignment, and peace of mind. *The Three-Account System* is not about minimalism for its own sake. It is about *functional simplicity*—a model that *respects complexity, but refuses to be governed by it.*

The Case for Structural Elegance

Let's begin with a simple truth: most people do not fail at budgeting because they lack discipline. They fail because their systems are structurally incoherent. They are trying to execute sophisticated intentions—invest more, save more, spend consciously—through fragmented mechanisms. Dozens of categories. Multiple dashboards. Inconsistent automation.

Budgeting becomes something you *revisit*, rather than something you *live*. It becomes reactive, not proactive.

The antidote is not more information. It is better structure. *The Three-Account System* offers that structure. Not through gimmicks or financial minimalism theatre, but by returning to behavioural fundamentals: clarity, intention, and repeatability.

The Anatomy of the System

At its core, the Three-Account System rests on a simple behavioural principle: *every financial decision falls into one of three core functions—spending, safeguarding, or growing.* We mirror these functions with three distinct, purpose-driven accounts:

1. **Spending Account** – This is your active, day-to-day account. It funds your present lifestyle—bills, food, fuel, fun. All income is initially deposited here before being distributed to the other two accounts according to your system.

2. **Safety Account** – This is your buffer against volatility. Emergency savings. Short-term planning. Unexpected events. It holds liquid cash only, not investments.

3. **Growth Account** – This is where long-term wealth is built. It houses your investments, retirement contributions, or any capital intended to increase over time through market exposure or business deployment.

Each account has a *clearly defined purpose*, making the system psychologically intuitive and financially actionable. This division doesn't just declutter your banking—it clarifies your relationship with money itself.

Why This Works: Cognitive Bandwidth and Behavioural Economics

Cognitive science has shown repeatedly that human willpower is not a bottomless well. As psychologist Roy Baumeister's research on decision fatigue illustrates, the more complex a system becomes, the more likely it is to break down—*not at the point of extreme stress, but in the quiet erosion of daily overwhelm.*

By reducing the number of financial surfaces you need to interact with—yet preserving the full spectrum of financial purpose—the Three-Account System offers a rare combination: simplicity *without* oversimplification.

You do not need twenty budgeting categories when three architectural anchors can perform the same role more efficiently.

This approach also aligns with the behavioural insight that *humans perform best in environments where feedback is clear and consistent.* When each account has a role, and only that role, you begin to associate decisions with purpose. You stop asking "Can I afford this?" and start asking "Does this align with the function of this account?"

It reframes budgeting from a surveillance tool to a *values mirror.*

Contrast: Category Overload and the Illusion of Control

Compare this with the prevailing method offered by most budgeting apps: a labyrinth of categories and sub-categories. Groceries, utilities, rent, transport, entertainment, fitness, subscriptions, donations, clothing, takeaways—each sliced, labelled, and assigned a fixed percentage.

But behavioural finance tells us that *humans do not think in granular categories when they spend.* They operate by emotional triggers, habits, and environmental cues.

This makes hyper-categorisation cognitively expensive but behaviourally ineffective. Users feel overwhelmed, then frustrated, then disengaged. It's the *illusion* of control, not actual agency.

In contrast, the Three-Account System trades micro-tracking for macro-alignment. It allows you to see the forest without obsessing over every tree.

Real-World Application: Case Study

Consider a professional in their late 30s. Income is stable, but they struggle to consistently save or invest. Expenses don't feel excessive, but at the end of each month, there's rarely anything left to move forward.

After implementing the Three-Account System:

All income enters their *Spending Account*, which is capped at a predefined lifestyle threshold (e.g. £2,500/month).

A fixed transfer (say, £1,000) is sent monthly to their *Growth Account*, which automatically invests in a passive portfolio.

A standing order sends £500 to their *Safety Account* until six months of living expenses are reached.

In three months, patterns become visible. The lifestyle cap feels manageable. The investment account grows without effort. The safety buffer provides peace of mind. Most importantly, *the sense of financial drift is replaced by deliberate rhythm.*

This is not because they are smarter. It is because the system is clearer.

Adaptability Without Bloat

A natural question arises: *What about goals that don't fit neatly into one of those three categories?* Holiday funds? A new car? Wedding expenses?

Here, the system flexes. Short-term, non-essential goals can be placed within a sub-pocket of the *Safety Account.* Larger aspirations—those with a timeline beyond three years—should live in the *Growth Account*, appropriately invested.

The power of the system lies in its clarity, not its rigidity. As long as each new goal passes through the lens of *"Is this for now, for protection, or for growth?"*, it will find a natural home.

Emotional Resonance and Habitual Trust

Perhaps the most underappreciated benefit of the Three-Account System is *the emotional separation it creates between different kinds of money.* You stop seeing all funds as fungible. You stop negotiating with your future every time a new purchase tempts you. You cultivate a sense of boundary.

Over time, this builds a kind of financial self-trust—*not just because your balances rise, but because your system reinforces your values.*

When your accounts are designed around your intentions, each transaction becomes a small expression of who you are and what you prioritise. That's not budgeting. That's identity alignment.

A System That Respects Your Time

Finally, and perhaps most practically, this system *respects your attention span.* Once configured, it requires no app updates, daily category tweaking, or hours of analysis.

Your role is simple: review monthly, adjust annually, and *live intentionally in between.*

The Three-Account System is not a financial trick. It is a *philosophical stance*—a refusal to be swallowed by complexity masquerading as competence. In its structure, you reclaim what modern finance often takes away: *clarity, confidence, and calm.*

In a world that sells you more tools, this system offers fewer distractions. And in doing so, it returns you to what personal finance was meant to be: *personal, purposeful, and powerfully simple.*

Portfolio Minimalism

A streamlined investment model that balances risk and return—without stress or guesswork.

Most investors don't fail because they pick the wrong stock. They fail because their portfolios are shaped by noise, not logic. Too many holdings. Too many opinions. Too many moving parts that obscure rather than clarify. In a world increasingly obsessed with optimisation, portfolio construction has become a performance art—dense with jargon, peppered with complexity, and loaded with false confidence.

Portfolio Minimalism is a deliberate departure from that culture. It doesn't argue for simplicity because it is fashionable. It argues for simplicity because it is *functional.* Because most of what modern investors do to feel "in control" is statistically irrelevant, behaviourally destabilising, and financially unproductive.

This model begins with a question very few investors ask: *What is the minimum number of moving parts required to achieve a long-term, evidence-based investment outcome that you can stick with—calmly, repeatedly, and without heroic predictions?*

When you strip away the ego, the news cycle, and the thrill of tinkering, the answer is: *not many.*

Complexity is a Cost, Not a Virtue

The finance industry thrives on opacity. Fund managers, private equity marketers, algorithmic traders—each one has a vested interest in convincing you that outperformance is a function of precision timing, exotic strategy, or insider nuance. But empirical data continues to paint a more sobering picture: *over long horizons, simplicity beats sophistication—not always in raw returns, but almost always in behavioural sustainability.*

Consider this: A Vanguard study spanning decades of retail investor performance found that the greatest predictors of long-term success were not product selection, market timing, or tactical allocation. They were: time in the market, regular contributions, and emotional detachment during downturns.

In other words, *the investor's temperament—not their toolkit—drives the outcome.*

So why the obsession with complexity? Because complexity gives us the illusion of control. It flatters our intellect. It makes us feel active in an arena where doing less often wins.

Minimalism in portfolio construction is a conscious rejection of this illusion. It is the art of *knowing what to ignore.*

The Anatomy of a Minimalist Portfolio

A minimalist portfolio is not sparse; it is streamlined. It does not sacrifice diversification; it targets only *meaningful* diversification. It consists of components that are uncorrelated enough to reduce risk, yet broad enough to avoid redundancy.

At its most elemental level, a minimalist portfolio often consists of three to five core building blocks:

1. **Global Equity Exposure** – Representing ownership in the world's businesses. Typically held via low-cost, broad-market index funds (e.g. FTSE Global All Cap or MSCI World ETFs).

2. **Government Bonds** – Adding a stabilising ballast. Depending on risk tolerance and interest rate environment, this could range from short-duration gilts to inflation-linked bonds.

3. **Cash Reserve** – Not for growth, but for optionality—emergencies, dry powder, or psychological buffer.

4. *(Optional)* **Real Assets** – Such as global REITs or commodities, added sparingly to hedge against inflation or systemic shocks.

That's it. No thematic ETFs, no leveraged instruments, no exotic asset classes requiring spreadsheets to decode. A structure that *you can understand in one breath, and manage with one hand.*

And it is precisely this simplicity that makes it resilient—*not because it maximises potential returns, but because it minimises behavioural error.*

Behavioural Design Over Asset Selection

Minimalist portfolios do not win by predicting. They win by *surviving.* And survival in investing is a behavioural game.

Every additional fund, sector, or strategy added to a portfolio is another variable demanding attention—another potential source of anxiety, narrative, or reactive decision-making.

When your portfolio consists of 15 funds, and five of them are underperforming, your instinct is to *intervene.* You check more often. You second-guess. You become less of an investor, and more of a manager. And managers under pressure make worse investors.

By contrast, a minimalist portfolio is designed not just to endure market volatility, but to *shelter you from your own volatility.*

It asks: "Can this be understood, maintained, and emotionally tolerated under stress?" If the answer is no, it doesn't belong.

A Historical and Empirical Foundation

Some of the world's most rigorous financial research—from Nobel laureates Eugene Fama and Harry Markowitz to practitioners like Jack Bogle and William Bernstein—has shown that broad diversification, low fees, and disciplined rebalancing outperform most active strategies over time.

This isn't ideology. It's statistical fact. Yet despite overwhelming evidence, the average investor continues to chase complex strategies that add marginal benefit at disproportionate risk.

Portfolio minimalism is the refusal to mistake intellectual stimulation for financial gain.

Take the example of the *Three-Fund Portfolio*, popularised by the Bogleheads community: one global equity fund, one international equity fund, and one bond fund. It has historically outperformed the average actively managed portfolio *precisely because it reduces friction and maximises participation.*

Add automatic monthly contributions and an annual rebalance, and you've captured 90% of the investable outcome with 10% of the cognitive load.

Practical Implementation: A Template

Let's consider an archetype for a minimalist investor—a 40-year-old professional with moderate risk tolerance and a 20-year investment horizon. A simple allocation might look like this:

60% Global Equity Index Fund (e.g. MSCI ACWI)

30% Government Bond Fund (e.g. UK Intermediate Gilts)

10% Cash (held in high-interest savings or premium bond equivalents)

This portfolio:

Is diversified across thousands of securities and geographies

Is rebalanced once or twice a year

Requires no market predictions

Has one job: compound steadily, with minimal drama

Over time, this structure has the uncanny ability to outperform portfolios ten times more complicated—*not always in peak performance, but in average performance, which is what most people actually live with.*

Counterpoint: "But What About Customisation?"

Minimalism is not one-size-fits-all. It is *fit-for-purpose.* For those with higher risk tolerance, the bond component may shrink or disappear. For those nearing retirement, the equity allocation may taper. But in each case, the principle remains: *streamline without sacrificing function.*

The goal is not to find *the* perfect portfolio. The goal is to find *your* durable portfolio—the one you can understand, commit to, and execute with calm consistency.

The test is not sophistication. It is *sustainability under pressure.*

The Hidden Benefit: Liberation from Noise

Portfolio minimalism is not just a technique—it is a lifestyle design choice. It liberates you from the constant churn of financial commentary, market updates, fund comparisons, and quarterly performance reviews.

When your portfolio is simple, intentional, and automated, you stop checking. When you stop checking, you stop reacting. When you stop reacting, *you start building.*

And in the long arc of financial progress, *calm persistence outperforms intermittent brilliance.*

Final Insight

Portfolio minimalism is not for those who want to "beat the market." It is for those who want to *participate in the market, continuously and peacefully*, for decades. It is for people who recognise that every extra layer of complexity may be stealing not just their returns, but their peace of mind.

In the end, your portfolio is not a showcase. It's a tool. It doesn't need to impress anyone. It needs to *work when you don't want to think about it.*

When properly designed, the minimalist portfolio becomes what all great systems are: *invisible, reliable, and quietly powerful.*

Decluttering Financial Clutter

Exercises and prompts to clean out dead investments, apps, accounts, and subscriptions.

The typical modern investor is over-diversified, under-focused, and—most critically—overwhelmed. Not by risk, but by *residue.* The residue of forgotten accounts, half-used apps, low-impact subscriptions, and once-promising investments that now float unmonitored in digital limbo. These are not just distractions. They are *taxes on clarity.* They dilute intention and reduce the signal-to-noise ratio in your financial life.

In personal finance, as in architecture, *elegance emerges through subtraction.* The more you remove what is no longer relevant, the more visible your values become. Decluttering is not cosmetic. It is *philosophical.* And it is urgent.

This subchapter is not about minimalism for minimalism's sake. It is about reclaiming bandwidth—cognitive, emotional, strategic—so that your capital aligns more directly with your actual aspirations. In a world engineered for maximum consumption and maximum distraction, *a tidy financial life is a form of rebellion.* It allows you to stop reacting and start directing.

The Case for Financial Hygiene

Before we discuss how to declutter, it's worth considering *why* clutter accumulates in the first place. The answer lies not in laziness, but in inertia. Every tool, fund, account or subscription begins with a decision—one that made sense at a point in time. But the half-life of usefulness is short, especially in personal finance. What served you well at age 28 may be obsolete at 38. But unless deliberately reviewed, it lingers. Unused credit cards remain open. Robo-advisors coexist with DIY brokerage accounts. Forgotten stock punts from a past bull market sit untouched. The result is *a fragmented identity.* You are not managing your finances. You are managing *versions* of your former self.

Financial clutter thrives in the space between intention and attention.

Decluttering reasserts control. It's not about organising what you have. It's about deciding *what no longer deserves to be there.*

Category One: Dead Investments

A dead investment is not simply one that has lost value. It is one that no longer has *purpose.* That purpose could be return, diversification, learning, or psychological comfort. Once that function dissolves, the asset becomes baggage.

Classic examples:

A thematic ETF you bought during a pandemic trend—now stagnant, and rarely monitored.

Shares in a startup you believed in, now directionless but emotionally sticky.

A high-fee mutual fund from a bank relationship you've long outgrown.

These holdings often persist because they're not *painful* enough to trigger action. They don't cost you monthly. They just erode mental sharpness.

The discipline here is not market timing—it's *portfolio hygiene.* Ask of each investment:

Do I understand what this does?

Is it still aligned with my current strategy?

If I didn't already own it, would I buy it today?

If the answer is no, it belongs in the *sell or consolidate* column. Not because it's "bad," but because it's no longer *you.*

Category Two: Redundant Accounts

Financial technology has proliferated faster than most people's ability to integrate it. You open a brokerage account to chase a trend. You download a budgeting app with good intentions. You sign up for a challenger bank because it offers 3% cashback. The result: *a forest of logins*, scattered across platforms, none of them fully trusted, many of them underused.

What this splintering does is create *friction.* You're less likely to review your holdings when they live in five different portals. You're less likely to act with confidence when your view is fractured.

The goal is not to delete everything. The goal is *consolidation with clarity.*

Recommended actions:

Consolidate brokerage accounts under a single platform where feasible.

Migrate savings into a unified high-interest account, segmented by purpose (emergency, holidays, home).

Close unused current accounts—even if they're "free." They cost attention.

Each reduction is a cognitive dividend. You reduce admin. You regain clarity. You know where your money lives—and *why*.

Category Three: Digital Distractions and Subscriptions

Less visible, but no less corrosive, is the clutter of *digital tools and subscriptions*. The proliferation of fintech has created an ecosystem of well-intentioned clutter: budgeting apps you never check, newsletter subscriptions you auto-delete, portfolio trackers that don't match your holdings.

While these are not "investments," they influence how you *feel* about your money. And feelings shape behaviour.

Two key filters to apply:

1. Does this tool or subscription *improve decision quality*?
2. Does it get used *reliably and consistently*?

If not, eliminate. Financial literacy does not require a dashboard. It requires *mental quiet.*

Run an annual audit. Create a master list of every app, tool, or paid resource related to money. Be ruthless. Retain only what delivers insight, peace of mind, or a clear edge.

Category Four: Lifestyle Leakage

Financial clutter is not only digital. It hides in forgotten subscriptions—gym memberships, magazine renewals, online learning platforms you haven't logged into for six months. The cumulative cost is less about pounds and more about *identity drift.* Each one is a commitment unkept. A silent vote for a version of yourself you no longer endorse.

The act of cancellation is clarifying. It says: "I am no longer pursuing that path." It creates both financial and psychological surplus.

A powerful frame: *Every recurring payment is a subscription to a belief. Do I still believe in it?*

This is not just frugality. It's alignment. It's the reduction of friction between what you spend on and what you stand for.

A Simple Ritual: The Financial Detox Day

Clutter cannot be eliminated reactively. It must be *scheduled.* Set aside one day each year—a Financial Detox Day. Block time. Approach it as an act of leadership, not admin.

Checklist for your detox:

Review all investments: sell, consolidate, or reaffirm.

Review all accounts: close or merge non-essentials.

Review all subscriptions: cancel those not used or loved.

Review all tools and dashboards: uninstall or recommit.

Review all financial habits: audit monthly rituals, recurring charges, auto-transfers.

You'll finish lighter. Sharper. More aligned.

The result is not just cleaner spreadsheets. It's *higher signal.* Your financial system begins to reflect your current identity, not your past experiments. Your capital allocation becomes a mirror of your intent—not a museum of outdated strategies.

Why This Matters More Than Ever

In a world of AI-generated noise, FOMO-driven investment forums, and hyper-targeted financial products, *the capacity to filter is more valuable than the ability to optimise.* Decluttering is a filter. It is how you reduce drag so that your real strategies—long-term compounding, intentional allocation, calm behaviour—can do their work without sabotage.

The opposite of clutter is not perfection. It's *clarity with momentum.*

Most wealth advice focuses on adding: add tools, add diversification, add strategies. But in reality, the ability to *subtract well*—intelligently, precisely, and without guilt—is what builds a sustainable system. Decluttering your financial life isn't a one-time clean-up. It's an operating philosophy.

Less, in this case, is not just more. It's better.

Chapter 6
The Automation Mindset

Most people handle their finances the way one might steer a car down an unfamiliar road in dense fog—tense, reactive, half-guessing at every turn. They check account balances with a flicker of dread, scramble after the latest tactic, and course-correct only once emotions—or markets—start spinning out. But the financially grounded, the truly wealthy in the structural sense, approach it all differently. They don't just manage their money. They choreograph it.

Not with obsessive micromanagement, mind you—but through quiet, deliberate design. Not with frantic willpower, but through built-in defaults. This chapter is about that shift: the movement from intention to infrastructure. It's about constructing a system in which financial progress unfolds almost inevitably, not as a result of daily strain but as a function of smart architecture.

Look at any field where performance matters—surgery, aerospace, defence. What drives excellence isn't brilliance in the moment. It's process. It's protocol. Personal finance, oddly, tends to reject this. We romanticise the lone genius, the savvy investor, the disciplined saver who outperforms the odds through sheer grit or intuition. But wealth—true, lasting, quietly resilient wealth—isn't forged in moments of heroism. It's grown through invisible rhythm. Boring, even. And that's the point.

Which brings us to the deeper truth of automation. It's not just a technical fix or a way to "set and forget." It's a worldview. A philosophy, even. It shifts your posture from reactive to generative, from fiddling with every variable to deciding once—clearly, confidently—and letting that decision echo across time.

Automation isn't abdication. It's authorship.

So, let's begin with a reframe: your salary, your income, your paycheque—whatever you call it—isn't just a pile of numbers to be sliced up each month. It's a narrative. A script. And the question is not "How should I spend it this month?" but rather, "What story am I writing with this money—again and again?"

This is what we mean by scripting your paycheque. Assigning every pound a role, on purpose. Not after the fact, when temptation and emotion have already taken the wheel—but at the outset, when clarity still has a fighting chance. You might automate your emergency fund top-up, your investment contributions, your bills. But beneath those mechanics lies something more personal: a signal to yourself that your goals are not negotiable. They're scheduled.

From here, we move to something less tangible, but arguably more enduring: the emotional residue of consistency. When your financial behaviour is repeated, reinforced, and aligned with who you believe yourself to be, it creates more than savings. It builds dignity. Self-respect. A quiet internal knowing that you're acting in accordance with your own standards—not the whims of the market or the pressure of comparison. We might call this Habitual Riches—not because the habits make you rich (though they might), but because they make you feel congruent. And that feeling, once rooted, is very hard to shake.

But let's not pretend that systems eliminate difficulty. Life will throw a wrench into your routines. Income changes, emergencies arise, energy dips. That's why the final pillar of this approach isn't just resilience—it's anti-fragility. A good system doesn't simply endure disruption. It absorbs it. Learns from it. Adapts. It gives you a protocol for the bad days, not just the good ones. It prevents a momentary lapse from becoming a long-term derailment.

This is the idea behind Fail-Proofing Your Progress. You build margin into your system. You allow for mistakes, because you've already expected them. Maybe that means keeping a slush fund for the irregular stuff. Maybe it means automating at 85% capacity instead of 100%, to leave breathing room. Maybe it's as simple as having a checklist for when things go sideways—so you're never left floundering. You don't have to feel strong to act wisely, if the system is holding you up.

Together, these three ideas—Scripting Your Paycheque, Habitual Riches, and Fail-Proofing Your Progress—converge around a single, liberating principle: automation isn't about surrendering control. It's about designing the environment in which control becomes unnecessary.

You still steer. But you've shaped the road beneath you.

The Illusion of Discipline

Let's confront a persistent myth: that wealth is built by people who are especially disciplined. The truth is far less flattering—and far more liberating. People who accumulate wealth consistently aren't usually more disciplined. They're just *less reliant* on discipline. They've built systems—automatic savings plans, recurring investments, default spending flows—that reduce the number of decisions they need to make in the first place.

The goal is not to be heroic. The goal is to be unavailable for chaos.

This matters because willpower is both finite and fickle. Your future depends on what happens when you're tired, distracted, or overwhelmed. Do your systems hold? Or do they break under pressure? Automation protects you in the moments you're least capable of protecting yourself.

The paradox here is elegant: *true financial freedom is built through constraint.* But it must be the right kind of constraint—chosen, not imposed. That's what this chapter equips you to create.

Scripting Your Paycheque: Money as Narrative

Every paycheque tells a story. For many, that story is muddled, reactive, and transactional. Bills get paid. Leftover money disappears. At best, a portion is saved—if there's energy left to care. But what if your income told a story *on purpose*? One where every pound had a defined role, one that mirrored your values, goals, and obligations—*without requiring monthly reinvention*?

This is where scripting comes in. Instead of manually juggling payments and ad hoc transfers, you architect a set of automated instructions that turn income into choreography. Your rent, utilities, savings, investing, and guilt-free spending are all pre-directed to their destinations. The result is a system where you no longer have to trust your memory—or your mood. You trust the script.

This is not budgeting in the traditional sense. It's something higher-order. It's allocating resources the way a great director casts actors: based on role, not presence. Once built, the system runs in the background. And more than that—it becomes a form of *financial storytelling.* You are no longer reacting to what's left over. You are defining what gets written.

Habitual Riches: When Systems Become Self

Automation only becomes powerful when it becomes *personal.* Anyone can set up a standing order. The transformation happens when those behaviours are seen not as tasks, but as *identity cues.* Every time you automate your investing, you're casting a vote for the kind of person who builds a legacy. Every time you pay yourself first, you reinforce the belief: "I am someone who takes my future seriously."

This concept—repeated in behavioural psychology and identity theory—is what makes automation stick. People don't change by wanting different outcomes. They change by *believing* different things about who they are. Systems help because they create consistency. And consistency, over time, builds evidence. Evidence builds identity.

A standing investment plan is no longer just a transaction. It's a ritual. A quiet, repeated act that says: "This is who I am." This is why automation is not impersonal. Quite the opposite. *It is deeply personal.* It encodes your values, crystallises your goals, and protects your energy from the volatility of life.

Automation becomes a scaffold for becoming who you meant to be.

Fail-Proofing Your Progress

No system is complete without contingency. Automation that lacks resilience is a trap waiting to snap. That's why this chapter doesn't just teach how to build default systems—it teaches how to *protect* them. From yourself. From the market. From the unexpected.

We explore how to use buffers—both financial and emotional. Why tripwires are essential: thresholds that alert you to drift before it becomes danger. Why automation should include *emergency flexibility*, not just blind persistence.

Think of this as designing for *minimum regret.* Not because regret is always avoidable, but because its intensity can be muted by design. Fail-proofing is not a lack of faith. It is *faith, informed by realism.* You don't automate because you're naïve. You automate because you're a human being in a complex world—and your best days should not have to carry the burden of your worst ones.

The Deeper Shift: From Control to Clarity

To automate well is not to control more. It's to *need less control.* It's to create a structure that serves you whether you're busy, tired, distracted, or simply uninterested in thinking about money that day. The more elegant your automation, the more energy you free up for things that actually require your full presence—your work, your family, your mind.

This chapter will not offer tips. It offers *infrastructure.* Scripting your paycheque. Embedding wealth behaviours into your identity. Designing buffers and correction paths that make staying on track the default, not the exception.

By the end, you won't just have tools. You'll have an operating system—one that allows you to live well now, and still arrive well-prepared for the future.

And perhaps most importantly: you'll stop confusing friction with discipline. *Your system will do the heavy lifting.* Quietly. Reliably. Unfailingly.

Because *wealth is not built by those who fight every battle.* It's built by those who set fewer traps—and walk fewer minefields—because their systems were smarter than their moods.

Wealth on Autopilot

How systems outperform motivation—and why designing your defaults may be the most important financial decision you ever make.

There is an enduring myth in personal finance—quietly reinforced by books, influencers, and well-meaning mentors—that wealth is a product of constant attention. That building a solid financial life means becoming a hyper-vigilant tracker, a spreadsheet devotee, someone who "just cares more" and "stays on top of things." But what if the opposite were true? What if the people most likely to succeed with money were not the ones who think about it constantly, but the ones who rarely need to think about it at all?

This subchapter challenges a central assumption of conventional wisdom: that *discipline is the engine of financial success.* It isn't. Systems are. Not only because they're more consistent—but because they're *designed to survive you at your worst.* When life gets busy, moods shift, motivation fades, or distractions multiply, systems don't flinch. Habits break. Goals dissolve. But systems—if built correctly—*persist.*

The promise of putting your wealth on autopilot is not effortlessness. It is *reliability.* Not perfection, but insulation—from your own inconsistencies and from the everyday frictions that derail most people's best intentions.

The Case Against Willpower

Let's begin with a reality backed by decades of behavioural science: willpower is a limited resource. Research in self-regulation

(Baumeister et al., 1998) has shown that human decision-making depletes over time. Each financial choice—whether to invest, spend, save, or budget—draws from the same cognitive reservoir you use to navigate work, relationships, and life's daily demands. By the time you get to your money, that reservoir is often dry.

This is where financial systems outperform humans. They do not fatigue. They do not second-guess. They do not negotiate with temptation. Systems remove the need for repeated deliberation by replacing *choice* with *default.* And in doing so, they shift the foundation of wealth-building from effort to design.

This isn't a fringe idea. The wealthiest individuals and most successful institutions rely on automation as a first principle. Consider pension funds. They don't ask participants to re-approve each monthly deposit. They design the contribution system to be invisible, recurring, and assumed. Why? Because the greatest risk to long-term investing is not market volatility—it's human inconsistency.

Put another way: *wealth is not what happens when you're at your best—it's what continues when you're distracted.*

Systems as Identity Engines

There's another underappreciated benefit to automation: identity reinforcement. Every time your system executes a behaviour—investing a percentage of your salary, allocating savings, or paying down debt—it reinforces the *kind of person you believe yourself to be.* And identity, more than outcome, is what sustains long-term behaviour.

This concept is supported by research from James Clear, Charles Duhigg, and BJ Fogg, whose work across behavioural psychology demonstrates that small, repeated actions are more sustainable when they reinforce a clear sense of *who we are*, not just *what we want.* Automating wealth is not about checking out; it's about *checking in*—

on a more profound level. You are building an infrastructure that aligns your external actions with your internal aspirations.

A person who automatically invests 10% of every paycheque isn't just saving. They're embodying a belief: "*I am someone who takes care of my future.*" That belief becomes increasingly robust—not through reflection, but through repetition.

Practical Design: The Core Mechanics of Financial Automation

To operationalise wealth on autopilot, several elements must converge: clarity, consistency, and constraints. These are not technical terms; they are behavioural imperatives.

1. Clarity
You cannot automate what is vague. Most people don't automate their finances not because they lack tools, but because they haven't yet made clear decisions about what they want their money to do. *Every pound must have a purpose.* If your goals are ill-defined—retirement "someday," savings "when possible"—then automation has nothing to anchor to.

Clarity precedes automation. Define the role of your income. Decide the percentage you'll invest. Choose the accounts that will receive funds. And commit to a sequence.

2. Consistency
The true power of automation lies not in its complexity, but in its *predictability*. When a system executes the same financial pattern month after month, the gains become structural. You're not just building a balance—you're building rhythm, and rhythm is the heartbeat of compounding.

This is especially critical in investing. Dollar-cost averaging (or pound-cost averaging, if you prefer local terminology) works precisely because it removes timing from the equation. You invest at regular intervals, regardless of market conditions. Some months the market is up, some down—but your system is agnostic. Over time, this reduces volatility and cognitive stress. The system succeeds by being boring.

3. Constraints

Automation thrives within boundaries. Without constraints—such as fixed investment percentages, spending limits, or account-specific roles—automation becomes either arbitrary or dangerous. Constraints are not restrictions. They are *guardrails.* They keep your financial machine from overextending, and they allow for course correction without collapse.

These constraints can take many forms:
– Emergency fund thresholds
– Credit card repayment ceilings
– Auto-transfers into tax-advantaged accounts
– Guilt-free spending caps

All are designed to ensure your automated system is not only efficient but *safe*—resilient in the face of change.

Case Study: The Invisible Investor

Consider the case of Maya, a 35-year-old project manager earning a moderate salary in London. For years, she kept meaning to "start investing properly" but always felt too busy or uncertain. She tinkered with different apps, tried budgeting tools, followed financial influencers—but nothing stuck. Each attempt added friction to her already full life.

Eventually, she set up a system:
– 15% of her salary auto-transferred to a low-cost global index fund monthly
– 5% went to a high-interest savings account for annual travel
– Another 10% was allocated to a "Future Self" fund—flexible, yet untouchable for present-day wants

She stopped checking her account obsessively. She didn't need to. The system did the heavy lifting. Over three years, she saved more than in the previous eight combined. Not because she changed her personality. But because she changed the architecture.

This is the subtle truth behind wealth on autopilot: it feels uneventful. But beneath that calm surface, something remarkable is unfolding. The old, chaotic variables—mood, distraction, economic noise—have been removed. What remains is progress, uninterrupted.

The Ethical Edge: Automation as Emotional Protection

We rarely talk about the emotional cost of financial decision-making. But it's real. Each money decision carries not just logistical weight but psychological load—guilt, shame, second-guessing. Automation doesn't eliminate those emotions, but it buffers them.

By removing the need to *choose* again and again, automation grants a quieter mind. It creates space between you and your financial past. You're not continually trying to overcome bad habits or "get back on track"—because the track is already built.

This matters especially for those who carry financial trauma or chronic anxiety around money. Wealth on autopilot is not a shortcut. It's a shield. It reduces exposure to the psychological toll of daily judgement and creates space to focus on higher-order financial thinking: planning, growth, purpose.

Final Thought: The Quiet Revolution

What makes automation powerful is not its novelty. It is, in fact, ancient. Farmers plant seeds in predictable patterns. Architects build structures with repeatable load-bearing designs. Pilots don't reconfigure their cockpit before each flight—they follow systems that guarantee safety.

Personal finance, when done well, follows the same logic. Wealth on autopilot is not a fantasy. It's a *discipline of design.* It is the quiet revolution of deciding once—wisely—and then letting that decision compound, unbothered, over time.

Automation, when elevated from convenience to philosophy, becomes something more than a feature of modern banking. It becomes a principle of modern living.

Because the smartest financial decision you'll ever make is the one you only need to make once.

Scripting Your Paycheque

How intentional income allocation creates identity, stability, and long-term momentum.

Most people don't realise that their salary is already telling a story. The question is: *Whose story is it?* For many professionals, even those earning respectable incomes, the arrival of a paycheque doesn't trigger intention—it triggers reaction. Bills are paid, purchases are made, and whatever's left—if anything—becomes an afterthought or an aspiration: "*Next month, I'll save more.*"

This subchapter introduces a radical but refreshingly practical proposition: *Treat your paycheque not as a lump sum, but as a narrative you are authoring.* Each unit of currency should not merely have a destination. It should have a *function*, a *meaning*, and—most importantly—a *role* in the larger script of your life. This is not budgeting in the traditional sense. It is *behavioural storytelling*, where you assign your money the task of reinforcing the person you intend to become.

The objective isn't to control every penny. It's to ensure that your income is aligned with your priorities by design—not by default.

Why Most Budgeting Fails (And What Scripting Fixes)

Traditional budgeting approaches suffer from two fatal flaws. First, they tend to operate retroactively—looking at what was spent, rather than deciding in advance what money should do. Second, they fixate on categories (groceries, utilities, entertainment) rather than *intentions* (freedom, security, growth). The result is a process that feels tedious, overly granular, and disconnected from purpose.

Scripting your paycheque flips the sequence. Instead of reacting to expenses, you *cast* each portion of your income in a role, ahead of time. Like a director assigning parts in a stage production, you determine how each pound will perform, ensuring the whole play leads to a coherent outcome. *Your financial life becomes dramaturgical—deliberate, rehearsed, and values-aligned.*

Consider the difference in tone between these two internal dialogues:

Budgeting Mindset: "I can only spend £150 on restaurants this month."

Scripting Mindset: "This month, I'm allocating £150 to shared experiences that build relationships."

Same amount, different frame. One restricts. The other *directs*.

The Psychological Edge: From Scarcity to Structure

Cognitive psychology reinforces the superiority of forward-thinking frameworks. Humans are *teleological creatures*—we're more engaged by goals and narratives than by rules and constraints. Studies on mental accounting (Thaler, 1985) have long demonstrated that people treat money differently depending on how it's labelled or mentally categorised. This means that scripting isn't just a logical structure—it's a psychological strategy.

By pre-assigning roles to your income—*before* the first debit hits—you're reducing decision fatigue, increasing alignment, and giving your brain a clear script to follow. This reduces the chance of impulsive spending, post-hoc guilt, or ambiguous trade-offs.

Importantly, scripting is not about perfection. It's about *intention backed by automation.* You're not micromanaging every variable—you're setting the direction, and letting well-designed systems do the rest.

The Structural Blueprint: Roles, Not Categories

The most effective paycheque scripts are based on *roles*, not rigid expense buckets. Think in terms of outcomes:

Security: Essential obligations that preserve your current life—rent, mortgage, insurance, utilities

Freedom: Contributions that expand future optionality—investments, emergency fund, pension contributions

Identity: Spending that reinforces who you want to become—education, fitness, relationships, charity

Joy: Conscious enjoyment that prevents deprivation-based backlash—travel, dining, hobbies

Notice what's missing: "Miscellaneous." In a scripted framework, there is no room for vagueness. Every role must justify its inclusion in the cast.

This approach is particularly empowering for salaried professionals because it reorients the paycheque as a tool for self-authorship, not just expense management. *You are no longer merely spending—you are staging a production.*

Case Example: The Conscious Engineer

Meet Ashwin, a 37-year-old mechanical engineer in Bengaluru earning ₹1.4 million annually (~£13,000). Though his salary was solid by local standards, Ashwin constantly felt behind: never quite saving enough, occasionally splurging out of stress, and rarely sure where his money actually went. He decided to experiment with scripting.

Each month, on the day his salary was credited, Ashwin enacted a pre-set script:

20% auto-invested in an index mutual fund (Freedom)

10% into a personal development fund for courses and conferences (Identity)

10% to a joint family account for elder care and gifts (Joy with intent)

5% to an emergency buffer (Security)

Remaining 55% flowed to two operational accounts—one for fixed costs, one for discretionary spending—with defined boundaries

By month six, something remarkable had happened. Ashwin wasn't just saving more. He felt *clearer*. His spending felt *earned*, not anxious. He reported lower financial stress despite no increase in income—because *his money now had a mission*. His income wasn't scattered across apps and whims; it was *scripted into values-aligned actions*.

This is the crux: *clarity is wealth, even before returns.*

The Ritual: Paycheque Day as Review Day

Another powerful element of scripting is that it turns income arrival into an *intentional ritual*. Too often, payday is treated passively—a number lands in the account, and the subconscious scripts take over: consumption, repayment, obligation.

Instead, scripting encourages a monthly review and reallocation. Not a labour-intensive audit, but a check-in. What's changed? Do my current allocations still reflect my evolving priorities? Has my spending aligned with last month's script?

Over time, this monthly ritual becomes identity-reinforcing. The very act of meeting your money with attention becomes a form of self-respect. *You are no longer managing money. You are managing alignment.*

Tension: Flexibility vs Fidelity

One of the most critical aspects of scripting is knowing when to deviate from the script—and when not to. Too much rigidity and the system becomes brittle. Too much flexibility and the narrative collapses into chaos.

The art lies in building a script that is *robust but breathable.* Include discretionary space. Design buffers. Expect the unpredictable. But maintain fidelity to core roles—particularly those tied to future self and identity.

For instance, even in months where unexpected expenses arise, prioritising your investment or education allocations (even if reduced) signals continuity. The script may adapt—but the story doesn't derail.

This is what distinguishes scripting from outdated budgeting. It's *alive.* It evolves with context, yet remains anchored in purpose.

Legacy Perspective: Scripts Outlive Salary

Perhaps the most overlooked benefit of scripting is its scalability. While designed for monthly cashflow, the framework extends to life stages. As income increases, scripts evolve—*not into greater complexity, but into greater intentionality.*

You might introduce new roles—*legacy*, *mentorship*, *community impact.* But the architecture remains. This constancy in structure allows fluidity in purpose. It ensures that money does not become a goal in itself, but remains a *medium of agency.*

When done well, scripting builds not just a financial operating system—but a narrative of your evolving values, aspirations, and identity over time.

Final Thought: Your Paycheque Is a Manuscript

The average person will receive hundreds of paycheques in their lifetime. Each one is a blank page. You can choose to let circumstance write your story. Or you can *script it yourself*—with clarity, alignment, and purpose.

Scripting your paycheque is not just a method for better money management. It is a discipline of self-authorship. A practice of turning income into intention. And over time, intention into identity.

Because wealth is not just what you accumulate. *It's what you consistently tell your money to stand for.*

Habitual Riches

Why true wealth is less about pressure—and more about identity.

Wealth, at its most practical level, is built transaction by transaction. But at its most enduring level, it is built habit by habit. The difference is crucial. Transactions are momentary. Habits are structural. One can be reversed by a bad month. The other becomes part of who you are.

Most financial advice starts with *what to do*—save more, spend less, invest wisely. But the more transformative question is: *Who are you becoming when you do these things?* This is the central premise of *Habitual Riches*—that long-term financial security and prosperity are not sustained by discipline alone, but by a shift in identity. If you adopt habits only as obligations, they will decay under pressure. If you embody them as extensions of your values, they become automatic, sustainable, and, over time, generative.

This is not behaviourism masquerading as personal finance. It is a fundamental reframing: financial habits are not tools to manage money—they are signals of identity, rituals of legacy, and the architecture of quiet compounding. They do not demand motivation. They produce *momentum.*

The Myth of the Grind: Why Pressure Fails Over Time

There's a reason why so many intelligent, even disciplined professionals struggle to stay consistent with wealth-building behaviours. The problem is not information. It's not even intention. It's *internal friction.* When actions like saving, investing, or budgeting are viewed primarily as chores or burdens, they compete with identity. You feel like you're *doing finance*, not *being someone.*

This tension exhausts willpower—and willpower is a famously unreliable fuel. Research by Roy Baumeister and others in the field of self-regulation demonstrates that habits driven by external pressure deteriorate rapidly under cognitive load. The person who saves out of fear or guilt will abandon the practice when emotional stress rises elsewhere.

Contrast that with the individual who views saving 20% of their income as an *unquestioned trait*—as automatic and identity-bound as brushing their teeth or locking their front door. For them, consistency is not heroic. It is habitual.

The goal, therefore, is not just to *do* wealth-building actions more often. The goal is to *become* the kind of person for whom these actions are natural, obvious, and identity-congruent.

Ritual, Not Routine: Embedding Financial Identity

In his study of behaviour, James Clear outlines a simple but profound distinction: every action you take is a vote for the type of person you wish to become. Applied to personal finance, this becomes a potent framework: *Each habit isn't just a tool. It's a declaration.*

Setting up an automatic SIP isn't just investing. It's casting a vote for being a "builder."

Checking your net worth monthly isn't just data tracking. It's casting a vote for being "aware."

Saying no to impulsive purchases isn't frugality. It's casting a vote for being "disciplined by design."

Ritualising financial habits elevates them beyond the domain of obligation. It connects them to the identity and future self you're investing in. And it embeds them, not just in your calendar, but in your character.

One useful frame is to name your habits. This may sound trivial. It's not. When you label your monthly investment review as "Wealth Alignment Day" or your Sunday expense check-in as "The Stewardship Hour," you give them ritual weight. They stop being tasks and start becoming acts of self-honouring.

Rituals survive where routines fail—because they carry meaning, not just mechanics.

Systems vs. Goals: The Superior Unit of Change

Many professionals set financial goals—buy a house in five years, reach X corpus by 50, pay off student loans. These are fine, even necessary. But they are *results-focused.* They do not, in themselves, create the mechanisms to get there.

What does? *Systems.*

A system is a repeatable, identity-aligned pattern that operates with or without motivation. You don't need to "want" to invest every month if your paycheque is scripted to do so. You don't need to "remember" to review your spending if your financial calendar brings it to you.

Systems relieve pressure. They reduce variability. They convert ambition into architecture.

In a study by Wendy Wood on habit formation, it was found that 43% of daily behaviours are enacted in the same location and context without conscious thought. What if wealth-building was engineered into that 43%?

Consider the contrast:

Goal: "I want to save £20,000 over three years."

System: "Every 5th of the month, 25% of my post-tax income is auto-routed to a high-yield savings account before I ever see it."

One requires constant attention. The other becomes background code—habits running quietly in the operating system of your life.

From Discipline to Identity: The Compounding Effect of Self-Definition

The financial world is obsessed with *compounding returns*. But perhaps the more powerful force is *compounding identity*. Every financial habit executed repeatedly deepens your sense of self as someone who handles money wisely. This is more than psychological fluff—it is functional capital.

Identity-based habits are *stickier*. They resist disruption. And most importantly, they scale. The person who consistently invests £100 a month for three years without fail will almost certainly find themselves investing £500 or £1,000 a month within the next five. Not because of income jumps alone—but because their internal story has changed.

This is what Stanford psychologist Carol Dweck called *self-signalling*: your repeated behaviours communicate to *you* who you are. Eventually, you begin to *live into that version*, and the effort decreases while the output expands.

This is not mysticism. It is neuroeconomics in motion.

Reframing Riches: Not Performance, but Continuity

The cultural image of "riches" often involves visible markers—cars, property, portfolios. But *habitual riches* aren't always visible. They show up in the person who can weather a recession without panic. The one who has six months' expenses stashed quietly. The professional who knows precisely how much is invested, where it's growing, and when it will be enough.

That clarity is not sexy. But it is *sovereign.* And it comes from habit, not hustle.

Here's the irony: the more embedded your habits, the less mental real estate they occupy. Wealth-building becomes *unremarkable.* You are not *doing rich things.* You are simply *being someone whose life generates surplus.*

This reframes success entirely. You are no longer pursuing riches. You are living *as a rich person behaves.* Not in consumption, but in quiet structure.

The Role of Legacy: Why Habits Outlive Hustle

The final shift in habitual riches is existential. Once habits are secure, and identity is defined, a deeper question surfaces: *What are these patterns building toward?* This is where the conversation moves from money to meaning.

Financial habits, at their peak, become *intergenerational anchors.* Your children may never see the spreadsheets. But they'll inherit the rhythm. They will live inside the security your automated behaviours generated. They will internalise the culture of calm, structure, and intention you modelled.

This is legacy, in the purest sense—not wealth transferred, but *worldview transmitted.*

Your habits, once invisible, become inheritance.

Closing Reflection: Wealth Without Worry

The opposite of wealth is not poverty. It is *perpetual financial worry.* Habitual riches cure this—not by maximising returns, but by minimising volatility in your behaviour.

The path to that state isn't paved with pressure, ambition, or hacks. It's grounded in quiet rituals. Monthly. Weekly. Daily. Executed not with urgency, but with dignity.

Because wealth that must be chased is never restful. But wealth that arrives habitually—anchored to who you are—is the kind that stays.

Let others chase performance. You're building permanence.

Fail-Proofing Your Progress

Designing systems to catch you when—not if—you stumble.

It is not discipline that makes people wealthy. It is structure. Every consistent investor, disciplined saver, or intentional spender you admire has one thing in common: not superhuman willpower, but environments engineered to catch lapses before they become spirals. The most resilient wealth-builders assume failure is part of the process—and they prepare for it.

This is the heart of *fail-proofing*: not avoiding setbacks, but disarming them in advance.

The assumption that progress must be linear is not only false—it's dangerous. It sets up a fragile system where any deviation feels like defeat. A single missed investment contribution, a splurge on a holiday, or an unexpected emergency becomes evidence of personal failure. From there, shame sets in, followed by avoidance, and eventually abandonment.

Fail-proofing flips the script. It replaces guilt with feedback. More importantly, it builds *buffers, tripwires, and self-correction mechanisms*—small, intentional designs that prevent temporary setbacks from becoming permanent losses.

The Psychology of Setbacks: Why We Spiral

Let's begin with a counterintuitive truth: *Setbacks don't derail progress. Our reactions to them do.*

Psychologists refer to this as the "What-the-Hell Effect." A dieter eats one forbidden snack and thinks, "Well, I've ruined it—might as well eat the rest of the packet." This effect isn't just emotional; it's neurological. In a 2014 study on self-control failure, researchers found that people who viewed lapses as "evidence of moral weakness" were significantly more likely to abandon long-term goals altogether. Conversely, those who had self-compassion—and, crucially, a path to get back on track—maintained behaviour far more consistently.

In personal finance, this manifests as missed savings targets, investment withdrawals during market dips, or unexpected expenses derailing a budget. What matters is not the event, but the *presence or absence of recovery systems.*

Fail-proofing, then, is not defensive. It's creative. It's how the system forgives without collapsing.

Tripwires: When to Intervene Before It's Too Late

Tripwires are predetermined signals that tell you: *pay attention now.* Think of them as financial motion sensors—designed not to stop you from acting, but to alert you before a small drift becomes a directional error.

Example: Imagine a professional who has set a monthly investment of £1,000. They miss one month due to a holiday. A tripwire might be: "If I miss two contributions in a row, I pause and review my cash flow and schedule a 15-minute recovery meeting with myself."

Tripwires should be:

Measurable: "If my emergency fund drops below £2,000…"

Actionable: "…I suspend discretionary purchases until it's rebuilt."

Emotionally neutral: They are not punishments. They are recalibrations.

By setting tripwires *in advance*, you make intelligent decisions during calm states—not reactive ones under stress. That distinction is everything.

Buffers: Creating Space for Error Without Consequence

If tripwires are about detection, buffers are about *absorption.* They give your system the grace to absorb shocks without failure.

A buffer is any financial reserve, margin, or redundancy that protects you from volatility—whether internal or external.

There are three key types:

1. **Time Buffers** – Automate savings and investments *a few days after* payday rather than immediately. This catches payroll errors or timing mismatches without compromising the strategy.

2. **Cash Buffers** – Maintain a modest balance in a separate "spillover" account—often a week's worth of expenses. If you overspend from your main current account, the buffer absorbs it silently, preventing overdraft fees or emotional panic.

3. **Psychological Buffers** – Label accounts not just by function, but by *emotionally resonant intent.* For example, "Stability Fund" is more protective than "Savings 2." When you feel emotionally attached to the purpose, you're less likely to violate it carelessly.

Importantly, buffers aren't about hoarding—they are about resilience. *A good buffer is one you rarely use, but always respect.*

Correction Paths: Making Recovery Frictionless

Most financial systems fail not because people don't know what to do—but because the act of resuming feels confusing, inconvenient, or guilt-laden.

A correction path is a *predefined protocol* for how to return to the system when you go off-course.

Here's how to structure an effective one:

Name the lapse neutrally: "Missed savings" not "I failed again."

Review without shame: What conditions caused the lapse? Were they structural, emotional, or calendar-based?

Resume with simplicity: Don't overcorrect. Don't punish. Just re-engage. For example, if you stopped investing for two months, don't try to catch up instantly. Resume your standard contribution. If possible, add a one-time top-up from discretionary funds—but only if it's emotionally sustainable.

This is the difference between *resilience* and *rigidity*. Rigid systems break. Resilient systems bend, self-correct, and endure.

The Role of Automation: Removing Willpower from Recovery

Where possible, automate the *return*, not just the contribution.

For instance, if you pause investments during a cash crunch, don't leave it to memory to resume. Schedule a 60-day "restart" transfer in your banking app or investment platform. Even better, tie it to a calendar event with a personal note: "Restart automated investing today—because your system protects you, not pressures you."

Automated fail-proofing has a distinct advantage: it reduces cognitive load. The fewer decisions required to get back on track, the more likely you are to do it. Recovery, like progress, benefits from *design over discipline.*

Anticipating Variability: Designing for Real Life

The financial industry often builds plans based on ideal behaviour: stable income, consistent spending, no emergencies. But real lives are messy, emotional, and cyclical. A durable financial system must accommodate:

Lumpy income (bonuses, freelance, commission)

Irregular expenses (school fees, holidays, emergencies)

Emotional seasons (burnout, grief, impulsivity)

Fail-proofing recognises that no one behaves perfectly, and no calendar is flawless. It incorporates *flexibility without fragility*. For example:

Allocate 5–10% of all bonuses to a "Re-alignment Fund"—used strictly for correcting system drift (not new spending).

Build a quarterly check-in, not just a yearly one. A bad March can be corrected by a good April—if spotted in time.

Progress doesn't demand precision. It demands recovery speed.

Philosophical Interlude: What You Protect Reveals What You Prioritise

Why bother with all this design? Because *what you protect*—through structure, automation, and foresight—*reveals what you value most.*

Fail-proofing is not just tactical. It is existential. It says: "This matters enough that I will not leave it to chance." It reclaims financial agency from randomness, ego, or impulse.

It also reaffirms the truth that success is not a product of perfection, but of *repeatable return to alignment.* As in aviation, where the autopilot makes thousands of tiny adjustments mid-flight, your financial system must be built to adapt—gently, intelligently, continuously.

Setbacks Are Part of the Architecture

To build a wealth system that lasts, assume setbacks are not anomalies. They are *fixtures.* The goal is not to prevent them entirely. The goal is to *design around them so they lose their power.*

This is what elite investors, quiet millionaires, and long-term thinkers do. They build portfolios and cashflows and habits that do not depend on daily excellence—but on monthly recovery.

Fail-proofing is, in essence, *respect for your future self.* It's a form of financial kindness. And it may be the most underrated wealth-building skill of all.

Chapter 7
Investing Without Obsession

Where clarity supplants control—and wisdom endures beyond the din

Wealth, contrary to the narratives spun in countless finance columns and trading apps, is rarely built by those glued to their portfolios. It's forged quietly, over time, by those who've learned to look away. Not because they're indifferent, but because they understand that true clarity often begins where obsessive control ends. If your investment plan requires constant tending—daily check-ins, mood-dependent tweaks, a steady drip of market news—then what you have is not a strategy. It's a strain.

This chapter takes a firm stand for the long-term investor's mindset—an orientation that has grown increasingly rare in a world designed to monetise your attention, gamify your fears, and turn patience into an antique virtue. The irony? The more tightly you clutch your portfolio, the less effective you become at managing it. Not due to a lack of intellect, but because preoccupation skews perspective. Like trying to read a book by holding it an inch from your face.

The root problem isn't a dearth of information—far from it. If anything, today's investor suffers from an excess. And yet, most financial advice keeps recycling the same surface-level fixes: better asset allocation, tighter risk modelling, tax efficiency. Useful? Certainly. Sufficient? Hardly. Because none of it reaches the real fault line—the emotional undercurrent that derails even the most technically sound plans.

Here lies the deeper issue: the conflation of obsession with commitment. Modern financial culture has mistaken vigilance for virtue. But relentless monitoring, far from being prudent, is often a form of quiet panic. It doesn't build resilience; it fractures it. The constant impulse to check, to tweak, to react—that isn't dedication. It's an erosion of your ability to stay the course.

Temperament, not tactics, is what separates consistent investors from reactive ones. And yet, temperament is the one thing most financial education glosses over—as though composure could be assumed, or outsourced. It cannot. It must be cultivated. That means creating distance. That means trusting the system you designed. That means acknowledging that, in the long run, noise is the real enemy—not volatility, not downturns, not missed opportunities. Just noise.

So what does it look like to reclaim your mental margin in this age of anxious investing? Not disengagement, but design. Not indifference, but boundaries. A portfolio you can forget about for weeks—or months—because it has been set up to weather the ordinary storms. A system that requires your presence only occasionally, not incessantly. That's not a lack of discipline; that's discipline evolved.

Because if your money is constantly demanding your attention, then it's not funding your life—it's running it. And in that scenario, you're no longer the investor. You're the asset being drained.

To invest well over decades, you don't need perfect timing. You need a system that survives your worst moods.

The Market Is Not a Mentor

The modern investor lives in a state of cognitive dissonance. On one hand, they are told to think long-term. On the other, they are bombarded with minute-by-minute performance metrics. Apps ping with portfolio updates. Headlines oscillate between crisis and euphoria. Everyone is either winning or losing. Rarely are they simply *investing.*

This creates a psychology of urgency—an addictive loop where one begins to equate activity with progress. In behavioural finance, this is known as the "action bias"—the compulsion to do *something*, even when doing nothing would be wiser. Studies from institutions like Vanguard and Morningstar consistently show that the most successful retail investors are often those who forget their account passwords.

But forgetting is not a strategy. *Designing a system that doesn't require daily vigilance is.*

This chapter introduces frameworks and tools to help you exit the performance treadmill and enter a state of strategic detachment—where you remain engaged, but not reactive; informed, but not obsessed.

The Long Game Ledger: Measuring What Actually Matters

Traditional performance tracking conditions us to prioritise short-term results: monthly returns, benchmark comparisons, leaderboards. But these metrics often reward luck, punish patience, and trigger emotional interference. They seduce us into managing optics rather than outcomes.

Enter the *Long Game Ledger*—a mental and (optionally) physical tool that flips conventional tracking on its head. Instead of logging returns, you record *alignment.*

Did I stick to my investment plan this month?
Did I avoid unnecessary tinkering?
Did I use new capital to build, not speculate?
Did I learn something that increased my investing maturity?

Over time, this ledger becomes a record of character, not just capital. It trains you to see success as consistency, not cleverness. It also builds psychological immunity: when you've documented a year of principled behaviour, a 7% drop in the market doesn't feel like a threat. It feels like noise.

The goal is not to track performance, but to witness process. It is process, not prediction, that compounds reliably.

Silencing the Market's Sirens: Emotional Sovereignty in a Reactive Age

The greatest risk to your wealth is not market volatility. It's your inability to remain unmoved by it. Behavioural economists have documented over 180 cognitive biases. Many of them show up when money and markets mix: loss aversion, recency bias, overconfidence, herd behaviour. These aren't flaws in your thinking—they're features of a brain evolved for survival, not statistical reasoning.

But these emotional reflexes can be trained. The key lies in *distancing mechanisms*—tools and habits that create space between stimulus and response.

You'll explore in this chapter how to build a portfolio you can observe without reacting to. That includes techniques such as pre-committed behaviour protocols, curated information diets, and reframing volatility as a *feature*, not a fault. You'll also learn the distinction between *data that informs* and *data that provokes*. Knowing the difference is not just an investing skill—it's a mental health practice.

Consider this: if you need constant reassurance that your portfolio is "okay," it probably isn't built for your psychology. True alignment is quiet. When your strategy reflects your temperament, *silence becomes confidence.*

Compound Wisdom, Not Just Interest

If your investment returns are the only thing compounding, you're missing the deeper payoff.

Every market cycle offers two returns: one financial, one behavioural. The former may rise or fall with external conditions. But the latter—how you respond, reflect, and revise—compounds internally. The most experienced investors are not those with the most exposure to risk, but those with the deepest reflections upon it.

This is where the concept of *investment mistakes as assets* becomes transformative. Most financial media encourages avoidance of error. Yet seasoned investors treat mistakes as meta-returns—each misstep, when consciously processed, increases decision quality going forward.

You will be introduced to a framework for post-mistake reflection—how to turn regret into resilience, and how to mine your own history for principles that are truly *yours*, not borrowed scripts from gurus or Twitter threads. The goal is not infallibility. The goal is *adaptive integrity*: acting in ways today that your future self would still endorse, even if the market doesn't.

Investing as a Moral Act of Patience

There is a final, more existential layer to this chapter—one not often discussed in books about money. To invest without obsession is not just a psychological strategy. It is a philosophical stance.

It is the belief that patience is not passivity. That choosing not to act is a form of agency. That meaningful outcomes can unfold *without constant interference.* And that your worth is not measured by daily growth curves, but by the continuity of your intent.

This is a radical position in a culture of immediacy. But it is a necessary one if you are to build wealth that survives not just inflation and taxation—but *your own attention span.*

To invest without obsession is to reclaim stillness in a system designed for stimulation. It is to say: "I am not ruled by every fluctuation. I do not need daily affirmation to know I am on track."

And when that becomes true—not just intellectually, but viscerally—you are no longer a speculator. You are a steward.

That is the shift this chapter offers.

The Anti-Day-Trader Philosophy

A manifesto for long-term investors tired of flashy predictions and financial noise

There is a quiet revolution underway—one not led by alpha-seeking traders, fast-talking pundits, or dopamine-fuelled screen-watchers, but by thoughtful individuals who are opting out. Out of the frenzy. Out of the noise. Out of the culture that equates activity with intelligence and volatility with opportunity. These individuals are not lazy. They are not uninformed. They are *anti-day-traders*—by principle, not ignorance.

The anti-day-trader philosophy is not merely a critique of short-termism. It is a deliberate commitment to a different intellectual posture: one that resists prediction, embraces time, and restores investing as a rational, identity-driven discipline rather than a recreational obsession. If day trading is theatre, this is architecture—measured, grounded, and designed to last.

Let's be clear: this is not about pitting "smart" investors against "dumb" traders. It is about recognising that the incentives, mechanisms, and assumptions that govern day trading are structurally at odds with wealth-building for most salaried professionals. What works in a high-frequency hedge fund with proprietary algorithms is not only irrelevant to the average investor—it is dangerous when imitated without context.

The anti-day-trader is not trying to win today. They are trying not to lose tomorrow.

The Tyranny of the Tick

The stock market, in its rawest form, is not an investing tool. It is a pricing machine. And what it prices, moment by moment, is not long-term value but short-term emotion—fear, speculation, crowd psychology. To treat this machine as a guide for personal financial strategy is like using a weather radar to plan a forest.

Day trading thrives on this emotional volatility. It sells the illusion of control—the idea that, with just enough information, timing, and skill, one can outwit the randomness. The research, however, is unequivocal. A landmark study from the University of California, Berkeley, found that the average active trader underperformed the market significantly, not due to poor strategy alone, but due to overconfidence and excessive turnover.

Even worse, this behavioural cost compounds. In attempting to capture small gains, many traders expose themselves to *constant decision fatigue, frequent tax events, and the mental exhaustion of perpetual vigilance.* The pursuit of edges becomes a treadmill. And as every long-term psychologist will tell you, even the most disciplined minds erode under sustained pressure when the game is never allowed to end.

Time vs Timing: The Foundational Divide

The anti-day-trader philosophy is anchored in a different logic. It does not assume that the world is predictable. It assumes that most of it isn't. And therefore, the only variables worth betting on are those we can control: our time horizon, our contribution rate, our asset allocation, and our response to volatility.

This is not ignorance of market cycles. It is *humility before them.* It is not a denial of opportunity, but a redefinition of what constitutes opportunity in the first place. While the day trader asks, "What is the market doing right now?", the anti-day-trader asks, "What matters ten years from now—and am I behaving in accordance with that?"

Warren Buffett once noted that his favourite holding period is "forever." That's not hyperbole—it's a strategic posture. Because when you stretch your timeframe far enough, noise becomes irrelevant. When you shorten it to hours or days, noise becomes your oxygen. And no meaningful wealth was ever built on noise.

Resisting the Spectacle

The real challenge for the long-term investor today is not data, strategy, or tools—it is *attention sovereignty.* We live in a media environment designed to destabilise patience. Financial content has morphed into entertainment. Clickbait thumbnails shout about the "next big crash," while social media celebrates wins with the enthusiasm of a casino floor.

This environment does not reward good investing. It rewards constant reaction. And reaction, by definition, is *the enemy of intention.*

To be an anti-day-trader is to resist this spectacle. It is to protect one's cognitive bandwidth. To deliberately consume less market commentary, not because one is uninformed, but because information is not neutral—it comes pre-loaded with emotional energy. The more often you check your portfolio, the more likely you are to act. And *every action demands justification—even when none is needed.*

Anti-day-traders set boundaries. They don't check their net worth daily. They automate their investments not just for efficiency, but for insulation. They build systems that eliminate unnecessary choices, so that *discipline becomes default*, not a daily negotiation with willpower.

Betting on Behaviour, Not Brilliance

The modern financial landscape offers endless products, strategies, and tactics. Yet study after study finds that the single greatest predictor of long-term investing success is not IQ, education, or access. It is *behavioural consistency.* And this is where the anti-day-trader philosophy reveals its power.

By removing the temptation to optimise every trade, rebalance every week, or react to every tweet, long-term investors preserve their most important asset: *psychological stamina.* They understand that markets reward those who are still standing—not necessarily those who guessed right.

A portfolio's greatest risk is not misallocation. It is misbehaviour. And this misbehaviour is most frequently triggered by hyper-engagement with market noise. Just as people who track their calories obsessively are more prone to disordered eating, investors who track their holdings minute-by-minute are more likely to override sound plans with impulsive moves.

To invest well is to rehearse calm. The anti-day-trader doesn't try to be emotionless. They build systems that make emotion irrelevant.

The Practical Manifesto

What does this philosophy look like in practice? It's not glamorous. It doesn't yield fast wins. But it builds wealth with remarkable reliability. Here are a few core tenets—expressed not as rules, but as deeply held postures:

Invest according to a strategy that you *can follow for decades*, not one that only works if perfectly executed in the next six months.

Make decisions at the *portfolio level*, not at the security level. You are not a hedge fund manager. You don't need to be.

Judge performance by *consistency of behaviour*, not by quarterly returns.

Define success by *alignment with your values*, not your proximity to the S&P 500.

This last point is especially important. Many investors unconsciously anchor their sense of success to benchmarks that have nothing to do with their goals or constraints. A person saving for a home in five years should not compare their outcomes to someone compounding for retirement over 40. The anti-day-trader philosophy invites a more *sovereign definition of success*—one that is internal, anchored in context, and resilient to external pressure.

Legacy Over Liveliness

The final distinction to make is this: anti-day-trading is not about passivity. It is about *purposeful quietness*. It is not the same as neglect, laziness, or inaction. It is *an act of resistance* against the cultural script that equates motion with meaning.

This is especially relevant for professionals who are building wealth alongside full-time careers, family responsibilities, and finite cognitive bandwidth. Your job is not to beat the market. Your job is to *not let the market beat you.* And the way you do that is not by becoming more active, but by becoming more intentional.

In the end, this philosophy is less about tactics and more about identity. It asks: *Who am I becoming through the way I invest?* Am I building a posture of patience, clarity, and self-trust—or am I becoming more anxious, reactive, and dependent on external validation?

If your investment strategy makes you feel less calm over time, something is wrong—not with the market, but with the relationship you've built to it.

To be an anti-day-trader is not to be a contrarian. It is to be a craftsman. Not of trades, but of temperament.

And in a world that celebrates the loudest players, it's often the quietest ones who build the strongest fortunes.

The Long Game Ledger

A simple yet profound tool to track not returns, but alignment with long-term goals

There is a quiet flaw in how we track our progress as investors. Not in the spreadsheets themselves—those are often precise—but in what we choose to measure. Most personal finance tools obsess over returns, balances, growth curves, and net worth. But these metrics, while numerically satisfying, are not always meaningful. They measure *performance*, not *progress*. They offer numbers, not narrative. And in doing so, they can obscure the one question that matters most: *Am I moving in the direction that matters to me?*

The Long Game Ledger is a direct response to this flaw. It's not a product or an app, but a reframing device—a behavioural and strategic tool that shifts the axis of measurement from "How much have I made?" to "Am I aligned with my actual goals?" It is minimalist in form but radical in function. Because while traditional tracking systems mirror the markets, the Long Game Ledger mirrors the investor.

It is not about returns—it is about *returning* to what matters.

Measuring the Wrong Game

Let's begin with the obvious: most investors know how to check their portfolio value, but very few know how to evaluate whether that portfolio is serving the life they're trying to build. There's a dangerous asymmetry in modern financial culture: precision in tracking market data, and vagueness in defining personal purpose.

For instance, if your primary financial goal is to achieve partial work independence in your 50s, but your portfolio is optimised for maximum capital growth through high-volatility assets with a 30-year horizon, there is a silent mismatch. Your spreadsheet might show green arrows and compounding charts. But your *life design* might be drifting further from feasibility.

Traditional investing tools do not alert you to this. They reward quantitative efficiency, not qualitative alignment. And so, you can be "winning" according to the dashboard while actually drifting, quietly and incrementally, from your true objectives.

The Long Game Ledger corrects this by making your future self the benchmark—not the market.

What Is the Long Game Ledger?

At its core, the Long Game Ledger is a structured, periodic reflection exercise—part journal, part decision review, part planning prompt. Unlike portfolio trackers, it doesn't ask what your investments have done. It asks what you've done with your investments. What decisions you made. Why you made them. Whether those choices were consistent with your stated principles. And whether those principles still hold.

It is a qualitative check-in system that operates alongside, not in place of, quantitative tools. And it does so on a human time horizon—monthly, quarterly, or semi-annually—rather than daily or weekly. Its format can be adapted, but its key dimensions usually include:

Clarity Review: Are your long-term goals still defined and visible? Have they shifted?

Behavioural Audit: Did your recent decisions reflect fear, excitement, or strategy?

Alignment Assessment: Are your current financial structures (automations, asset mix, liquidity access) still optimised for your life stage and values?

Regret Minimisation: Is there anything you would undo or rethink, not because of outcomes, but because of process?

Forward Posture: What small refinement will increase alignment without increasing complexity?

In this format, the Ledger becomes a quiet ritual of realignment. It puts *life context* back at the centre of wealth-building.

The Philosophy Behind It: Financial Eudaimonia

What the Ledger truly represents is a philosophical pivot—from outcome-centric finance to *eudaimonic finance*. That is, wealth defined not as accumulation, but as the capacity to live in accordance with one's values and potential. Aristotle's eudaimonia referred to human flourishing—something cultivated over time through congruence between intention and action.

Modern investing often loses sight of this. Chasing better yields, clever funds, or market timing strategies might serve portfolio growth, but they can also become distractions from the deeper work:

building a financial life that enhances agency, optionality, and emotional stability.

The Ledger confronts this head-on. By asking whether your behaviour is becoming more aligned with your identity and aspirations, it protects you from the dangerous illusion that more data equals more wisdom. It replaces *reaction* with *reflection*. And it ensures that strategy is always interpreted through the lens of the self—not through the ticker.

Case Study: Two Portfolios, Two Realities

Consider two hypothetical investors, both in their late 30s.

Investor A has built a £400,000 portfolio aggressively tilted toward tech stocks. Her returns over the last five years have outperformed the S&P 500 by 3% annually. She tracks her accounts weekly, reallocates quarterly, and follows market trends via multiple newsletters. She experiences regular swings between pride and anxiety depending on recent performance.

Investor B has a £280,000 portfolio divided across three globally diversified index funds and a 12-month emergency reserve. He hasn't touched his allocation in 18 months. His annual return trails Investor A by 2%. But each quarter, he reviews a one-page Ledger that documents: a) his updated financial goal timeline (partial retirement at 55), b) a note on why no changes were made, and c) his current alignment rating (on a 1–10 scale) with key principles: simplicity, time freedom, and peace of mind.

Objectively, Investor A has "better numbers." But Investor B has *better clarity*. And, crucially, he has fewer behavioural risks over the next 20 years. His system is grounded in internal feedback loops, not external signals. He is less likely to panic-sell in a downturn or chase yield in a bull market. Because his metric of success isn't monthly returns. It's *continued alignment* with his life arc.

The Ledger gives him something the spreadsheet can't: narrative coherence.

Avoiding False Certainty

One of the greatest risks in long-term investing is mistaking statistical precision for strategic certainty. Historical backtesting, Monte Carlo simulations, and asset correlation charts are helpful—but they do not guarantee lived outcomes. Your future will include job changes, family shifts, health surprises, policy changes, and emotional weather.

In this dynamic context, the most effective system is not the one that maximises return projections. It's the one that creates the most *resilient alignment* over time.

The Long Game Ledger thrives under uncertainty. Because it teaches you to ask a deeper question: *Given who I am becoming, is this financial path still right-sized for the life I want to live?*

That's not a question a graph can answer. It requires introspection. And systems that prioritise behaviour over bravado.

Alignment as a Living Practice

The Ledger is not static. Like a good financial plan, it evolves as your life does. In your 20s, it might focus on habit-building and identity clarity. In your 30s and 40s, it becomes a strategic map—coordinating children, mortgages, career evolution, and wealth-building. In later decades, it transforms into a legacy tool—helping ensure that financial decisions support continuity, autonomy, and stewardship.

Its power lies in simplicity. The act of pausing, writing, and reflecting every quarter forces a confrontation with the core question: *Are my actions aligned with what I say matters?*

This alone inoculates against one of the most common investor failures—not losing money, but losing orientation.

From Tracking to Thinking

We are not suggesting investors abandon numbers. Metrics matter. But they are not enough. When you over-index on return tracking, you outsource your self-awareness to the market. The Long Game Ledger is the opposite: a way of *internalising strategy* by embedding it into the rhythm of your thinking life.

And this is perhaps its deepest function—not just as a tool for better financial outcomes, but as a mirror for becoming the kind of person who makes decisions from conviction, not compulsion.

Silencing the Market's Sirens

Psychological skills to ignore the panic and euphoria that derail steady investors

Every investor begins with good intentions. They sketch out long-term goals, build a balanced portfolio, and nod approvingly at the wisdom of patience and compound growth. Yet, when markets spike with irrational exuberance or crash under the weight of sudden fear, those same investors often abandon their principles. The pull is visceral. Newsfeeds glow red. Voices of urgency multiply. And rational plans are swiftly replaced by impulsive reactions.

What derails most investors is not poor knowledge—it is *emotional interference.* The mind, under pressure or promise, begins to misinterpret noise as signal. The problem is not information scarcity, but the *misweighting* of information. A tweet feels louder than a long-term trend. A news headline feels heavier than a well-formed financial plan. In these moments, investing becomes less about strategy and more about *survival theatre*—where action feels like safety, and stillness feels like negligence.

To build enduring wealth, one must acquire not only financial knowledge, but *emotional insulation.* The ability to stay calm—not because the market is calm, but because *you* are trained to withstand its seductions and scares. That is what this subchapter is about: the cognitive muscles and behavioural techniques that allow long-term investors to ignore the sirens—and stay anchored.

The Sirens Are Real: A Historical Prelude

In Homer's *Odyssey*, the Sirens lured sailors to their death not with threat, but with song—sweet, seductive, promising truths the listener most wanted to believe. Odysseus, forewarned, had his crew plug their ears with beeswax and tied himself to the mast. It wasn't brute strength that saved them. It was pre-commitment.

Modern financial markets are filled with digital sirens—constant, melodic, and psychologically engineered. Market pundits make definitive predictions. Apps send alerts in red fonts. Influencers declare the next "unmissable" opportunity. It is not a lack of data that threatens investors—it is *over-attunement* to data that is emotionally arousing but strategically irrelevant.

What makes the modern sirens harder to ignore is their personalisation. Algorithms feed us precisely the kind of information that has previously triggered us. Your panic is not accidental. It is *targeted.* And unless you install deliberate cognitive defences, you will act not as an investor—but as prey.

The Psychology of Market Panic

Fear and greed are not abstract concepts. They are deeply embodied reactions, wired into our evolutionary inheritance. When an investor sees their portfolio down 20%, the brain doesn't run a Monte Carlo simulation. It activates the amygdala, which primes the body for flight or fight. Cortisol levels rise. Sleep is disrupted. The idea of "riding it out" feels like abandonment.

This is not weakness. It is *biology*. But it means that investing well requires training the brain to override its own instincts. You cannot "think" your way out of a panic in real time unless you've *pre-trained* for it. The market rewards discipline, but it punishes those who believe discipline is the same as intelligence.

Behavioural finance has mapped dozens of biases that contribute to poor investing decisions—recency bias, loss aversion, herd behaviour, overconfidence. Yet knowledge of these biases is not protective unless accompanied by *practice.* Knowing you're likely to panic is different from preparing your environment to prevent that panic from taking over.

This is the art of silencing the sirens.

Technique 1: Decouple Performance from Identity

One of the most damaging illusions in investing is the fusion of self-worth with portfolio performance. When markets rise, investors feel clever. When markets fall, they feel foolish or ashamed. This emotional yo-yo is not just exhausting—it distorts decision-making.

To invest steadily, one must decouple *identity* from *market outcomes.* This does not mean detachment. It means realignment. You are not a good investor because your portfolio rose. You are a good investor because your process was sound—regardless of what the market did this quarter.

A helpful reframe: judge yourself not by *performance*, but by *process adherence.* Did you stick to your principles? Did you rebalance when you said you would? Did you resist reacting to headlines? If yes, then you succeeded—even if your portfolio temporarily shrank. Letting the market become the measure of your discipline is like letting the weather define your fitness.

Technique 2: Time Horizon Rehearsal

Humans are present-biased. We overemphasise short-term events and underweight long-term consequences. One powerful corrective is *time horizon rehearsal*—a mental exercise in which you imagine your future self looking back on today's decisions.

Ask: How would my 65-year-old self view this moment? Would they thank me for panic-selling a diversified portfolio in response to one year of underperformance? Or would they admire the calm?

By rehearsing the long view—habitually—you create a buffer against short-term emotion. You install a higher self as a kind of internal compass. This doesn't eliminate stress, but it gives you a reference point beyond the daily noise.

Technique 3: Intentional Information Fasting

Information is not inherently helpful. Unfiltered information—especially in excess—can paralyse or mislead. One of the most powerful tools a long-term investor can adopt is *structured ignorance.* That is, the deliberate decision to not know certain things, or to know them *less often.*

For example: check your portfolio once per quarter. Subscribe to only one source of market commentary, and read it weekly—not daily. Turn off push notifications. Delete trading apps from your phone. Build *informational firewalls* that protect your brain from volatility masquerading as relevance.

The irony is profound: in an age of infinite access, wisdom often comes from *selective blindness.* If your investment plan is long-term, then most short-term information is not just noise—it is sabotage.

Technique 4: Anchor to First Principles

When you feel drawn into market emotion, return to your own plan. Why are you investing? What are your goals? What is your asset allocation, and why was it chosen? Often, panic arises not from genuine threat, but from *forgetfulness.*

Writing down your investment principles—and revisiting them during times of market drama—is a powerful anchor. It reminds you that you made decisions based on strategy, not moods. And it gives your current self a chance to respect the wisdom of your past self.

This is not rigidity. It is fidelity. You are allowed to evolve your plan—but not abandon it mid-storm because of noise you didn't account for.

Technique 5: Create Emotional Circuit Breakers

Sometimes, even preparation isn't enough. That's why it's useful to install *circuit breakers*—pre-agreed behavioural constraints that prevent impulsive damage.

Examples:
– A 48-hour rule before executing any major portfolio changes.
– Requiring a written justification before making a trade.
– Speaking to a financial coach or accountability partner before altering your plan.

These are not signs of weakness. They are safeguards against *temporary irrationality*. Elite investors don't just trust their judgement—they distrust it *strategically* in high-stress moments. And they build systems accordingly.

The Cost of Obsession

The final siren is not panic—but obsession. Watching the market too closely, even when it rises, creates a form of psychic entrapment. It breeds overconfidence, breeds reactionary thinking, and installs false urgency as a default mental mode.

You were not made to monitor fluctuations by the hour. Nor does wealth multiply faster because you worry harder. The goal of investing is not to be *engaged* all the time—but to be *structured* enough to disengage.

Wealth is built not only through compound interest, but through *compound calm.*

Silencing the market's sirens is not about tuning out the world. It's about *retuning your internal world* so that outer noise no longer dictates your inner state. This is a psychological skill, not a technical one. It's a shift from fragile reactivity to practiced resilience.

In a world that celebrates reaction and reveres instant commentary, this is a radical act. But it is also a necessary one. Because the investors who stay grounded are not the ones who knew the most—but the ones who could *remain themselves* when others forgot who they were.

Compound Wisdom, Not Just Interest

Positions every investment mistake as an asset—if reflected upon, not avoided

The greatest return on investment is not always financial. While spreadsheets quantify growth in percentages and charts display compounding over time, there is another curve—less visible, more personal—that can be even more consequential: the compounding of insight. In the realm of personal finance, the idea that mistakes are liabilities to be minimised is as common as it is limiting. A more fruitful premise is that errors, when examined with clarity and discipline, are *intellectual assets*—tools to refine your judgement, deepen your understanding, and elevate your investing acumen far beyond what smooth success ever could.

This subchapter is not about making peace with mistakes. It is about extracting *equity* from them. The investor who learns to compound wisdom—not just interest—is the investor who becomes resilient, anti-fragile, and quietly formidable. Because money grows when it is left alone. But *judgement* grows when it is not.

The Asymmetry of Learning: Why Mistakes Matter More Than Success

One of the cognitive illusions that afflicts even intelligent investors is the assumption that success teaches more than failure. But in investing, the opposite is often true. Success, particularly early success, tends to reinforce overconfidence and survivorship bias. It encourages the mistaken belief that outcomes are primarily the result of insight, rather than luck or favourable conditions. Failure, on the other hand, punctures illusion. It demands scrutiny. It compels an investor to ask: *What did I miss? What assumption did I carry that proved false?*

The neuroscientist Daniel Kahneman warned of *hindsight bias*—the tendency to view past events as more predictable than they were. This is particularly corrosive when investors look back on losses and tell themselves, "I knew it would happen." That false clarity protects ego but prevents growth. Real learning begins when the ego is bypassed in favour of post-mortem curiosity.

The real tragedy of investing errors is not the financial cost. It is the intellectual waste when those errors are ignored, denied, or explained away. *Every financial loss contains potential tuition.* But tuition is only useful if you actually attend the class.

Case Study: The Tuition of the Tech Bubble

Consider an investor who bought aggressively into technology stocks in 1999, riding the wave of optimism that surrounded the dawn of the internet age. By March 2000, their portfolio had ballooned. Then, the crash: the NASDAQ Composite lost nearly 78% of its value by 2002. If that investor walked away from the experience bitter, resolved never to invest again, the cost was total—both financial and intellectual. But suppose they asked: *Why was I so confident? What did I misunderstand about valuation? Why did I ignore warnings?*

Those questions, honestly examined, become compounding filters for future decisions. That investor may later resist overexposure to cryptocurrency during the speculative peaks of 2021. They may demand better reasoning before following a trend. They begin to see exuberance not as excitement—but as a caution signal. In this way, *the mistake pays again*—not in dollars, but in better decisions.

Wisdom accrues fastest when it is metabolised from failure.

The Metacognition Advantage

Metacognition—the ability to think about one's thinking—is the distinguishing trait of investors who get sharper over time. Many people increase their wealth through timing or exposure. Far fewer increase their *decision quality* consistently across cycles.

A metacognitive investor asks, after every major financial decision:

What was my reasoning at the time?

Which signals did I prioritise? Which did I ignore?

What was emotionally driving me that I may have mistaken for insight?

These are not academic questions. They are performance diagnostics. Just as elite athletes study video footage to refine technique, elite investors review their own behaviour—not to assign blame, but to *systematise feedback*. It is not enough to note a mistake. You must *classify* it. Was it an error of information, interpretation, emotion, or execution? Only then can you build safeguards that reduce its recurrence.

The irony is sharp: The most valuable tool in investing is not a calculator. It is a journal.

From Shame to Strategy: Reframing the Role of Error

The language we use around mistakes matters. Many investors feel shame around loss-making decisions. They describe themselves as "foolish," "impulsive," or "incompetent." But shame paralyses. It shuts down inquiry. A more productive framing views mistakes as *data-rich events*—inputs to a broader learning system. Instead of asking

"What was wrong with me?", the more generative question is, "What was incomplete about my model of the world?"

Consider the work of philosopher Karl Popper, who argued that the strength of a theory lies not in how often it is confirmed, but in how vulnerable it is to falsification. A strong investment thesis should have clear parameters for what would disprove it. If it fails, that falsification becomes a pivot point—not a personal failure.

The most skilled investors are not error-free. They are *reflection-rich*. And over time, they compound not just their capital, but their *clarity*.

The Feedback Flywheel

Once reflection is integrated as habit—not occasional crisis response—it becomes a *flywheel*. Insights gained from one mistake prevent a dozen others. Better yet, those insights often apply *outside* of investing. They improve hiring decisions, negotiation strategy, career moves. Because the mental models you refine—risk management, incentive analysis, delayed gratification—are broadly transferable.

This is the overlooked truth: *Your worst investments, if properly analysed, may produce your best insights.* Not because they failed, but because they left you no choice but to grow.

Building a Reflection Protocol

To make the compounding of wisdom systematic, not incidental, consider adopting a post-investment reflection protocol. It needn't be elaborate. It might include:

Writing a short memo before making any major financial decision, capturing your rationale and expectations

Reviewing that memo 6 or 12 months later to identify what played out differently

Tracking patterns of overconfidence, misjudged risk, or emotional override

Translating those findings into *operational changes*—whether in how you filter advice, how often you check performance, or how you diversify

In doing so, you convert each decision into *a learning loop*. Over time, the loops get tighter. You recognise danger signals sooner. You correct faster. You trust yourself more—not because you're perfect, but because you *know how you learn.*

The Mistake Dividend

The value of a mistake is proportional to your willingness to interrogate it. For investors, that interrogation must go beyond the superficial ("I shouldn't have sold") and penetrate deeper levels: *Why did I sell? What fear was I managing? What belief did I hold that proved false?* Only then does the mistake begin to pay its true dividend—not as a tax, but as a teacher.

We often speak of compound interest as the eighth wonder of the world. But compound wisdom may be the ninth. It pays not annually, but *per insight.* And while interest is limited by capital, *wisdom has no ceiling.* It scales with attention. It multiplies with humility. It protects against not just losses—but stagnation.

To become a wise investor is not to eliminate error. It is to *harvest it.* Every market cycle offers tuition. Most ignore it. A few pay for it but skip class. And the rarest kind of investor? The one who turns each error into *mental equity*—an asset class with no expiry, immune to inflation, and capable of compounding indefinitely.

You don't need to win every trade to build wealth. But you must learn from every one that goes wrong. Because when wisdom compounds, so does *peace of mind.* And over time, that may be the highest return of all.

Chapter 8
The Wealth Conversation

Silence, contrary to popular belief, isn't neutral. More often than not, it is a quiet kind of consent. Nowhere does this ring truer than in our widespread hesitation to speak openly, wisely, and humanely about money. In many households, financial matters are either a recurring battleground or a topic carefully avoided. Offices wrap it in professional decorum, where tension simmers just below the surface. Among friends, it's a minefield of unspoken comparison and polite distance. And within families—especially between generations—money tends to be shrouded in secrecy, passed down more as mystery than meaning.

This chapter is an attempt to dismantle that silence—not by amplifying the noise of money talk as we currently know it (the status signalling, the speculative banter, the performative spreadsheets), but by reimagining the conversation altogether. By raising the tone, widening the lens, and asking better questions.

Real, durable wealth has never been just a number. Its truer measure lies in how clearly we understand it, how confidently we engage with it, and how well we pass its lessons forward. If wealth is to serve its purpose, then we must begin treating it less as a private battleground and more as shared terrain—a living, evolving conversation that carries values across time, cements trust, and brings coherence to the lives we are building.

Because when money goes unspoken, it doesn't disappear—it calcifies. It becomes legend, loaded with assumption and secrecy. But when brought into the light, into conversation, money becomes what it ought to be: a tool, not a mystery. Something that can be taught, understood, adjusted. Something we shape—rather than chase.

The real question isn't whether we should talk about money. That's long settled. The question is whether we can begin to talk about it in ways that nourish rather than shame, illuminate rather than intimidate. Can we speak of wealth without falling into spectacle or silence?

This chapter argues that we need a new language for wealth—one rooted not in flash or volume, but in maturity of thought, clarity of heart, and depth of purpose. A vocabulary that treats money not as the centre of life, but as one of its instruments. Not the goal, but the means. Not the measure of worth, but a reflection—imperfect but telling—of what we value most.

It's time, then, to bring wealth back into conversation. Not louder. Just better.

From Taboo to Toolkit: Teaching Money Before It Teaches You

Let us begin where too few financial conversations do: with children. Not in a didactic, rules-based way, but through quiet exposure to autonomy, generosity, trade-offs, and time. Financial literacy is not something to be installed like software when a child turns eighteen. It is a language, a lens, and a logic that must be embedded through stories, observations, and—most powerfully—*participation.*

Studies in developmental psychology have long shown that children as young as seven begin forming money beliefs based on observed behaviour. Not what they are told—but what they witness. If a child grows up seeing money as a source of stress, secrecy, or status, those impressions calcify into habits. But if a child is shown that money can be discussed, planned, and shared thoughtfully, it becomes a neutral, navigable part of life—not a source of fear or guilt.

Financial autonomy doesn't begin with a bank account. It begins with *consequence.* Letting a child allocate part of their allowance to spending, saving, and giving—not as a test, but as a tool for *identity formation.* The point isn't precision. It's narrative. Each financial act teaches a story: about enoughness, about trade-offs, about *values with real-world implications.*

We are not raising account managers. We are raising future decision-makers. And decision-making is trained not in one-off lectures, but in the repeated small acts of resource allocation, stewardship, and reflection.

Wealth in Relationship: The Shift from Isolation to Shared Intelligence

There is a quiet fallacy embedded in most personal finance narratives: that the path to wealth is individual. The solo investor. The self-taught genius. The frugal outlier. While independence is useful, isolation is not. Financial competence may start alone—but financial *durability* is social.

Humans are pattern-seeking, emotionally reactive, and cognitively biased. We are especially vulnerable to financial mistakes when we are *untethered*—without context, without feedback, without accountability. A well-designed wealth life includes others—not as dependents or competitors, but as *mirrors and mentors.*

This does not mean outsourcing decisions. It means building *networks of context*: trusted peers who understand your financial philosophy, your risk tolerance, your long-term vision. It means engaging in transparent, shame-free conversations about what's working, what's confusing, and what's changing. And critically—it means *reciprocity*. A collective wealth model is not a pyramid scheme or groupthink. It is *co-learning*. You offer perspective and receive it. You become literate not just in your own decisions, but in the mistakes and experiments of others.

Modern tools—investment clubs, accountability partnerships, financial therapists—are all evidence of a cultural hunger to talk about money without posturing or panic. But the deeper opportunity is this: to normalise financial dialogue as a core competency of adulthood, not a crisis-driven sidebar. When intelligent people speak intelligently about money, it raises the standard for everyone.

The more money is talked about wisely, the less it needs to be worshipped blindly.

Redefining Pride: Wealth as Quiet Stability, Not Loud Performance

What if wealth wasn't something to show—but something you could feel? Not in the form of dopamine hits from luxury or applause, but in the form of *quiet, internal orientation.* Knowing your obligations are covered. Your values are funded. Your future is not a guess, but a graph you trust.

The cultural signals around wealth are noisy: luxury, dominance, speed. But the lived experience of real wealth is different. It feels like *margin.* Like *optionality.* Like being able to say no—without drama. Like being able to help—without depletion. These forms of wealth rarely show up on social feeds, but they endure far longer than their performative cousins.

The "quiet pride of wealth" is a reframing worth adopting, especially in a time when visibility is often mistaken for substance. Wealth does not require branding. It requires *consistency.* It doesn't ask you to prove yourself. It invites you to *know yourself*—and to construct a financial life that reflects that knowledge, privately and powerfully.

This pride does not preclude generosity. In fact, it enables it. Quiet pride is not secrecy. It is sovereignty. It is the internal satisfaction of *alignment*—knowing that your wealth practices mirror your beliefs, not someone else's expectations.

The Invitation: Become the Author of Your Own Financial Culture

Every person inherits a financial culture—sometimes silently. Messages about money flow through family habits, community norms, media saturation, and economic circumstance. But few are taught to examine that culture, let alone *reconstruct it.* This chapter invites you to become an author, not just a recipient. To design a personal and familial financial culture that is *intentional, legible, and durable.*

This may include new scripts with your children, new rituals with your partner, new alliances with peers, or new practices of reflection and review. It may include vulnerability. Almost certainly, it will require practice. But the reward is generational: *a family, a circle, a legacy where wealth is neither idolised nor ignored—but understood, nurtured, and shared.*

That is the wealth conversation worth having.

And it starts, quite simply, by deciding: *we talk about money here.*

Breaking the Money Taboo

Guides readers on initiating honest money conversations with partners, children, and ageing parents.

Silence around money is rarely neutral. It's a form of avoidance that breeds misalignment, confusion, and often, regret. Across families, partnerships, and generations, the unspoken norms surrounding finances do not protect relationships—they quietly erode them. What's left unsaid about money tends to show up elsewhere: in tension, mistrust, or unintended consequences. This subchapter is an argument—not just for financial literacy—but for *financial dialogue* as a core form of emotional maturity and relational health.

Money is not merely arithmetic. It is autobiographical. Our financial behaviours and anxieties are shaped by family histories, personal traumas, socio-economic positioning, and the stories we inherit about success, security, and self-worth. That complexity is precisely why most people don't want to talk about it. But that complexity is also why we must.

The ability to initiate honest conversations about money—with partners, children, and ageing parents—is not just a tactical advantage. It's a moral one. It respects the reality that financial life is rarely lived in isolation. It acknowledges that even solitary earners are part of relational systems, where decisions ripple outward, sometimes for generations.

To break the money taboo is to stop treating wealth as a private obsession or shameful secret and begin treating it as a shared resource—a source of collaboration, not control; of alignment, not avoidance.

Why Money Is So Hard to Talk About—Even for Smart, Mature Adults

The resistance is rarely intellectual. It is emotional. Money conversations are loaded not because the maths is hard, but because the meanings are. Talking about finances often stirs feelings of guilt, inadequacy, fear, or perceived judgment. It invokes buried beliefs—about independence, generosity, failure, or identity.

In partnerships, it can feel like vulnerability: *What if they see how disorganised I've been? What if they don't agree with my choices?*
In parenting, it can feel like responsibility: *Am I teaching the right lessons—or projecting my fears?*
With ageing parents, it can feel like role reversal: *How do I bring this up without implying incapacity?*

Psychologically, these conversations tap into some of the deepest parts of our personal narratives. The economist is not exempt, nor is the therapist. It is not knowledge but *self-awareness and courage* that determine the success of these dialogues.

The taboo persists not because money is unimportant, but because it is too important—and we lack a script for dealing with that complexity directly.

With Partners: Aligning Values, Not Just Expenses

No topic triggers more undercurrents in romantic partnerships than money. Not because of greed or materialism, but because money so often proxies for values: freedom, security, generosity, identity. Yet many couples manage finances without ever directly discussing these foundations. They talk about the "how"—who pays for what, how much to save—but rarely the "why".

The risk here is quiet misalignment. When one partner sees money as a source of safety, and the other as a tool for spontaneity, no budget will resolve that until the values are clarified and respected. Harmony in financial life is not merely logistical. It is philosophical.

This doesn't require full agreement on every item—but it demands transparency. What are we optimising for? What scares us about money? How do we define *enough*? What are our long-term commitments, and what trade-offs do they imply?

It can help to treat these discussions as periodic audits—not just in times of conflict, but as part of relationship maintenance. Ideally, they're held when emotions are stable, not inflamed; when time has been carved out with intention, not squeezed between errands. Done well, they become rituals of shared clarity, not episodes of confrontation.

The aim is not to eliminate tension, but to *understand its origin.* Most couples don't disagree on whether money matters. They disagree on what it *means*.

With Children: Teaching Financial Maturity Without Inheritance of Fear

The great paradox of money and parenting is that we're told to teach children financial responsibility, but rarely shown how to do it without projecting our own wounds. Many adults, raised in environments of scarcity or secrecy, find themselves over-correcting: either shielding their children completely from financial topics or involving them too early, too forcefully.

But children don't need details—they need *exposure*. They need to see money being discussed calmly, intentionally, and ethically. They need to understand that spending choices reflect values, that generosity is as real as accumulation, and that saving isn't deprivation—it's *prioritisation.*

One effective frame is age-appropriate transparency. For younger children, this might involve decisions at the supermarket—"We're choosing not to buy that today because we're saving for something important"—rather than "We can't afford it." For adolescents, it can involve explaining household costs or inviting them to co-manage a modest budget. The goal is not control but *dialogue*—letting them ask, disagree, and develop their own reasoning, under the guidance of experience.

The deeper invitation is to model a non-anxious relationship with money. Not perfection. Not wealth. But *thoughtfulness.* When children see that money can be discussed without fear or judgment, they are far more likely to grow into adults who are neither avoidant nor obsessed—but balanced.

With Ageing Parents: Navigating Role Reversal with Dignity

Perhaps the most emotionally complex financial conversation is with one's parents. The dynamic is charged: parents may feel shame, pride, or defensiveness. Adult children may feel guilt, anxiety, or helplessness. Add cultural taboos around mortality, inheritance, or dependence—and it's no wonder these conversations are delayed, if not entirely avoided.

Yet delaying these discussions rarely improves outcomes. Too often, adult children discover the truth—about debt, medical costs, or estate ambiguity—only when a crisis occurs. By then, options are constrained. Emotions are heightened. Misunderstandings abound.

The key here is *framing* and *timing.* Rather than positioning the conversation as a critique or interrogation, it can be introduced as *collaborative planning.* A frame such as, "I want to make sure I honour your wishes and support you well in the future. Can we set aside time to talk about what that might look like—financially and practically?" is far more likely to be received with dignity.

These conversations may need to happen incrementally, especially if your parents are reluctant. But starting them is a sign of *respect*, not intrusion. It recognises that financial well-being in late life is not just a private matter—it is a shared responsibility. And addressing it early can prevent both logistical chaos and relational strain.

To speak about finances with ageing parents is not to usurp their autonomy, but to secure their agency while time and clarity still allow for it.

Practical Considerations Without Oversimplification

While each context—partner, child, parent—requires its own sensitivity, several principles remain consistent:

1. **Lead with values.** Anchor the conversation in what matters, not just what costs.

2. **Ask before advising.** Curiosity disarms defensiveness. "What's your thinking behind that?" is more effective than "That doesn't make sense."

3. **Normalise discomfort.** Acknowledge openly that money is hard to talk about—for *everyone*. This levels the playing field.

4. **Return to the topic.** One conversation rarely suffices. Normalisation comes through repetition, not resolution.

And perhaps most critically: *Model what you hope to invite.* If you want your partner to share more transparently, start by doing so yourself. If you want your children to think long-term, narrate your own trade-offs and savings decisions. If you hope your parents will open up, begin by asking for their wisdom—not just their numbers.

Breaking the Taboo as an Act of Generosity

To talk honestly about money is to offer others a gift: the gift of context, of clarity, of shared decision-making. It is not merely a rational act. It is a *relational one.* You're saying: "I trust you enough to let you in. I respect you enough to include you. I care enough to plan, not just react."

These conversations won't all go smoothly. But their absence carries a greater cost. Mistrust, confusion, avoidable conflict—these are the consequences of silence. Honesty about money isn't a guarantee of harmony, but it is a prerequisite.

Ultimately, breaking the money taboo is not about scripts or spreadsheets. It's about courage. The courage to name what matters. The courage to be seen without polish. The courage to build a financial life that is not just numerically sound, but relationally resilient.

It is an act of intelligence—and of love.

Raising Financially Fluent Kids

Simple, age-appropriate ways to teach children autonomy, generosity, and long-view thinking.

Most adults arrive at financial literacy through trial, error, and emotional scar tissue. They learn not because someone taught them early, but because someone didn't. The bills arrived. The overdraft fees accumulated. The missed investments lingered in hindsight. And then, belatedly, financial adulthood set in.

What if we could interrupt that cycle? Not with lectures or alarms, but with clarity, autonomy, and deliberate exposure—starting not in university, but in childhood. Not with complex spreadsheets, but with simple systems that reflect how money actually functions in adult life: as a medium of value, a reflection of priorities, and a test of long-term thinking.

Teaching children about money is not about creating miniature capitalists. Nor is it about burdening them with financial stress prematurely. It is about *building a relationship*—between the child and the concept of money—that is calm, thoughtful, and resilient. One that avoids both overindulgence and austerity. One that positions financial literacy not as a shield against hardship, but as a foundation for freedom.

The ultimate goal is not control, but *confidence.* Not early savviness, but *early awareness.* Because children who understand the mechanics and meaning of money are more likely to become adults who can think clearly in the face of financial complexity—and act wisely in the presence of temptation.

Why Most Financial Education Comes Too Late

The vast majority of financial education is either absent or abstract. Schools rarely teach budgeting, opportunity cost, or delayed gratification with the same rigour they apply to algebra or grammar. When money is addressed at all, it is often detached from lived reality—reduced to inert lessons about coins, banking terms, or pretend scenarios that rarely map to the decisions adults actually face.

By the time students encounter real money—through a part-time job, student loans, or online purchases—their habits have already started to form, typically modelled subconsciously from the adults around them. But these models are inconsistent. Some children grow up seeing wealth handled responsibly but never discussed. Others witness stress, secrecy, or compulsive spending with no explanation. Silence teaches, too—but often the wrong things.

The point is not that schools or systems are failing. The point is that *parents and caregivers are uniquely positioned to fill the gap*—not through perfection, but through intentional, candid engagement.

The Psychological Foundations: Autonomy, Generosity, and Time Perspective

Before any child grasps compound interest or budgeting tools, they need to internalise three foundational financial dispositions:

1. **Autonomy** – the sense that they can make decisions and live with the outcomes.

2. **Generosity** – the practice of allocating some portion of resources toward others, not because they're told to, but because they *value* it.

3. **Long-view thinking** – the ability to imagine trade-offs across time and prioritise future benefits over present impulses.

These aren't financial lessons per se—they are *identity lessons* taught through the medium of money. And they're most effectively absorbed not through instruction, but through involvement.

Let's explore each more fully.

Autonomy: Letting Them Spend—and Err—Within Boundaries

A foundational mistake well-intentioned parents often make is over-orchestrating their child's spending. They direct every purchase, rescue every poor decision, and inadvertently teach that money flows only through authority. While this may preserve resources in the short term, it inhibits the very skill the child needs most: *financial decision-making* under real constraints.

The counterintuitive truth is this: *a controlled mistake in childhood is far less costly than an untested instinct in adulthood.* The child who wastes £10 today and reflects on the emptiness of the purchase is better positioned than the one who enters adulthood having never weighed cost against value.

A healthy approach involves giving children real money—through allowance, earned tasks, or gift funds—with defined boundaries and *no bailouts*. That last part matters. If children are to develop financial autonomy, they must learn that every pound spent is a pound not available for something else. That trade-off is the essence of budgeting—and it can only be *experienced*, not merely explained.

It also helps to narrate trade-offs aloud in your own life. "I'd love to upgrade the car, but we're choosing to put that money towards a family trip instead. It's about what matters most." These statements do not require formal lessons. They simply demonstrate that money reflects values—not moods.

Generosity: Modelling and Enabling Financial Kindness

Children do not become generous because we lecture them about sharing. They become generous because they *observe generosity being treated as joyful, voluntary, and integral* to a meaningful life.

This is why structured giving—where children set aside a small percentage of their money for donation or gifting—can have profound developmental effects. The key is not the amount, but the intentionality. Letting the child choose the cause, discuss the reasoning, and even see the impact (where possible) helps them understand that wealth is not solely for accumulation or indulgence. It is a tool for contribution.

Importantly, generosity should be decoupled from guilt. It's not a correction for privilege, nor a moral tax. It's a value, like curiosity or gratitude—something that requires expression, not obligation.

When parents model giving openly and involve children in that process—even occasionally—they plant the idea that *money is part of how we show care for others*. This framing outlasts any financial tip.

Long-View Thinking: Training Patience in a World of Speed

Perhaps the hardest financial skill to teach—because it's the hardest to live—is long-term thinking. We are all, adults included, wired for immediate gratification. But in money matters, *delayed gratification is disproportionately rewarded.* From saving for a holiday to compounding an index fund, the patient investor almost always beats the impulsive spender.

So how do we teach this, without moralising or punishing?

The best tool is *a visible, time-linked goal.* For a younger child, this might be a toy that costs more than their weekly allowance, prompting them to save for several weeks. For a teenager, it might be planning a trip, buying a device, or even investing in a custodial account they monitor.

The goal is to let them *feel the reward of waiting*—not just know it. Abstract encouragement ("saving is good") rarely competes with tangible alternatives ("you could buy that now"). But if they experience the satisfaction of achieving something they saved toward, the lesson embeds far deeper than any rule.

Many parents also find that using visual tools—like a goal tracker or spending journal—can reinforce this lesson. But again, the most powerful influence is seeing adults make thoughtful trade-offs. When a child sees you skip a discretionary purchase and explain, "We're putting this toward our anniversary trip instead," they witness long-view thinking in action.

Age Appropriateness Without Infantilisation

A common mistake is underestimating children's capacity to engage with money meaningfully. At age 5, they can understand trade-offs. By 10, they can begin budgeting. By 15, they can grasp investing principles. What matters is not making them "financial geniuses" early—it's *normalising financial thinking* as part of everyday life.

This requires a delicate balance: avoid overwhelming details, but don't reduce everything to slogans. Be honest about your own thinking process. Share your mistakes. Ask for their input. Invite discussion.

Financial literacy thrives where curiosity is welcome and shame is absent.

Building Systems, Not Just Moments

Teaching financial fluency is not about a few big talks—it's about *systems of exposure* that unfold gradually:

A weekly allowance with flexible categories: spend, save, give.

A family budget conversation once per quarter, with simplified categories.

A savings goal sheet or app the child updates themselves.

A "family generosity fund" where children can nominate charities or causes.

Occasional real-world financial planning sessions—planning a birthday party, shopping with a budget, comparing mobile plans, etc.

These aren't lessons. They're *invitations to participate* in the economic life of the family. They help children see that money is not mysterious, forbidden, or intimidating. It is a tool—sometimes complex, often emotional, but always approachable with thoughtfulness.

Why This Matters More Than Ever

In a world of gamified spending, algorithmic persuasion, and near-instant gratification, the ability to navigate money wisely is both rarer and more necessary than ever. Schools may teach coding. Influencers may preach side hustles. But the deeper work—of cultivating children who are thoughtful, grounded, and value-oriented in their financial life—falls to families.

This isn't about turning children into savers, investors, or financial planners. It's about *raising humans who understand that every pound they control is a decision about the life they're shaping*. And that autonomy, when paired with values, is the foundation of freedom.

Financial fluency is not a skillset. It is a mindset. One best learned early, modelled consistently, and reinforced with calm, conscious intention.

It starts not with the numbers, but with *the conversations*.

Collective Wealth, Not Isolation

Encouraging networks of accountability and shared knowledge—without pyramid schemes or hype.

The notion of wealth as a solitary pursuit is both deeply embedded and deeply flawed. Across modern culture, financial success is still narrated as an individual conquest: the lone investor who beat the market, the self-made entrepreneur who rose through grit, the frugal genius who gamed the system. These are seductive stories—but they're structurally misleading. They obscure a quieter, often more powerful truth: *sustained financial progress is rarely made alone.*

To build wealth intelligently and ethically in today's world requires more than effort or information. It demands *connection.* Not dependence, not blind trust, but deliberate networks—spaces where knowledge is exchanged honestly, blind spots are revealed constructively, and momentum is shared, not sold.

And yet, many otherwise thoughtful professionals attempt to navigate personal finance in near-complete isolation. They download budgeting apps they never revisit. They read investment books they never discuss. They make decisions that feel right, but they second-guess them in silence. Why? Because the culture surrounding money often makes openness feel *risky*. The moment finance is discussed among peers, it seems to invite comparison, discomfort, or performative advice.

This is not an accident. It's the product of a financial culture designed to monetise isolation.

Why Financial Isolation Persists

Financial isolation thrives on two psychological loops: *shame* and *confusion.* Shame about past mistakes or perceived shortcomings creates silence. That silence breeds confusion, since there's no healthy feedback loop. And confusion feeds new mistakes—which compound the shame.

Unlike fitness, where group accountability is widely accepted (think gyms, running clubs, training apps), or professional growth (study groups, mentorships, seminars), money often operates in a shadowed zone. It's simultaneously hyper-visible (through status symbols and lifestyle marketing) and hyper-concealed (few people disclose their true net worth, let alone their money anxieties).

Even in friendships, conversations about finances are more likely to orbit *around* the topic than into it. People share tips ("you should try this savings hack"), anecdotes ("crypto made me anxious"), or passive judgements ("I don't get why people still rent"), but rarely disclose the full texture of their financial life—how they budget, what mistakes they've made, what trade-offs they've accepted, and what goals feel uncertain.

Without shared context or collaborative reflection, wealth-building becomes lonelier and riskier than it needs to be.

What *Collective Wealth* Actually Means

The phrase *collective wealth* is often misused. It has been co-opted by multilevel marketing schemes, financial influencers with opaque incentives, and "community" investment platforms that prioritise hype over substance. But the principle itself is valid—and historically powerful.

Collective wealth is not about pooled finances. It's about shared clarity. It means building and participating in networks where financial knowledge, perspective, and accountability circulate freely—without hidden agendas or transactional layers. These networks do not require shared bank accounts, income levels, or investment strategies. They require shared *intentions*—to grow not just money, but understanding.

In practice, collective wealth looks like:

A group of friends meeting quarterly to discuss financial goals, not just net worth.

Siblings openly planning for the financial care of ageing parents.

Peer circles that exchange investment insights and question each other's blind spots.

Communities that normalise talking about money *without performance*—no flexing, no shaming, no pitching.

These interactions are not just socially enriching. They produce tangible benefits: better decisions, fewer regrets, more resilient planning. Research in behavioural economics consistently shows that *people make wiser, more future-oriented financial choices when they feel observed—not judged, but witnessed.* Accountability, in the right setting, elevates clarity.

Historical Precedents: Finance Has Always Been Communal

Throughout history, the idea of individual financial autonomy was the exception, not the norm. From rotating savings and credit associations (ROSCAs) in Africa and Asia, to informal lending circles in immigrant communities, to religious tithing systems that operated as mutual support structures—wealth, and its management, was communal by necessity.

In these models, money flowed through relationships. Reputation, trust, and reciprocity were more powerful than algorithms or contracts. The communities that practised this didn't always have much in material terms—but they had *systems* for resilience. The collapse of one member didn't spiral into a family-wide crisis because others stepped in. Knowledge wasn't hoarded, it was passed on.

Today, despite our vastly more sophisticated tools, we've regressed in this regard. Financial literacy is fragmented, often self-directed, and heavily influenced by commercial interests. But that doesn't mean the communal model is obsolete. In fact, it's more necessary than ever—precisely because financial products have become more complex and marketed narratives more misleading.

Building the Right Kind of Financial Community

Here's the challenge: not all communities improve financial outcomes. Some amplify noise, chase trends, or entrench shame. The key lies in the *design* of the financial circle and the *norms* it reinforces.

A meaningful financial circle should be:

Non-judgmental – Mistakes are treated as learning data, not moral failings.

Disclosure-driven – Members are willing to share real numbers and honest concerns.

Non-commercial – There is no selling, pitching, or hidden monetisation.

Process-oriented – Focus is on habits, systems, and intentions—not outcomes alone.

When these conditions are met, the results can be transformative. People feel less alone. They iterate faster. They course-correct earlier. And they start to see money less as a measure of success, and more as a lever for intentional living.

This isn't theoretical. Studies on peer accountability groups—whether in debt reduction, financial independence, or behavioural change—show significant improvement in outcomes when individuals feel *seen* and *supported*, not just informed.

Technology Can Help—But Only With Guardrails

The digital age offers unprecedented tools to facilitate financial communities. Group chats, budgeting apps with sharing features, co-investing platforms, and online forums have made it easier than ever to connect around money.

But ease of connection is not the same as *quality* of conversation. Many online financial spaces are gamified, adrenaline-fuelled, or dominated by voices with something to sell. They incentivise attention, not reflection.

The solution is not to avoid technology, but to *curate it consciously*. A group of three trusted friends using a shared spreadsheet or budgeting app for quarterly check-ins is infinitely more valuable than 300 strangers on a speculative trading Discord. What matters is *intentionality and trust*, not scale or flash.

Shared Knowledge vs. Shared Dogma

One of the hidden dangers of financial communities is the potential for groupthink. When everyone in a circle shares the same strategy—whether it's property, passive income, or FIRE principles—critical thinking can erode. The moment doubt becomes disloyalty, you are no longer in a community; you are in a cult.

True collective wealth welcomes diversity of thought. It makes room for disagreement, experimentation, and reversal. It says: "Here's what worked for me. What did you see when you tried it?" It invites critical curiosity rather than reinforcing a single orthodoxy.

This is especially important in an age where financial influencers—many without credentials or regulatory oversight—build cult-like followings around their content. The antidote is not cynicism. It's *discernment*, sharpened through honest dialogue with peers who are also navigating complex choices.

Accountability Without Pressure

A final nuance: collective wealth is not about competition or urgency. It's not about "keeping up" with a group's savings rate, investment returns, or property milestones. Healthy accountability is *inward-facing*. It helps you stay aligned with *your own* values and goals, not someone else's trajectory.

A well-designed financial circle doesn't breed comparison. It cultivates clarity. It reminds each member, again and again, that wealth is a personal story—but one best edited with feedback.

Towards a Culture of Financial Dialogue

If the first wave of financial independence was about information access—books, blogs, tools—the next wave must be about *relational competence.* Can we talk about money with nuance, not noise? Can we build networks of accountability that elevate insight without ego? Can we replace secrecy with context?

Collective wealth begins here—not in pooled assets, but in *shared attention.* Not in formulaic strategies, but in honest, evolving conversations. Wealth is not a competition to be won. It is a landscape to be navigated—better with maps, better still with companions.

The myth of the solo financial genius must give way to a more grounded truth: most sustainable wealth is quiet, relational, and guided by thoughtful dialogue. Not everyone needs a financial advisor. But *everyone* needs a financial sounding board.

And that starts not with a spreadsheet, but with a sentence: *"Can we talk about money?"*

The Quiet Pride of Wealth

Reframing financial success as humble, stable, and deeply personal—not loud or performative.

There is a curious irony at the heart of modern wealth: the more money some people have, the more invisible it becomes. Not because they hide it, but because they no longer *need* it to speak for them. This is not humility in the performative sense—frugal billionaires who fly private but wear plain T-shirts. Nor is it the aesthetic minimalism that signals status through understatement. It is something more grounded, more personal: *a form of financial confidence that requires no applause.*

Quiet wealth does not deny its own power. It simply refuses to make power the performance.

For salaried professionals, especially those navigating careers within structured hierarchies and finite pay scales, the cultural noise around wealth is deafening. Influencer culture, speculative investing, luxury marketing, and social media narratives all conspire to define wealth as *visible success*: the car you drive, the holidays you take, the properties you buy, the watches you wear, the announcements you make. These expressions are seductive precisely because they are tangible and recognisable. They signal to others that you've made it—even when the underlying reality is more fragile than it appears.

But when wealth becomes a theatre, sustainability tends to be the first casualty.

The Danger of Performance Wealth

Public displays of wealth, while culturally normalised, often distort personal decision-making. They skew financial priorities towards optics: investing for bragging rights rather than long-term alignment, buying to signal rather than to serve, and measuring success in relative rather than absolute terms. This creates a feedback loop of anxiety—where personal satisfaction is held hostage to perceived social benchmarks.

Consider the well-documented phenomenon of "wealthy broke" professionals: high-income earners with impressive lifestyles but razor-thin buffers. Their portfolios may contain real estate, equity, and private placements, but their day-to-day finances are stretched, and their long-term resilience is questionable. What went wrong? Not intelligence, not access, but *orientation.* Wealth became something to showcase, rather than something to structure with care.

Performative wealth is ultimately fragile because it is externally defined. Quiet wealth is robust because it is internally aligned.

Wealth as a Private Discipline

The quiet pride of wealth is not about being secretive. It is about reclaiming the right to define financial success on your own terms—without the need for external validation. It is about designing a life where money enables autonomy, not anxiety. Where financial systems hum in the background, rather than dominate the foreground. Where you can afford to say no—not just to things, but to people, decisions, and timelines that don't serve your longer arc.

This pride is *earned*, not announced. It comes from habits that don't look glamorous: automated transfers, boring investments, thoughtful budgeting, and values-driven trade-offs. It reveals itself not in possessions, but in posture—how you respond to volatility, opportunity, and uncertainty. It's not loud because it doesn't need to be. Its confidence is structural.

Philosophically, this view aligns more closely with *eudaimonia*—Aristotle's concept of flourishing—not in the sense of hedonic pleasure, but in the quiet fulfilment of living well by living wisely. Wealth, reframed through this lens, is not a trophy but a tool. And its effectiveness depends not on scale, but on stewardship.

Signals vs Systems

One of the most important mental shifts in building quiet wealth is the ability to distinguish *signals* from *systems*.

A signal is designed for others: it is a display. A system is designed for you: it is a foundation. Most performative wealth relies on signal logic—cars, clubs, credentials, curated holidays. These are not inherently bad. But when signals replace systems—as they often do in consumerist environments—they hollow out your financial infrastructure. You can look rich while being brittle.

By contrast, systems are invisible but powerful: regular rebalancing, cash flow management, low-fee diversified portfolios, layered insurance, estate planning, intentional giving. These don't post well on Instagram. But they protect, preserve, and expand your options quietly and exponentially.

One does not need to reject all outward signs of success. But *anchoring your identity in systems rather than signals* is the difference between lasting autonomy and cyclical stress.

Wealth as Identity Infrastructure

If the first half of wealth-building is numerical—how much you earn, save, and invest—the second half is psychological: *what that money means to you, how you relate to it, and how you let it shape—or not shape—your sense of self.* And it is in this second domain that the idea of *quiet pride* finds its strongest footing.

Wealth is not just a financial resource; it becomes, over time, a piece of identity infrastructure. We may not consciously define ourselves by our bank balance, but we *do* define ourselves by the freedoms—or restrictions—it affords. A person with quiet wealth is often less reactive, less desperate to win an argument, less prone to envy or overextension. Why? Because the scaffolding of their life is already aligned with their deeper values. They do not need to reach for status to feel secure. Their pride rests in having created a system they trust.

This is a different psychological posture from either consumer hedonism or financial asceticism. It does not moralise wealth. It *integrates* it—*neither worshipping nor rejecting it, but using it as a reflection of intentional living.* In that way, quiet wealth is less a finish line and more a filter. It sharpens your judgement, not your jewellery.

The Cultural Collision: Visibility vs. Stability

We live in a visibility-obsessed culture. What is shared is often valued more than what is stable. But quiet wealth offers a form of resistance to this cultural logic. It asks a different question—not "How does this look?" but "What does this *allow*?" That question redirects the purpose of wealth away from the social mirror and back toward personal agency.

This is not an argument for hiding or shrinking. Rather, it is an argument for *anchoring*. To be anchored in your financial life means your decisions are internally consistent, not externally dictated. You are no longer flinching at market headlines, comparing pay slips, or feeling pressure to justify your spending. You've earned the ability to operate below the noise.

This cultural contrast becomes particularly visible in middle- to high-income communities, where lifestyle creep is normalised, and wealth signalling is thinly disguised as aspiration. You may live on a street where everyone drives imported cars and upgrades kitchens every five years. But what you cannot see is *who is actually solvent, who is leveraged, and who is quietly building a future immune to surface-level status inflation.*

Quiet wealth does not abstain from enjoyment. It simply *disconnects the enjoyment of life from the appearance of affluence.* That separation—small as it may seem—is what gives it both psychological power and structural durability.

Profiles in Quiet Wealth

To understand quiet wealth more vividly, consider three archetypes—not fictional, but distilled from real behavioural patterns seen in long-term investors and financially mature professionals.

The Architect: This person uses their income not as a tool for performance, but as a mechanism for design. Their wealth plan is not a series of hacks, but a deliberate architecture—automated investments, ethical insurance cover, living trusts, regular rebalancing. Their goal is not speed, but symmetry: each part of their financial life supports the others.

The Steward: This is the person who finds fulfilment not in accumulation, but in careful allocation. They give regularly—not just for tax planning, but as an expression of values. They invest in time-richness for their family. Their wealth is structured to outlast them—not in grandeur, but in *goodness*. Their pride is in what they protect, not in what they project.

The Strategist: This person has cultivated a kind of financial emotional intelligence. They know their trigger points: when they're likely to overspend, chase trends, or react to market hype. So they design systems to override those impulses: spending caps, accountability partners, blackout periods for investment decisions. Their wealth is quietly fortified through behavioural engineering, not just portfolio returns.

None of these archetypes are about radical self-denial. Each demonstrates a form of *conscious authorship*—a refusal to outsource financial direction to cultural trends, peer pressure, or emotional volatility.

The Ethics of Enough

One of the least discussed virtues of quiet wealth is the ethics embedded in it. Not in a sanctimonious sense, but in a practical, lived sense. When you structure your wealth around sufficiency rather than spectacle, you make different kinds of decisions—not just for yourself, but for others.

You may choose not to exploit every tax loophole available, because *compliance and conscience are not always enemies*. You may avoid aggressive returns if they come tethered to companies whose business models harm the vulnerable. You might decide that working one less day a week to be present with your children is worth more than climbing one more income rung.

These are not anti-ambition stances. They are *post-ambition decisions.* They reflect a sense of *"enoughness"*—where wealth stops being a proving ground and starts being a platform for responsibility.

This reframing can only happen when you no longer need money to declare your identity to others. That is the quiet pride: to live in such a way that your finances speak to your integrity, not your insecurity.

The Emotional ROI of Quiet Wealth

There's a final, often overlooked benefit to this orientation: *psychological spaciousness.* When your money is working quietly behind the scenes—automated, diversified, purposeful—you reclaim the bandwidth to think about things that matter more. You stop checking your portfolio daily. You stop budgeting reactively. You stop overthinking every discretionary purchase.

Instead, you have the emotional capital to be present—with your work, your relationships, your community. You make decisions from calm, not compression. And over time, that mental spaciousness compounds. Not unlike interest, but more deeply felt.

That's the kind of return you can't benchmark. And yet, for many, it's the only kind that really matters.

Part 3: Designing a Life That Doesn't Need Proving

There's a crucial distinction between being *wealthy* and being *seen as wealthy.* The first is a financial condition. The second is a social performance. Quiet wealth begins where the need for the second fades—and what remains is the capacity to design a life that feels coherent, principled, and internally satisfying.

This isn't asceticism dressed up as minimalism. It's not about romanticising frugality, nor is it a passive rejection of luxury. It's about intentionality. *What do you really want your money to do?* What is it building—beyond your lifestyle? If financial planning is merely a future-facing spreadsheet, then quiet wealth is the layer underneath it: the *why* behind the *what.*

In practical terms, this means treating financial decisions not as consumer expressions, but as design acts. You are not buying a bigger home just because your peers have. You are not investing in startups to seem "visionary." You are not buying the latest phone out of boredom. Each choice has a logic—and that logic is personal, not performative.

Over time, this way of operating creates not just stability but congruence. Your outer life—your expenses, your investments, your routines—mirrors your inner values. And when there is less distance between the two, life becomes lighter. Not less ambitious. Just less conflicted.

From External Validation to Internal Metrics

The modern financial environment tempts us with endless points of comparison. Someone's net worth is trending on social media. Someone else's startup just went public. There are property portfolios to admire, crypto portfolios to envy, and lifestyle aesthetics to replicate.

Quiet wealth is not indifferent to these signals—it simply *replaces* them with internal metrics. *Am I living below my means? Am I investing in what I understand? Is my wealth aligned with the life I actually want—not the life I feel pressured to perform?* These questions don't erase ambition. They *purify* it. They remove the parts borrowed from others.

This move toward internal calibration is profoundly liberating. It allows for unorthodox paths. Maybe your wealth goal is not early retirement, but meaningful work without financial anxiety. Maybe it's funding an art school, not a pension. Maybe it's intergenerational stability, not maximal extraction of returns.

When you define wealth in your own terms, you reduce the likelihood of wasting years chasing someone else's prize.

Reclaiming Privacy in a Hyper-Visible Age

There is also a quieter—yet equally essential—dimension to this philosophy: the preservation of privacy. As wealth becomes more digitised, financial transparency is increasingly demanded, often under the guise of "openness" or "community." But for many, *privacy is not secrecy—it's sovereignty*. It's the ability to manage your affairs without exposing them to scrutiny, envy, or unsolicited advice.

Quiet wealth reclaims that boundary. It rejects the conflation of "personal brand" with personal identity. Your money decisions are yours. Your assets need not be narrative devices. Your success need not be shared for it to be real.

This privacy is not paranoia. It is a conscious *counterweight* to the performative norms of the digital economy. It creates the space for unfiltered decisions—and a more grounded relationship with your own success.

Practical Anchors for Quiet Wealth

While the philosophy of quiet wealth is largely psychological, it expresses itself through concrete design choices. For those seeking to operationalise these ideas, consider the following anchors—not as prescriptions, but as provocations:

Automated systems that reduce noise: Investments made monthly, not monitored daily. Contributions that require no discipline, only design.

Simplified portfolios: Fewer moving parts. Fewer exotic instruments. Greater transparency of purpose.

Values-led spending rules: A self-defined set of categories you prioritise—whether that's books, travel, education, health—and permission to ignore trends elsewhere.

Deliberate invisibility: Resist broadcasting milestones. Let your success unfold inwards, not upwards.

Legacy scaffolding: Structures that extend impact beyond your lifetime—without tying your identity to grandiosity.

None of these practices require radical wealth. What they require is a clear sense of authorship. When you are no longer optimising for applause, you can optimise for alignment. And that shift—quiet though it may be—changes everything.

The Final Word: Status is a Shadow, Substance is the Light

In the final analysis, the choice is not between being rich or poor, seen or unseen. The real choice is between *alignment and distortion.* Between a life designed for meaning and a life bent toward mimicry. Between the noise of status and the substance of strategy.

Quiet wealth is not a marketing concept. It's a structural lens through which to build a life that doesn't wobble under the weight of appearances. It doesn't promise social recognition. It doesn't traffic in virality. But it delivers something rarer: *trust in your own system.*

And for the thoughtful investor—one who is not trying to impress, but to endure—that trust may be the most valuable asset of all.

Chapter 9
Financial Self-Defence

The financial world is brimming with advice—slick platforms, charismatic influencers, well-packaged products—all lining up to tell you what to do with your money. Some promise foolproof certainty. Others dangle speed and shortcuts. A few cloak their pitch in the language of mentorship or "just trying to help". But peel back the layers and what often remains isn't seasoned wisdom—it's self-interest.

And so, the modern investor, no matter how thoughtful or numerate, needs something that rarely appears in investment guides or budgeting apps: defence. Not the sort born of cynicism, but of steady pattern recognition. A quiet readiness. The ability to see through gloss and get to the heart of intent.

Financial self-defence is not alarmism. It is the calm, grounded practice of not mistaking visibility for credibility, charm for competence, or pressure for potential. It means understanding, deeply, that persuasion is now industrialised—streamlined, gamified, endlessly optimised to hijack attention and manufacture urgency. In that kind of environment, the single most valuable skill is not just knowing what to do, but knowing what to ignore.

This chapter doesn't aim to catalogue every scheme or swindle—it's not a list of warning signs or headlines to fear. Instead, it offers something sturdier: a behavioural operating system. A mindset that doesn't merely react to danger but anticipates distortion. One that equips you not to spot this scam or that trap, but to inhabit the posture of someone who rarely falls for them in the first place.

Discernment, in this context, is not the same as technical prowess. It's more foundational. It's about stepping out of the reactive trance that financial culture so often induces—and pausing long enough to ask: "Who benefits if I believe this?" or "Would I still make this choice if nobody knew I had?"

Because, if we're honest, most financial harm doesn't arrive with flashing warnings. It comes slowly. Through overconfidence nudged by envy. Through half-truths wrapped in aspiration. Through voices that echo your hopes just enough to feel trustworthy. And before you realise it, your decision-making is no longer yours—it's been shaped by someone else's metrics, someone else's momentum.

That's the deeper risk—not a single con, but the quiet erosion of your own logic. The gradual shift from autonomy to imitation. From stewardship to performance.

And so, what's offered here is not a shield, but a compass. A way of thinking that brings you back—again and again—to your own values, your own reasoning, your own rhythm. Because in a landscape built to seduce, staying grounded isn't just a matter of prudence. It's a discipline. A way of walking through noise without being moved by it.

Why Smart People Still Get Taken

There's a popular delusion that scams only affect the naïve. That a sharp, educated person could never fall for something as crude as a Ponzi scheme, a misleading product, or a hyped-up investment narrative. But history—and psychology—say otherwise.

In 2008, Bernie Madoff's clients included Nobel laureates, financial professionals, and globally respected institutions. In the 2020s, hundreds of thousands of professionals were lured into meme stocks, unregulated crypto schemes, and influencer-led trading platforms. These people weren't ignorant. Many were brilliant. They simply underestimated *how susceptible they were to emotional contagion, cognitive blind spots, and perceived credibility*.

That's the paradox. The smarter you are, the more dangerous it can be to assume you're immune. Intellectual arrogance—disguised as confidence—often creates the perfect opening for manipulation. The antidote isn't self-doubt. It's *structured scepticism*—a mode of decision-making that respects the complexity of the landscape without succumbing to cynicism or paralysis.

From Defence as Reaction to Defence as Design

Many investors only think defensively after damage is done. The contract has been signed. The portfolio has been rearranged. The money has vanished. But true financial self-defence is not reactive—it's preemptive. It's baked into your operating system.

You do not wait to feel uncertain to start asking questions. You do not rely on your memory to spot patterns—you document them. You do not outsource your instincts to popularity, credentials, or hype cycles. Instead, *you build habits, tripwires, and guardrails that make bad decisions harder to make—even on a bad day.*

This chapter will show you how. Not just what to reject, but how to recognise the social and psychological levers being pulled in every high-pressure pitch. We'll explore what it means to define your own opportunity criteria—and stick to them. You'll learn to navigate the subtle line between curiosity and susceptibility, between optimism and overreach.

The Psychology of Predation

Financial predators do not wear warning signs. They often wear suits. Or brand themselves as disruptors. They may speak in polished frameworks or strategic acronyms. What unites them is not their script—but their psychological choreography.

They understand that if they can move your emotional state, they can bypass your analytical defences. Fear of missing out. Urgency. Exclusivity. Complexity masquerading as intelligence. They work to collapse your time for reflection, often by presenting you with a binary: act now or lose everything.

The rational response is not to trust no one. It's to understand the patterns. To develop a calm fluency with tactics designed to hijack your thinking. The goal is not suspicion—it's *composure*. You are most vulnerable when you believe there's no time to breathe, verify, or consult. Financial self-defence is about reclaiming that pause—and protecting it with rules.

Designing a "No" that Protects Your "Yes"

One of the most underdeveloped financial skills is the artful, confident "no." Not a vague delay. Not a mumbled excuse. But a precise, values-aligned rejection of ideas, offers, or strategies that violate your mental model.

To do this consistently, you must first *have* a model. Most investors don't. They operate from a loose collection of instincts, anecdotes, and heuristics. Which is why they remain vulnerable to narratives that sound just credible enough to override their hesitation.

In this chapter, we introduce decision frameworks—practical, repeatable tools that let you assess any financial idea against your priorities, not someone else's. Whether it's a business proposal from a colleague, a hot tip from a friend, or a message from a financial influencer, you'll know what to ask, what to probe, and how to exit with integrity.

Because every "yes" to the wrong idea is a "no" to something better, quieter, and more aligned. And defence, at its core, is about *protecting your ability to say yes to what matters.*

The Long-Term Game Isn't Just Math. It's Temperament.

Finally, we turn to the subtlety of behavioural self-defence. Not against others, but against ourselves.

Most poor financial decisions aren't made during periods of clarity. They are made in moments of desperation, envy, euphoria, or fatigue. No tool, checklist, or framework can fully eliminate those states—but we can *design around them.*

This chapter concludes with the profile of the Scam-Proof Investor. Not someone who's never made a mistake, but someone who has internalised a mental operating system that detects, defuses, and de-escalates emotional surges before they translate into irreversible action.

The strongest financial defence, ultimately, is *a life that doesn't run on adrenaline*. One that moves deliberately. Listens more than it speaks. And holds its ground in a world built to push, prod, and pull at your attention.

Insurance as Emotional Armour

Redefines insurance not as fear-based, but as a dignified shield for your future self.

The average person thinks about insurance the way one might think about fire extinguishers or seatbelts: obligatory, precautionary, slightly annoying. It is often purchased under duress, filed under paperwork, and then mentally shelved until crisis calls. The emotional narrative surrounding insurance—especially among salaried professionals—is often one of reluctance. It's something we *have to do*, not something we *get to do*. But this framing is intellectually thin and psychologically misleading.

What if we reimagined insurance not as a bet against catastrophe, but as an expression of quiet self-respect? What if it wasn't a purchase rooted in fear, but a practice anchored in foresight? What if insurance, properly understood, became a pillar of dignity—not paranoia?

That is the argument of this chapter. Not merely that insurance is necessary, but that it is profoundly misunderstood. Not that it should be embraced uncritically, but that it deserves better than the narrow, transactional treatment it often receives. Financial self-defence is incomplete without it—but not for the reasons typically marketed. Insurance is not just financial protection. *It is emotional armour*. And it becomes most powerful when we stop treating it as an afterthought and start treating it as a psychological and philosophical decision.

Against the Cultural Backdrop of Denial

Most people do not buy insurance because they anticipate a specific misfortune. They buy it because they were either mandated to, scared into action by a near-miss, or advised by a third party. This reactive posture has created an emotional culture around insurance that is simultaneously cynical and passive. As a result, policies are often chosen with minimal attention, under-covered in crucial areas, and over-funded in others.

But what's underneath this resistance? Psychologists point to *optimism bias*, the well-documented human tendency to believe that bad things are more likely to happen to others than to ourselves. Paired with *present bias*—our tendency to overweight immediate gratification over long-term benefit—we find ourselves perpetually underprepared for contingencies that are predictable, if not precisely knowable.

Insurance, in this light, becomes a mirror. It reflects how well we've internalised the idea that *not everything can be controlled, but many things can be cushioned.* To reject it out of hand is not a gesture of bravery—it is often a signal of unresolved anxiety, disguised as confidence.

Insurance as a Signal of Maturity, Not Anxiety

In wealth-building cultures that prize assertiveness and autonomy, insurance can appear to stand in contrast with entrepreneurial optimism. Why hedge when you can charge forward? Why prepare for failure when you could visualise success? This binary is unhelpful.

Mature investors—and financially literate individuals more broadly—know that confidence is not the absence of contingency planning. It is its by-product. To have insurance is not to assume disaster is imminent. It is to recognise that part of adulthood is decoupling your financial stability from sheer luck.

Consider two professionals with equal incomes. One views insurance as a bureaucratic tax. The other sees it as a structure that allows their future self to grieve, repair, or pivot without scrambling. Who is more resilient? Who is more likely to respond to disruption with composure, rather than panic?

This is not a theoretical question. It plays out daily in the aftermath of accidents, job losses, health diagnoses, and legal entanglements. The difference isn't always in the event. *It's in the preparedness—and the posture that preceded it.*

The Anatomy of Emotional Armour

What does it mean to call insurance "emotional armour"? It is not a metaphor. It is a literal mapping of financial tools to psychological burdens.

Life insurance: not a payout for death, but a continuation of care. It protects dependents from the compounding trauma of grief *and* destabilisation. It affirms that your role in their life was more than symbolic—it was structural.

Health insurance: not merely a hedge against illness, but a means of accessing treatment without delay, guilt, or impossible trade-offs. It creates *permission* to seek care early, rather than permission withheld by affordability.

Disability insurance: often ignored, yet potentially more valuable than life cover, especially for young professionals. It says: *your earning capacity is your most vital asset—and worth defending.*

Liability insurance: protection not just from lawsuits, but from the moral erosion that comes when a single accident dismantles decades of prudence.

Each type of insurance *reduces the emotional volatility* of life's worst days. It acts as a stabiliser—not just financially, but mentally. This stabilisation matters. Studies from behavioural finance consistently show that people under financial distress have degraded decision-making capabilities. *Insurance does not just pay bills—it protects clarity under stress.*

A Philosophy of Insurance Selection

Too often, the process of purchasing insurance becomes a race to the bottom: lowest premium, least coverage, minimal interaction. This is partly a response to an industry that has failed to build trust, cluttered by jargon and often stained by mis-selling. But a truly empowered investor refuses to be boxed in by institutional mediocrity.

The antidote is not cynicism—it's *deliberate literacy.* A financially competent individual does not outsource their discernment entirely to an agent or algorithm. They ask questions rooted in their own life model:

What are the events I cannot afford to self-fund?

Who depends on my income, time, or presence?

If this event happened, what kind of life would I want my loved ones—or my future self—to have access to?

This reframing leads to a surprising insight: *the best insurance is not always the cheapest. It is the most stabilising.* The product is not a policy—it is peace of mind.

The Problem with Over-Insurance and Performance-Based Products

Just as under-insurance is a risk, *so is over-insurance.* This chapter would be incomplete without addressing the proliferation of performance-linked policies: unit-linked plans, market-tied life insurance products, and investment+insurance hybrids.

These are often sold under the premise of "killing two birds with one stone." But more often than not, they deliver on neither promise convincingly. They blur the lines between protection and speculation. And they distort the purpose of insurance, which is not to *grow wealth*, but to *preserve dignity in its absence.*

True insurance *doesn't need to perform.* Its worth is not found in a return table—it's in its presence at the exact moment when all other bets fail.

For professionals who are building diversified investment portfolios elsewhere, insurance should remain a pure form of risk transfer—not a backdoor into the equities market via opaque wrappers.

Reclaiming the Language of Dignity

If we are to restore insurance to its rightful place in the architecture of financial confidence, we must also reframe its language. The terms often used—"burden", "cost", "requirement"—treat insurance as a nuisance. But the language of dignity changes the frame:

"This is a monthly gift to my future self."

"This is how I preserve choices for the people I love."

"This is the mechanism by which I stay calm when others panic."

None of these statements require catastrophising. They invite maturity. And they return control to the person making the choice.

The highest version of wealth is not about constant gains. It is about maintaining your equilibrium when gains become unavailable. That is what insurance offers—not a payout, but a pact. A promise you make to your own stability. One that holds even when markets fall, health fails, or chaos strikes without warning.

How to Recognise Predators

Spotting red flags in financial advisors, schemes, and bad online advice masquerading as insight

It is no longer just the desperate or the uninformed who fall prey to financial predators. Increasingly, it is the intelligent, the busy, the self-assured. Not because they lack intellect, but because they overestimate their immunity. *Today's financial predator is not a cartoonish con artist or a shadowy fraudster with broken English and offshore accounts.* They are articulate, credentialled, tech-savvy—and very often, legally compliant.

That is what makes this chapter necessary. Not as a list of generic warnings, but as a forensic analysis of *how manipulation is modernised, and how insight is counterfeited.* The predator of today wears a professional suit, has a verified Instagram account, or may even carry a job title sanctioned by financial regulators. They exploit a psychological landscape, not just a regulatory one.

To protect yourself, you must develop what might be called *cognitive self-defence*: the ability to detect asymmetries in information, motive, and emotional influence—*before* the maths even begins. True protection is not about finding the perfect advisor or avoiding all risk. It's about *recognising manipulation in its earliest, most seductive form.*

The Misconception of Malice

One of the most dangerous myths about financial predators is that they must be malicious. Many are not. They are simply incentivised in ways that conflict with your interests. They may not *intend* to deceive—but their business model requires that they obscure trade-offs, oversell upside, or gloss over complexity. This is not malevolence. It is structural misalignment. And *it is no less dangerous.*

An insurance broker paid by commission is likely to push high-premium, low-value products—*not because they are evil, but because their paycheque depends on it.* A content creator touting obscure cryptocurrencies may be compensated in coin—*which only rises in value when others buy in.* A wealth manager charging assets under management (AUM) fees may discourage you from paying off your mortgage—*because debt repayment shrinks their billable base.*

These people may be polite, educated, and well-intentioned. But the incentives are louder than their ethics. If you are not discerning, *your future will be shaped by someone else's bonus structure.*

Modern Schemes are Psychologically Engineered

Predators no longer operate in alleyways or unsolicited emails. They live in platforms that reward visibility over veracity. YouTube, TikTok, Instagram, even LinkedIn—these are not neutral landscapes. They are *amplifiers of extremity*. What trends is not what's thoughtful. It's what's emotionally arousing.

This makes the modern scam psychologically invasive. It doesn't sell you a product—it manufactures urgency. It tells you:

You're already behind.

Everyone else knows this secret.

Only this community can make you free.

This framing mimics cult psychology. It creates insiders and outsiders. It builds loyalty around identity, not evidence. And it *makes you feel like scepticism is a sign of ignorance*, not intelligence.

Consider this when you hear phrases like:

"Banks don't want you to know this."

"This one stock will 10x by year-end."

"Passive income secrets they won't teach you in school."

These are not insights. They are emotional triggers disguised as financial advice.

The Red Flags You Can't Afford to Ignore

While there is no single diagnostic checklist, certain signals should be treated as *hard brakes*—not mild concerns. These include:

Non-transparent compensation: If an advisor or seller cannot clearly explain *how they are paid* and *by whom*, you are not in a conversation—you are in a transaction disguised as one.

Overuse of urgency: Pressure to act fast—before a deadline, before a price change, before the "window closes"—is not just unprofessional. It is manipulative. True opportunities welcome scrutiny.

Excessive secrecy or jargon: Complex structures with vague explanations often mask products that are either overpriced, illiquid, or unregulated. If you cannot teach the product back in plain terms, you don't own the knowledge—you've leased someone else's pitch.

Emotional mirroring: Watch for advisors who mimic your fears rather than challenge them. A good guide *stabilises* you. A predator *amplifies* you, because *a distressed client is a pliable one.*

Promises of certainty: Anyone who guarantees returns in a variable market is either lying or deluded. Uncertainty is not a flaw of investing—it is its fundamental condition. Confidence should come from *robust reasoning*, not bold predictions.

The Illusion of Professionalism

Many predators present themselves as "certified" or "qualified," invoking titles like "financial coach," "wealth strategist," or "retirement architect." These may sound impressive, but most are *unregulated terms*. They are not evidence of competence. They are marketing.

Even regulated professionals—those with fiduciary obligations or formal licences—are not immune to conflicts. This is especially true in systems where "fiduciary" means "suitable," not "optimal."

The appearance of legitimacy is not proof of alignment. Always ask: *Whose problem does this person solve? And whose incentives does that serve?*

The Economics of Desperation

Financial predators thrive in environments of desperation: job loss, family pressure, late-stage retirement anxiety. When people feel out of time, they become susceptible to "one-shot" solutions. This is not a character flaw. It's a neurological fact. *Stress shortens time horizons. Fear disables reasoning. Urgency suppresses due diligence.*

One of the most effective ways to avoid being scammed is *not about recognising external signs*, but *controlling internal states.* Never make major financial decisions when:

You are emotionally charged (fear, greed, grief)

You are feeling rushed

You are isolated or embarrassed about your finances

The more stable your inner world, the less vulnerable you become to false solutions.

Cognitive Immunity Is Your Only Real Shield

No regulatory agency, software, or product label can fully protect you. The landscape of scams evolves faster than legislation. The only durable protection is *epistemic immunity*—your ability to think critically under pressure.

This includes:

Understanding base rates: How many people actually achieve the returns being promised?

Requesting source material: Can this person cite verifiable, third-party data?

Deconstructing incentives: Who benefits if I act on this advice? And who is liable if it fails?

Seeking disagreement: Can I find a credible expert who *disagrees* with this position? If not, I am likely inside an echo chamber.

These tools are not paranoia. They are *intellectual hygiene.* And in a world where manipulation is scalable and digital, they are not optional.

What the Best Advisors Actually Do

If the predators of finance seek to inflame your emotions, *true professionals seek to centre them.* A real advisor:

Spends more time asking questions than giving answers

Says "I don't know" without shame

Encourages second opinions and independent research

Accepts delay as part of wise decision-making

Makes themselves dispensable—not indispensable

They are not selling urgency. They are building understanding. And their credibility is evident *not in how persuasive they are—but in how calm you feel afterwards.*

Closing Thought: Financial predators do not look like villains. They look like shortcuts.

To resist them, you do not need paranoia. You need clarity. And that clarity is forged not in mistrust of others, but in a rigorous trust of your own reasoning.

The Art of Saying No to "Opportunities"

Building a decision framework to evaluate pitches, ideas, and shiny distractions

Every financially secure person eventually masters a particular kind of courage—not the courage to take big risks, but the courage to decline alluring ones. In personal finance, the difference between momentum and misstep is rarely about knowledge. It's about discernment. It's about *learning to say no early, decisively, and without apology.* Not just to scams or bad advice, but to legitimate-sounding opportunities that are mismatched with your long-term goals.

The truth is simple but uncomfortable: *not every opportunity is an opportunity for you.*

This chapter is not about cynicism. It's about *precision.* It offers a framework—not just to detect what's fake, but to decide what's irrelevant. Because the modern financial world does not lack possibilities; it suffers from *pathological overchoice.* Pitches arrive daily in email inboxes, in WhatsApp groups, on social media feeds, or through well-meaning friends. And most of them are designed to bypass your analytical filters by appealing directly to your emotions—*urgency, fear of missing out, ambition, or insecurity.*

You don't need a better nose for risk. You need a clearer lens for alignment.

When Every Offer Sounds Smart

The financial industry—and its unregulated cousin, the "wealth influencer" economy—is deeply invested in packaging ideas that sound intelligent. They borrow language from economics, borrow confidence from marketing, and borrow urgency from speculation.

A "pre-IPO placement," a "tokenised real estate fractional investment," or a "next-gen smart contract ETF" might all be real products. But being real does not make them relevant. Or useful. Or suitable.

The tragedy is not people falling for nonsense. The tragedy is people rearranging their financial lives around things they barely understand, simply because they were afraid to miss out.

Understanding this problem means starting from a place of psychological awareness. You are most vulnerable to bad opportunities not when you are uninformed—but when you are insecure about your current progress.

The Cognitive Cost of Always Listening

Every unsolicited offer you entertain, every idea you "keep an open mind" about, imposes a cognitive cost. It fragments your attention. It introduces variables into an otherwise clean plan. It injects noise into what could have been a silent compounding machine. You don't need to vet every pitch to be thorough. You need to be *selectively deaf.*

That is not narrow-mindedness. It is a form of strategic filtration. *Financial health is not about information breadth. It is about decision depth.*

Constructing a Personal Decision Filter

The most resilient investors are not always the most knowledgeable. They are the most *filtered.* They have created for themselves a lens—deliberate, custom, and ruthlessly applied—to decide what earns their consideration. Here is how to build one that functions in real life:

1. Purpose Fit:
Does this opportunity support or dilute my existing long-term financial goals? If you can't link the idea to a pre-existing strategy, it probably doesn't belong. *Strategy should precede excitement.*

2. Emotional State Check:
Am I evaluating this idea calmly, or am I responding from fear, urgency, or envy? No high-quality decision is made from a compromised emotional state. If you feel adrenaline while considering a proposal, walk away for 72 hours.

3. Complexity-to-Transparency Ratio:
The more complex the pitch, the simpler the explanation should be. If the person presenting the opportunity cannot explain its risk, reward, liquidity, cost structure, and regulatory context in plain English, you are not under-informed—you are being misinformed.

4. Opportunity Cost Audit:
What am I not doing because I am entertaining this option? Is this

displacing higher-confidence strategies like debt reduction, index investing, or building cash reserves? Remember, *every "yes" is a "no" to something else.*

5. Source Integrity:
What is the track record, incentive structure, and bias of the person or entity presenting this idea? Discard titles and charisma. Ask: *What would this person gain if I say yes? And what would they lose if they are wrong?*

The Cult of Possibility

Modern financial culture suffers from an *optimisation addiction.* It tells you that if you don't chase every new product, trend, or tip, you're leaving money on the table. This is not wisdom. It is *manufactured scarcity.* The paradox of healthy wealth-building is this: *you often gain more by ignoring more.*

True opportunity is not loud. It is often *boring*, slow, and unrewarding in the short term. But it fits. It aligns. And most importantly, it doesn't require you to contort your plan, your ethics, or your peace of mind.

Why Saying "No" is a Muscle, Not a Mood

Declining a proposal is not just a one-time act. It is a *practice.* Like any muscle, it strengthens with repetition. At first, saying no might feel like missed potential. With time, it will feel like intellectual sovereignty.

This applies not just to strangers selling you "pre-seed equity placements" or rental arbitrage tools. It applies to friends, relatives, even professionals. If your financial planner is constantly "bringing you new ideas," they are not building strategy. They are building churn.

You are not obligated to explore everything. You are only obligated to protect the integrity of your financial future.

Learning from Anti-Models

Sometimes, the best evidence for saying no is found in the wreckage of those who said yes too often. Consider the following:

Professionals who diversified into 12 asset classes but never built a cash buffer.

Parents who cashed out pensions to fund their child's friend's crypto startup.

Seniors who fell for annuity schemes cloaked in "guaranteed returns."

Young earners who got locked into unaffordable property through "no money down" gimmicks.

Each of these examples began with what looked like an opportunity. The downfall was not ignorance. It was a failure to pause, vet, and say: "This is not for me."

Strategic Apathy Is a Strength

You will not become wealthy by chasing better products. You will become wealthy by *ignoring 97% of the noise* and compounding boring choices over time. That includes choosing index funds over private placements. Saying no to leveraged bets. Opting out of trendy asset classes because they don't fit your plan—even if they're working for others.

This kind of restraint is often mistaken for laziness or fear. It is neither. It is *financial maturity*. And it is rare.

The Confidence to Not Be Excited

A well-designed portfolio should not make you feel adrenaline. It should make you feel *calm*. That's the benchmark. If every offer you consider makes you feel alive, it is not an opportunity—it's a dopamine trap.

You do not need more excitement. You need more alignment. And that comes not from learning how to say yes faster—but from learning how to say no earlier.

Resisting temptation is not passive. It is an active decision to honour your plan over someone else's pitch.

Your financial future deserves more than enthusiasm. It deserves rigour.

The Scam-Proof Investor

A behavioural checklist to ensure you never invest from desperation or dopamine

There is a recurring delusion that financial scams are the domain of the naive, the elderly, or the uninformed. But history—and behavioural science—paint a more uncomfortable picture: *scams succeed not because people are uninformed, but because they are human.* Behind every successful con is a moment of emotional vulnerability—a cocktail of hope, haste, and the seductive illusion of certainty.

To be scam-proof is not to be cynical. It is to be *disciplined in how you feel, not just how you think.*

This chapter presents a behavioural framework designed not merely to help you spot scams after they happen, but to insulate you from the mindset that makes you vulnerable to them in the first place. Because most scams don't look like scams at the start. They look like shortcuts. And shortcuts are most appealing when we're tired of playing the long game.

Desperation and Dopamine: The Twin Engines of Poor Investment Decisions

Let's be clear: the vast majority of investing errors—whether they end in outright fraud or simply underperformance—can be traced to two psychological states: **desperation** and **dopamine**.

Desperation distorts risk perception. It makes promises feel like plans and options feel like obligations. A person trying to "make up for lost time" or "catch the next big thing" is often a prime target—not because they are foolish, but because they are *hurting.*

Dopamine, on the other hand, creates the illusion of control and the intoxication of novelty. It thrives in the speculative corners of finance: meme stocks, altcoins, hot tips, pre-IPO chatter, leverage platforms promising triple-digit returns. But it is not limited to fringe investments. Even seasoned investors chasing yield can fall into this trap when their strategy becomes more about stimulation than sustainability.

The scam-proof investor does not just resist bad offers. They are vigilant about *why* they're drawn to them in the first place.

Why We Still Fall For It—Even Now

In 2022, more than £1.3 billion was lost to investment fraud in the UK alone—much of it through regulated platforms or scams that used *credible language and professional design.* The scammers are no longer shadowy figures in alleys. They're influencers. They're webinars. They're inside your phone.

But we must resist the temptation to frame scams as purely external threats. The more powerful threat lies within: *our own psychological architecture.* Overconfidence, social proof, sunk cost bias, authority bias, urgency triggers—these are the levers that scammers pull. They don't create the levers. *We carry them in by default.*

That's why traditional fraud warnings—"if it sounds too good to be true..." etc.—are insufficient. What's needed is not just knowledge, but a behavioural audit. A checklist. A filter that functions even under emotional duress.

The Behavioural Checklist of a Scam-Proof Investor

This isn't about building paranoia. It's about building *emotional systems* that precede technical analysis. Each point below is a friction layer—an intentional pause that disrupts impulsive, hope-driven decision-making.

1. Time Check: Do I feel urgency or time scarcity right now?
If the opportunity is marketed as time-limited, exclusive, or reserved for early access, slow down. The best investments are rarely urgent. *Urgency is the predator's preferred disguise.*

2. Status Audit: Am I trying to prove something?
Scams often succeed because they are tied to identity. If your interest in an investment rises when others are watching—or when you imagine sharing it—you're not investing. You're signalling. And *signalling is bait.*

3. Language Filter: Can I explain this investment in plain English?
Clarity is not optional. If an opportunity relies on jargon, layered instruments, or overly optimistic forecasts to make sense, discard it. *Complexity is not sophistication—it's camouflage.*

4. Alignment Review: Does this serve my actual financial plan?
Every investment should be a servant of your pre-defined goals, not a detour from them. If the offer demands that you "reconsider your strategy," it's probably not compatible with it. *Fit precedes upside.*

5. Cost and Liquidity Check: What am I giving up—time, control, or access?
Illiquid investments, high lock-in periods, exit penalties—these are fine when managed deliberately, but are a red flag when hidden. Ask: *How easy is it to get out? What happens if I change my mind?*

6. Source Scrutiny: Who profits even if I lose?
Track incentives. Does the person presenting the opportunity earn commission, referral fees, or undisclosed compensation? Are they selling access, not just ideas? *If they win no matter what, you're the product.*

7. Peer Review: Have I asked someone who will challenge me, not validate me?
Every investor needs a skeptic in their life—someone who asks hard questions, not out of pessimism, but protection. If you're avoiding those people because they'll "just not get it," you've already been emotionally compromised.

8. Emotional Check-In: How does this make me feel?
The strongest signal of a pending mistake is emotional volatility. Euphoria, fear, thrill, envy—none of these are wise investment partners. *A good investment feels boring. It feels calm. It feels quiet.*

Real-World Applications: Case Studies in Psychological Failure

It's easy to think: "This wouldn't happen to me." But consider three brief examples of intelligent individuals making emotionally driven investment choices:

A London-based doctor, frustrated by years of modest returns, invests £30,000 in an unregulated FX scheme pitched by a fellow healthcare professional on Instagram. The loss was not financial only—it was reputational, relational, and psychological.

A young engineer, flush with bonus earnings, buys into an NFT project promoted by a celebrity without reading the whitepaper. Within months, the platform is abandoned. The regret is not just about the money—it's about *how easily he suspended his usual discernment.*

A retiree, chasing yield in a zero-interest environment, puts his pension into a "secured" peer-to-peer lending platform that collapses. He later admits: "It wasn't that I believed the numbers. I just didn't want to be left behind."

These are not cautionary tales about foolishness. They are *case studies in what happens when good people invest from emotion, not from design.*

Becoming Behaviourally Defensive

To be scam-proof is not to be invincible. It is to have mechanisms that activate under pressure. It's about rehearsing your *inner no*—so that when dopamine or desperation strike, you already have a counter-response.

This is why *intentional inertia*—the act of pausing before action—is so powerful. In a world wired for immediacy, delay is defence. Build a 48-hour rule into your financial habits. Make it non-negotiable. Let excitement cool before you act.

The Role of Boredom in Financial Maturity

Most sustainable wealth strategies are deeply unsexy. They involve index funds, cash buffers, reasonable debt, and diversified risk. What they don't involve is *constant novelty*. If your portfolio excites you every week, you're not investing—you're gambling.

The scam-proof investor is often bored. That boredom is not a bug. It's a feature.

Designing an Internal Compass

Ultimately, protection is not procedural—it's philosophical. The truly scam-proof investor is someone who has *decided in advance* what kind of life they want to fund, and what values they will not compromise to get there faster.

They don't chase ROI at the expense of sleep, ethics, or simplicity. They are not looking to impress, outperform, or dominate. They are looking to *align*—their money, their method, and their mindset.

Closing Thought:

To be immune to scams is not to be more intelligent than others. It is to be *less reactive*. It is to recognise when you are no longer reasoning but reaching. Because the most dangerous scams aren't the ones we don't see—they're the ones we *secretly want to believe.*

Chapter 10
Freedom as a Feeling

For most, the pursuit of financial freedom isn't really about money—not in the deepest sense. What they're chasing is something more elusive, more psychological: relief. Relief from the pressure to perform, from the unpredictability of life's next chapter, from that persistent internal monologue whispering, "You're falling behind," or "It still isn't enough." And unless we pause to interrogate that voice—where it came from, what it feeds on, and what it quietly demands—we may find ourselves devoting years, even decades, to building wealth without ever tasting the freedom we imagined it would deliver.

This chapter offers a deliberate shift—away from fixating on external milestones and towards something far more meaningful: the experience of felt financial freedom. Not net worth as status insulation. Not passive income as a ticket out of obligation. But a state of living in which money recedes respectfully into the background—functioning quietly, effectively—while your energy returns to the foreground, to the things that actually make life rich.

It's a vision of wealth not as spectacle, but as serenity. A life in which you are not defined by what you can afford, but liberated by what no longer controls you. A life where decisions are made in alignment, not under pressure. Where money becomes the means, never the measure.

What follows isn't a roadmap to luxury, nor a manifesto for retirement at thirty-five. It is something more grounded—and more useful: a practice-based, emotionally attuned reimagining of wealth as something you live, not just accumulate. A kind of richness that has little to do with numbers and everything to do with how free you feel in the life you're already building.

The Myth of "When I Get There"

Much of modern personal finance is built on the lie of *arrival.* The idea that one day, after a series of strategically optimised decisions, you will reach a place where anxiety stops, desire quiets, and peace sets in. But the neuroscience of contentment doesn't support this fantasy. Nor does the lived experience of high-net-worth individuals, many of whom report the same internal restlessness—just with nicer backdrops.

The problem is not that we haven't earned enough. It's that we haven't defined *what enough actually looks or feels like.* In the absence of that clarity, our goals default to whatever the loudest voice in our social or professional circle is pursuing. More property. More leverage. More leverage on property. And so the game continues—evolving not toward freedom, but into ever more complex forms of performative insecurity.

This chapter aims to interrupt that cycle. Not with vague inspiration, but with concrete redefinitions.

Defining *Your* Enough

In the subchapter "Designing Your Enough," we'll explore how to build a personal blueprint for sufficiency—one that's emotionally grounded, visually clear, and resilient to comparison. You'll learn how to shift your internal conversation from "What should I want?" to "What's truly sufficient—for me, right now?"

Drawing from behavioural psychology and practical journaling exercises, this section introduces a structured reflection process to help you decouple your financial aspirations from cultural scripts. Because *freedom is not earned by hitting a number—it is earned by refusing to outsource your definition of success.*

The Micro-Freedom Method

Big wins are intoxicating. But it's often the small, repeatable upgrades that reshape how free we feel day-to-day. Whether it's buying back an hour of time each week, eliminating a friction point in your home life, or unsubscribing from the kind of digital noise that triggers financial anxiety, micro-freedoms compound.

This chapter doesn't offer productivity hacks disguised as financial strategy. Instead, "The Micro-Freedom Method" teaches how to identify *leverage points of liberation*—places where modest intentionality yields outsized improvements in quality of life. We'll look at real-world examples where people reclaimed autonomy through simplicity, not spending. And we'll challenge the belief that luxury is the ultimate signal of freedom. *It rarely is. Often, it's a costume people wear when they feel least in control.*

Micro-freedom is not minimalist asceticism. It's the deliberate redistribution of attention away from status signals and toward soul signals.

Living Rich, Staying Real

There's an entire industry now built around looking wealthy. Social media portfolios. Lifestyle entrepreneurs. Branded abundance. But the quietest forms of wealth are the most enduring: time sovereignty, relationship integrity, emotional self-containment, and the ability to sleep soundly regardless of market conditions.

In "Living Rich, Staying Real," we unpack how to spend, share, and enjoy your money without slipping into performance. This isn't about asceticism. It's about *reclaiming dignity in the experience of prosperity*. It's the quiet decision to live well without needing anyone to *know* how well you're doing.

Here, we'll study modern case examples—high-earners who remain grounded, as well as modest earners who have engineered lives of deep satisfaction. We'll revisit historical perspectives on wealth's relationship to virtue, pride, and humility, from Roman Stoicism to 20th-century Japanese aesthetic minimalism. And we'll ask the uncomfortable but vital question: *Would your financial life still make sense if no one else could see it?*

From Measurement to Meaning

Much of conventional financial advice revolves around quantification—savings rates, target income multiples, investment growth projections. These tools have their place. But they are incomplete if untethered from *subjective wellbeing*. What's the point of doubling your net worth if your stress levels double with it? What's the value of an 8% return if you're emotionally bankrupt from lifestyle inflation?

Throughout this chapter, you'll be asked not just to do financial planning—but to *feel your way through it.* Not as a rejection of rationality, but as a recognition that *money is an emotional object*, entangled with identity, safety, status, and love. You'll learn how to detect when your financial habits are rooted in fear rather than strategy, in control rather than connection.

This is not about anti-capitalist romanticism. It is about *deweaponising money*—transforming it from a silent tyrant into a trusted servant.

Beyond Autonomy: The Psychology of Financial Equanimity

True freedom isn't constant excitement. It's *equanimity*—a quiet mind in the presence of options. It's being able to say no without guilt, and yes without fear. It's knowing your financial architecture supports your real priorities, not your insecurities or impulses.

In the final section, we explore the subtle emotional shifts that occur when a person exits survival mode, resists performance pressure, and begins to trust that what they have is not just *enough*, but *appropriate.* You'll learn how to cultivate financial calm, how to protect it from erosion by consumer culture, and how to use money not as a mirror of worth, but as an instrument of alignment.

A Chapter Worth Returning To

This chapter will not promise you passive income, early retirement, or a six-figure side hustle. What it will offer is harder to measure but infinitely more valuable: *an internal sense of sufficiency that is resilient to noise, comparison, and manipulation.* You'll emerge not with a bigger balance sheet, but with a quieter inner life.

Because at the highest level of financial literacy, freedom is not a number. *It's a feeling.* And the sooner we begin designing for that feeling—consciously, personally, and courageously—the sooner we stop chasing mirages and start living lives we respect.

The False Finish Line

Questions the retirement myth and introduces alternative visions of financial freedom that start now.

Retirement, for much of the modern world, has become a ghost story told in numbers. Work hard for forty years, invest sensibly, avoid major mistakes, and—if markets, health, inflation, and governments cooperate—you'll finally get to *live.* This is the "finish line" version of financial planning: a promise that real life begins once the spreadsheet says it can. But like many inherited economic beliefs, this vision of retirement is not only outdated—it's conceptually broken. *It postpones agency in favour of an illusion.*

This chapter interrogates that illusion. Not with disdain for planning or discipline, but with a more sophisticated lens: one that asks *what we're really waiting for,* and whether the trade-offs we make in pursuit of the traditional retirement dream serve our well-being—or erode it.

A Legacy Built on Scarcity

The modern retirement construct emerged in the late 19th and early 20th centuries, when industrial economies needed to manage ageing workforces. Otto von Bismarck's introduction of retirement benefits in Germany (at a time when life expectancy barely exceeded 65) was not a celebration of freedom—it was a practical response to political pressures. In the United States, the Social Security Act of 1935 followed suit, providing a modest financial floor for the elderly who had few options.

These were *stopgap systems*, not life goals. Yet over the decades, the idea of retirement became romanticised: the golden years, the great escape, the reward for a life of loyalty. This mythology was amplified by mid-century corporate culture, which offered pensions in exchange for decades of dedication. The dream made emotional sense. But it was *never structurally designed to support 25- or 30-year leisure phases*—especially as lifespans grew, pensions shrank, and costs of living outpaced conservative returns.

The problem isn't just that the math no longer adds up. It's that the whole framing traps people in an extended waiting game. *Freedom becomes a product you buy later, instead of a way you relate to money today.*

The Psychology of Deferred Living

One of the most damaging by-products of the traditional retirement narrative is the mindset it cultivates: *postponement as discipline.* We learn to suppress present needs, desires, and curiosities for a future that is, at best, uncertain. This delay strategy masquerades as prudence, but in many cases it creates deep psychological strain—what psychologists call "existential postponement."

Studies in behavioural economics and positive psychology consistently show that *we're poor predictors of what will make us happy decades from now.* Preferences shift, identities evolve, priorities reorder. Yet many continue to organise their entire financial architecture around a version of their future self that may no longer exist by the time the finish line arrives.

This isn't an argument for short-term thinking. It's a call to *reclaim financial autonomy in the present.* To stop living as if our worth, dignity, or lifestyle must be delayed until the system validates us with a gold watch and a fixed income.

Freedom as a Practice, Not a Payout

To move beyond the retirement myth, we must adopt a more nuanced concept of freedom—one that isn't tied to cessation of work but to the *expansion of choice.* Financial freedom, properly understood, is not about quitting your job forever. It's about creating the space to say "yes" or "no" without fear. It's about *working with agency, not obligation.*

This shift in mindset reframes retirement not as a destination, but as one possible *expression* of financial confidence. Some people may still choose to step away from work entirely. Others may pivot into creative pursuits, mentorship roles, slower schedules, or location independence. The point is: the metric of success is no longer absence of labour—it's *presence of alignment.*

And that alignment can start *long before* you hit your investment targets. In fact, it must—because financial independence is not a moment; it's a curve. And you can begin climbing it today.

Designing Mini-Retirements and Financial Intermissions

A growing number of professionals are rejecting the binary of "work now, live later" and replacing it with intermittent financial sabbaticals. These are intentional pauses, often lasting several months to a year, that allow people to recharge, explore, study, or simply *test-drive their future lifestyle choices.*

Mini-retirements require planning, yes. But they also require *permission*—the internal validation that you don't have to earn your break with burnout. Writers like Tim Ferriss have popularised the idea, but its roots go deeper, drawing from Stoic principles of moderation and Buddhist ideas of non-attachment to a fixed career identity.

Some may scoff at the practicality. "Not everyone can afford to take a year off." True. But that's the wrong question. The better one is: *What kind of financial ecosystem would make that possible for you within the next five years?* That's what this subchapter helps you examine—not by rejecting work, but by challenging its monopoly over your calendar and self-worth.

The Hidden Costs of the Traditional Model

Holding out for retirement also invites hidden opportunity costs: lost time with family, deferred creativity, compromised health, and—perhaps most tragically—*the erosion of your sense of self outside your profession.* If your identity is fused entirely with your career, then stepping away, even voluntarily, often induces a crisis of meaning.

Philosophers from Aristotle to Frankl have observed that meaning is derived not from rest alone, but from *purposeful engagement.* Retirement, without a parallel investment in identity and relationships, can become a vacuum. One where time is abundant but meaning is scarce.

This is why rethinking retirement is not just a financial conversation. It is a philosophical one. *It forces us to ask what makes a life feel rich—and whether that richness is really about what we've accumulated, or how deliberately we've lived.*

Alternative Models of Financial Fulfilment

There is no one-size-fits-all alternative. But several viable models are emerging:

Blended Lifestyles: Professionals who downshift to part-time consulting, allowing more space for travel, caregiving, or community involvement.

Purpose-Led Portfolios: Investors who design their finances not for maximum return, but to fund specific values—such as funding a child's education, supporting climate initiatives, or underwriting a spouse's career transition.

Career Sequencing: Individuals who work in high-intensity fields for a set period, then pivot into slower, more values-aligned work—using money as a bridge, not a finish line.

These models are not utopian. They require planning, negotiation, and trade-offs. But they allow people to *shape their lives while they still have full agency*, rather than waiting for a day when time is ample but vitality is diminished.

A Call to Financial Immediacy

The central argument of this subchapter is simple, though not easy: *Do not design your life around a finish line that may never come—or worse, that may come and feel hollow.* Instead, use your money to practice autonomy incrementally. Create space now. Reclaim hours, not just decades. Measure success by your ability to live in integrity with your values—not by your distance from an arbitrary retirement date.

This is not a rejection of long-term planning. It is an insistence that *living well is not a deferred reward.* It's a discipline—one that begins not with more wealth, but with deeper clarity about what freedom feels like today.

Designing Your Enough

Helps readers define what 'enough' means to them, with visual tools and journaling exercises

Wealth, in the cultural imagination, is often framed as a destination without coordinates. The number keeps moving. The ceiling rises just as we approach it. "More" is the unspoken metric of success, even when we don't know what it's in service of. *But without a clear internal definition of 'enough', no financial strategy—however sophisticated—can deliver a sense of arrival.*

This subchapter makes the case for designing your own definition of enough: a qualitative and quantitative map that clarifies what you value, what you want to protect, and what you're willing to release. It is not a moral argument for modesty, nor a minimalist manifesto. It is a strategic framework for reclaiming authorship over your financial narrative. *Because if you don't decide what enough looks like, the market will keep deciding for you—and it never says stop.*

The Tyranny of Undefined Goals

Many financially literate individuals can articulate how much they want to earn, save, or invest. Fewer can tell you how those numbers relate to their lived well-being. And even fewer can explain why an additional £100,000, or another rung on the career ladder, would make a meaningful difference beyond status signalling or anxiety buffering. This disconnect has serious consequences.

Undefined financial goals tend to default to social comparison. We benchmark against peers, influencers, media narratives, or outdated family expectations. This creates a moving target of desire, which undermines both contentment and clarity. *You can have a net worth of £2 million and still feel behind if your internal compass was outsourced to someone else's standard.*

Defining enough, then, is not about capping ambition. It's about *calibrating ambition to values.* It's how you avoid building a life you don't actually want, just because it looks impressive on paper.

Financial Planning Without Self-Knowledge Is Just Arithmetic

Traditional financial planning models are technically robust but often philosophically shallow. They excel at projecting returns, optimising tax efficiency, and stress-testing scenarios. What they often fail to do is interrogate the assumptions behind the numbers: *What is this plan really buying? Whose life is it optimising for? What trade-offs are baked into its success?*

Designing your enough starts not with calculators, but with *questions*. What does safety mean to you—not just economically, but emotionally? What activities and relationships do you want time to prioritise? What kind of schedule feels most energising? When do you feel most free?

These are not abstract musings. They are strategic inputs. *Every financial decision—spending, saving, insuring, investing—should map back to these answers*. If they don't, then even a technically successful plan will feel hollow.

The Enough Spectrum: A Visual Framework

To clarify the concept of enough, consider creating a three-tier visual spectrum:

Survival: What are your baseline needs for housing, food, healthcare, and essential stability?

Sufficiency: What level of income and assets would allow you to live well, with dignity, autonomy, and periodic indulgences?

Surplus: What exists beyond sufficiency—optional luxuries, legacy ambitions, aspirational purchases?

By explicitly naming these tiers—and sketching real numbers against each—you can begin to *see* your enough. You may find, for instance, that your sufficiency number is far lower than you assumed. Or you may recognise that you're aiming for surplus out of habit, not alignment.

This framework also helps in times of financial stress. Rather than spiralling into binary thinking ("I'm failing" vs "I'm rich"), you can *adjust your position on the spectrum* and strategise accordingly. That psychological flexibility is its own kind of resilience.

Journaling as a Tool for Financial Clarity

Numbers without narrative are insufficient. To deepen your understanding of enough, integrate journaling exercises that probe beneath the financial surface. A few prompts worth revisiting:

When did I last feel truly content? What contributed to that feeling?

What purchases or investments have brought the most lasting satisfaction—and which left me feeling empty?

What fears drive my desire for more? Are they evidence-based or inherited?

Who am I trying to impress, and at what cost?

If I had to halve my income but keep my joy, what would I change?

These questions aren't easy. They require discomfort. But they also reveal what no spreadsheet can: *your lived relationship with money*—its emotional charge, its psychological significance, its symbolic roles.

This self-knowledge is not indulgent; it's *instrumental.* It informs everything from risk tolerance to estate planning to lifestyle design.

Historical and Philosophical Anchors

The concept of enough is not new. It's deeply embedded in ancient wisdom traditions, though often marginalised in contemporary economic discourse.

The Stoics, for instance, viewed freedom not as the absence of hardship but as the absence of insatiable desire. Seneca warned that "It is not the man who has too little, but the man who craves more, that is poor."

Similarly, Buddhist economics—articulated most notably by E.F. Schumacher—frames enough as a moral and environmental good. Unlimited accumulation, in this view, is a form of violence: to the self, to others, and to the planet.

More recently, behavioural finance has offered empirical backing for these insights. Studies show that after a certain threshold of income (often cited around £70,000–£90,000 annually in Western contexts), emotional well-being plateaus. What increases beyond that tends to buy insulation, not joy.

Enough, then, is not just a personal milestone. It's a societal corrective. It counters the myth that all growth is progress, and it reclaims contentment as a legitimate financial metric.

Strategic Benefits of Knowing Your Enough

Contrary to the myth that defining enough will blunt your ambition, the opposite tends to be true. People who can articulate their enough often make *bolder* decisions, not smaller ones. Why? Because they know what they're optimising for.

They're more willing to leave unfulfilling jobs, take creative risks, or downshift strategically. They resist status traps because they've already done the work of self-definition. They can say "no" with conviction—because they've already said "yes" to what matters.

They also tend to invest more thoughtfully. Instead of chasing the market or the next big thing, they build portfolios designed to support their *actual* lives. This is a profound shift. It moves the centre of gravity from fear and greed to clarity and purpose.

The Role of Enough in Legacy Planning

Your definition of enough doesn't just impact your own life—it ripples into your family, your community, your causes. When you stop aiming for infinite accumulation, you can start *allocating with intention.* That might mean funding education, underwriting someone else's dreams, or supporting systemic change.

It also means modelling a different kind of wealth ethic for the next generation. *You show that money is not the measure of worth, but a tool for expression.* That's a legacy more powerful than any asset.

Closing Argument: Enough Is Not a Limit—It's a Liberation

Designing your enough is not about settling. It's about setting *terms*. It's the act of replacing vague striving with intentional design. It protects you from overwork, underfulfilment, and financial performativity. It turns money from a master into a mirror.

Ultimately, enough is not a number. It's a relationship—with time, with self, with society. It is cultivated, not calculated. And once you define it, you stop waiting to feel free.

You begin *practising freedom now*.

The Micro-Freedom Method

Introduces small lifestyle upgrades that cost little but increase perceived wealth and control

What if the feeling of freedom wasn't a grand milestone, but a series of subtle, repeatable decisions? What if personal autonomy—so often postponed until after retirement, a major raise, or the sale of a company—could instead be constructed, piece by piece, within your existing life structure? This is the premise behind the Micro-Freedom Method: the idea that a sense of financial agency can be designed in increments, not windfalls. And when done well, these small interventions yield something money alone cannot guarantee—*a felt experience of control*.

In a world increasingly obsessed with scale—more income, more assets, more followers—the Micro-Freedom Method makes a contrarian case: that *quality of life often improves not through expansion, but through precision*. It doesn't require radical minimalism, nor extravagant spending. Rather, it involves carefully engineering small freedoms—temporal, spatial, psychological—that align with your values and restore a sense of authorship over how you live and work.

Why Micro-Freedom Matters More Than Ever

Despite record-breaking levels of household income in many developed economies, surveys consistently show rising financial anxiety. Part of this paradox stems from the mismatch between wealth and *control.* You can earn a high salary and still feel time-starved. You can own a beautiful home but be tethered to a commute you resent. You can have investments in five countries and still lie awake at night wondering if you're behind.

Freedom is not the absence of obligation; it is the presence of choice. And choice, especially in modern adult life, is constrained as much by habits, scripts, and narratives as it is by actual finances. Micro-freedoms create space within those constraints—not to escape life, but to edit it deliberately.

The Psychology of Perceived Wealth

Behavioural science offers compelling support for the power of micro-freedoms. In research published in the *Journal of Consumer Psychology*, individuals who exercised "temporal control"—for instance, choosing when to work or take breaks—reported significantly higher life satisfaction than those with higher incomes but fixed schedules. The subjective feeling of *agency*, it turns out, is a stronger predictor of well-being than many objective financial metrics.

Moreover, the psychology of *relative advantage* plays a role. A £15 daily coffee habit, often derided in financial media, may represent an outsized source of pleasure or ritual agency for someone whose day is otherwise scripted. Conversely, a six-figure salary locked into 70-hour weeks may provide fewer perceived options than a modest income paired with time autonomy.

This isn't an argument against wealth creation. It's a reminder that *wealth, to be meaningful, must translate into freedom.* And freedom begins with how we use what we already have.

Designing Micro-Freedoms: Four Domains of Intervention

1. **Time Reclamation**

The first—and often most transformative—micro-freedom is time-related. Even 15-minute increments reclaimed from reactive obligations can yield a measurable shift in perceived control. For example:

Replacing a 40-minute round-trip gym commute with a home workout

Carving out two hours weekly for "unstructured solitude" (a space to read, write, walk, or simply think)

Implementing a personal "no meetings before 10 a.m." rule once a week

These decisions may seem trivial in isolation. But over time, they accumulate into a powerful signal: *My time is mine to design.*

2. **Spatial Autonomy**

Where you work, eat, think, and rest has profound effects on your mental state. Micro-freedoms here might include:

Creating a designated "sacred space" in your home—a corner or table reserved for thinking, journaling, or focused work

Using noise-cancelling headphones or curated music to reclaim control over your sensory environment

Negotiating one remote workday per week, thereby restructuring your geography of effort

Again, the goal isn't disruption—it's *curation.* When your space supports your inner pace, freedom becomes more than a concept. It becomes embodied.

3. **Cognitive Bandwidth Protection**

Financial freedom is often imagined as the absence of worry. In practice, it is the reduction of *mental clutter*. Micro-freedoms in this domain focus on reducing unnecessary decision fatigue:

Automating bill payments and savings transfers to avoid monthly deliberation

Instituting a uniform wardrobe for workdays to reclaim decision energy

Blocking certain hours as "input-free"—no email, no media, no messages

These are not minimalist affectations; they are practical shields. Every mental shortcut you design in advance frees up emotional energy for higher-order decisions.

4. **Permission-Based Spending**

Finally, there's the question of financial freedom itself. Here, the Micro-Freedom Method encourages *conscious spending aligned with your personal definitions of wealth and joy*. That might include:

Giving yourself a "frivolity fund" of £50/month to spend without justification

Pre-committing to an annual solo trip—even if modest—because solitude enriches your mental wealth

Choosing to pay for convenience (e.g. grocery delivery, laundry service) in areas that free up time for your priorities

These are not indulgences. They are *investments in autonomy*. When you give yourself permission to spend according to values—not performative frugality—you stop outsourcing freedom to some future state.

Philosophical Anchors: Freedom as Praxis

The Micro-Freedom Method has roots in philosophical as well as psychological traditions. Existentialist thinkers like Jean-Paul Sartre and Simone de Beauvoir contended that freedom is not granted, but enacted. *To be free is to choose, to assume responsibility for one's choices, and to live with intention—even within constraints.*

Likewise, the ancient Stoics differentiated between *external liberty* and *internal freedom.* While external conditions matter, they argued, one's capacity to frame reality, respond to it with composure, and live in accordance with reason is a deeper form of liberation. The Micro-Freedom Method brings these concepts into modern financial life. It asserts that autonomy is not a luxury good—it is a design problem.

The Cumulative Impact: From Micro to Meaningful

Individually, these small freedoms may seem inconsequential. But as in compounding interest, the effect is exponential. Over time, your daily rituals, time use, and spatial arrangements begin to reinforce the identity of someone *in control.* And this identity shapes every future financial decision—from career changes to asset allocation.

More importantly, it guards against the all-too-common fate of deferring life until "later." Later becomes a moving target. Retirement ages rise. Market downturns interrupt plans. Energy levels fluctuate. But if freedom is practiced in increments, not deferred to endpoints, you don't need to wait to feel wealthy. *You just need to feel awake to your agency.*

Common Objections—and Their Rebuttals

Some may argue that these micro-freedoms are insufficient in the face of systemic inequality, wage stagnation, or real constraints. That is a fair and necessary critique. The Micro-Freedom Method is not a substitute for policy reform, labour protections, or structural change. But it is a form of *personal resistance*—a way to carve out autonomy even when larger systems feel immovable.

Others may see micro-freedoms as "too small to matter." Yet the same could be said of savings contributions, sleep hygiene, or habits of attention. What all these share is *consistency.* And consistent alignment with values is the architecture of meaning.

Final Provocation: Define Freedom for Yourself, Then Practise It Daily

To practice the Micro-Freedom Method is to accept the premise that freedom is not merely the absence of constraint, but the presence of intentional design. It is to notice where your life is on autopilot—and intervene gently. It is to refuse the narrative that you must wait until your mortgage is paid, or your net worth hits seven figures, to *feel free.*

Freedom is not deferred. It is designed. And it begins, not with escape plans, but with micro-choices—small edits to your days that restore the sense that your life is yours.

Living Rich, Staying Real

Discusses how to enjoy money with dignity and intentionality, without performing wealth

At a glance, modern wealth is louder than ever. Luxury is no longer merely owned—it is broadcast. Holidays are curated for social media. Watch collections and car garages populate YouTube channels. Even philanthropy is gamified through gala optics and Instagram-ready cheque handovers. But behind this performance is a quieter, deeper reality: *many of the world's most financially secure people don't act like it.*

To live rich and stay real is to decouple wealth from theatre. It is to reject the external validation loop that confuses consumption with self-worth. And it is to return to a more grounded definition of prosperity—one rooted not in symbols, but in *substance.*

The Performance Problem: When Money Becomes a Costume

Sociologists have long studied the phenomenon of "conspicuous consumption," first named by Thorstein Veblen in the late 19th century. Veblen observed that people often use luxury goods to signal status rather than to satisfy genuine needs. The car is not just a car; it is proof of ascension. The handbag is not just functional; it is tribal identity in leather. But the modern version of this phenomenon is more pervasive—and more performative. In a social media age, wealth must now be curated, photographed, filtered, and validated by peers. *It is not enough to be rich; one must be seen to be living richly.*

This performance is not only exhausting—it is corrosive. It distorts the purpose of money. It shifts attention away from *what wealth enables internally*—freedom, optionality, self-respect—and onto *what it communicates externally*. The problem is not enjoyment. It is theatre.

Living rich without performance means returning to an older ethic: *money as a quiet enabler of a deeply personal life—not a stage prop in someone else's narrative.*

Wealth as a Tool, Not an Identity

One of the clearest markers of financial maturity is the ability to see wealth as a tool, not a trophy. This reframing has profound implications. When wealth is viewed as identity, any threat to it—real or imagined—feels existential. A market dip becomes a self-worth crisis. A peer's windfall triggers insecurity. But when wealth is framed as *utility*, a means to expand autonomy or security, it is liberated from performance demands.

Consider a retired engineer who owns a modest home, travels occasionally, and supports their grandchildren's education. By conventional online metrics, this lifestyle may seem "boring." Yet it reflects a quiet richness: *the ability to live according to one's own values without external permission.* This is not austerity. It is clarity.

The Dignity of Financial Privacy

The decision to keep one's financial life private is not timidity—it is dignity. In a culture where oversharing is default, choosing to treat wealth as personal is a radical act. It affirms that not every gain must be declared, not every asset disclosed.

More importantly, privacy creates psychological insulation. It allows you to explore preferences without social interference. It shields your financial life from gossip, judgement, or pressure. And it reinforces the truth that *your money is nobody's entertainment.*

For professionals, this privacy is especially vital. Displaying wealth prematurely can compromise negotiating power, invite requests, or create workplace tension. Silence, in this context, is not withholding—it is strategic restraint.

Real Enjoyment vs. Symbolic Display

True enjoyment of wealth looks different from public assumption. It is often subtle, even invisible. It may take the form of:

Spending a weekday afternoon with your child without asking for leave

Sleeping peacefully at night because your emergency fund is intact

Paying for your parents' healthcare without financial stress

Knowing you could quit your job tomorrow—and being at peace if you don't

These moments do not photograph well. They are not likely to trend. But they are *indicators of lived wealth*, not performed affluence. And unlike status goods, they do not depreciate.

Contrast this with symbolic display. A £10,000 handbag might impress momentarily. But it cannot fix a toxic work environment. Nor can it compensate for time lost chasing admiration. Real wealth doesn't shout. It supports.

Financial Intentionality: Spending with Self-Respect

To live richly and stay real, spending must align with self-respect. That means interrogating each major outlay: *Is this purchase a reflection of who I am—or who I want to be seen as?*

This is not an anti-luxury argument. There is nothing inherently wrong with beautiful objects or experiences. But intentionality distinguishes *indulgence from insecurity*. You can buy a £300 dinner with zero guilt—if it reflects your values, relationships, or joy. But buying the same meal to keep up with colleagues whose values you don't share? That is financial theatre at its worst.

Intentionality also sharpens resource allocation. If private coaching brings you peace, but a new iPhone doesn't, the choice becomes obvious. If solo travel recharges your spirit more than designer wear, spend accordingly. Wealth, after all, is a *means to customise your life around your truth—not to mimic someone else's script.*

Historical Models of Quiet Wealth

Throughout history, the wealthiest families and thinkers have often adopted understated lifestyles. The Rothschilds were famously frugal despite immense fortune. Warren Buffett has lived in the same home since 1958. The Stoics—who shaped foundational thinking on self-sufficiency—championed internal peace over external accumulation.

These examples share a common ethic: *money should serve life, not distort it.* They also reinforce the insight that *status is inversely related to the need to prove it.* The more grounded your wealth, the less you need to telegraph it.

Contemporary Applications: Wealth in the Digital Age

Today, the temptation to perform wealth is turbocharged by digital culture. Influencers monetise lifestyle aesthetics. Crypto millionaires flaunt Lamborghinis. Even investment accounts are screenshotted for praise. But what if you opted out?

Imagine using wealth to design an intentionally offline weekend. Imagine deleting apps that spark envy instead of curiosity. Imagine building a life so satisfying internally, you forget to document it.

This is the paradox of modern richness: the less you feel the need to prove it, the more truly you've arrived.

Choosing Real Over Impressive

Real wealth isn't always impressive to others. It might look like an old car that's fully paid off. A simple flat owned outright. A weekend spent doing nothing—and loving it. These are not performative victories. They are quiet revolutions against a culture of constant display.

Choosing "real" over "impressive" is not a downgrade. It is an *upgrade in self-trust.* It is the confidence to live in accordance with your own metrics of success—even when no one's watching.

What Will You Use Wealth For?

If the purpose of wealth is merely to impress, then it will never feel like enough. Someone will always have more. The applause will always fade. But if wealth is used to craft a life of dignity, authenticity, and joy, then even modest amounts become powerful.

To live rich and stay real is to ask better questions:

What do I want money to protect?

What do I want money to enable?

What kind of life do I want to build quietly, without explanation?

These are not easy questions. But they are the right ones.

Because the richest life is not the loudest. It is the one most aligned with who you truly are—and the one that feels no need to apologise for being quiet about it.

Chapter 11
Legacy Without Ego

If your wealth disappears the moment you do, was it ever truly wealth? Not in any lasting or meaningful sense. Real legacy, the sort that leaves a quiet but persistent echo, isn't counted in bank statements or balance sheets—it's carried in stories, in values passed forward, in the subtle imprint of a life well-lived. It reaches beyond the solicitor's ledger and into the marrow of memory.

For many, legacy arrives as a late-life consideration—something to be drafted in a will, carved into donations, or packaged in trusts. Yet this is a narrow lens. Legacy is not paperwork. It's pattern. It's presence. It's the sum of decisions made when no one is watching, and the tone you set in rooms you'll never enter again. It begins far earlier than we like to think, and more often than not, it's already taking shape while we're still busy thinking we're just "getting started."

In this chapter, we'll set aside the polished veneer of achievement—the titles, the wealth milestones, the strategic bequests—and turn toward something quieter and far more consequential. We'll ask not how much we've accumulated, but what our lives are actually modelling. What messages, intended or not, we're sending through the way we spend, give, save, and speak. What we'll be remembered for—not in eulogies or formal tributes—but in behaviour quietly repeated by those we've influenced.

And perhaps most importantly, how to offer those who come after us something genuinely enduring—not a blueprint for replication, nor a mandate dressed up as tradition, but a rich, principled way of being. Something worth inheriting, even if there's not a penny attached.

What Is Left When the Numbers Fade?

The modern wealth narrative, in its default mode, is transactional. It centres on accumulation, preservation, and eventual distribution.

But what it often fails to interrogate is *meaning*. The assumption is that if we distribute enough financial assets, we've "done our duty." But that's a shallow metric for something as profound as a life.

Consider two heirs: one receives £1 million with no context, no preparation, and no ethical compass. The other receives £100,000 along with letters, rituals, practices, and life lessons about how to handle wealth with grace. Which one has inherited more?

In truth, *money without memory is often squandered; but money anchored to meaning can grow in all directions.*

The Myth of the Monument

Much of what passes as legacy planning today is closer to monument building—structures meant to preserve a name, not guide a life. Buildings are named, donations are publicised, and often the subtext is permanence. But permanence is not influence. A building may hold your name, yet a story told at the right time, a behaviour consistently modelled, may shape a person for decades.

This chapter rejects legacy as performance. It proposes legacy as *continuity*: the transmission of clarity, character, and care. We explore how your financial life can serve as a long-form letter to those who follow—not by creating awe, but by building understanding.

The Everyday Curriculum

Every time you discuss a budget with a child, share your reasoning on a career change with a sibling, or decide to fund a cause privately instead of broadcasting your generosity, you are teaching. Quietly. Continuously.

And that is the crux of real legacy: *teaching through your life, not your lecture.*

Legacy without ego does not require dramatic gestures. It asks instead for lived alignment. Children may forget what you gave them. They rarely forget what you stood for, especially if it cost you something. A decision to stay debt-free, to never invest in what you don't understand, or to quietly help a friend in need—all these build reputational residue. This is the curriculum of financial ethics. Not theory. Not inheritance seminars. Practice.

And what makes this form of legacy radical is its accessibility. You do not need millions to create it. You need clarity, consistency, and a refusal to outsource your values.

The Value Will

This chapter introduces the concept of the *Value Will*—a living companion to the legal will. It doesn't dictate who gets what; it expresses why it mattered. It's where you articulate not just the *distribution* of assets, but the *spirit* in which you hope they're used.

You can include letters to heirs explaining financial decisions. Notes of caution around common pitfalls. Lists of the books or ideas that changed your view of money. Even instructions on how to celebrate your life in a way that feels right to you.

What emerges is not a doctrine, but a compass. A framework for financial stewardship that is *human*, *relational*, and enduring.

Ritual Over Riches

Rituals are the cultural mechanisms through which values outlast individuals. They're repeatable, shareable, and sticky. One family may read a specific poem before financial meetings. Another might donate to a shared cause on birthdays. These rituals, seemingly small, *carry more meaning than a branded foundation ever could.*

Because they don't seek applause. They seek continuity. *The family story matters more than the family statement.*

The idea of the Everyday Heirloom is powerful here. Not jewellery, but practices. Not paintings, but principles. The weekly phone call. The holiday tradition. The dinner table questions. These are the practices that hold legacy like vessels. They are culture, passed quietly but potently.

And they are not subject to probate.

Why Ego Ruins Legacy

To be remembered fondly is not to be remembered extravagantly. Ego warps legacy into a theatre of control. It demands that your name survive, your rules endure, and your worldview prevail. But this is not legacy. It is micromanagement from beyond the grave.

Legacy without ego, by contrast, honours *choice*. It says: here's what I learned; take what serves you. It doesn't demand mimicry. It models possibility. It doesn't say "be like me." It says, "Here's how I tried to live with integrity, even when it was hard."

This restraint is often the most generous act. It respects the autonomy of those who follow. It acknowledges that *your lessons are only as valuable as their freedom to interpret them.*

The Real Test of Legacy

How will your grandchildren describe your life? Not your career or your net worth—but your decisions? Your laughter? Your grace under pressure?

This chapter invites you to begin answering that question now—not as a eulogy exercise, but as a clarity tool for how you want to live today. Because the truth is: *we do not leave a legacy; we live it, daily, through a hundred small choices.*

You will leave behind more than assets. The only question is whether what you leave behind will be *understood.* Will it guide? Or will it merely be distributed?

In the pages that follow, you will encounter practical tools for documenting your values, designing meaningful heirlooms, and reflecting on your financial decisions as pedagogical tools—not performances.

This is legacy without ego: grounded, generous, and human. Built not to impress, but to endure.

The Future You're Funding

Wealth is often defined in static terms: a net worth on a spreadsheet, a graph of returns, a tidy dashboard of accounts. But real financial power is not merely the ability to accumulate; it is the ability to *shape what comes next.* At its most meaningful, money is not just something we earn or protect—it's something we *aim.* The quiet but consequential question that every investor, professional, and saver must eventually confront is not simply, *"Am I growing my wealth?"* but rather, *"What future am I funding?"*

This is not a rhetorical flourish. It is a diagnostic. It asks us to treat our financial plans not as abstractions, but as active blueprints—concrete choices that, compounded over time, either enable or disable the life we imagine for those we love, the causes we support, and the legacy we leave.

Most people, even the financially literate, struggle to connect the dots between today's habits and tomorrow's consequences. Not because they lack intelligence, but because they are never prompted to *visualise money as a tool for building a specific vision.* Without clarity of purpose, we default to accumulation for its own sake. We chase numbers in isolation—retirement targets, investment yields, asset benchmarks—without fully grasping their endgame. The danger isn't just misallocation of funds. It's misallocation of *life.*

Money as a Mirror of Values

What you finance is what you prioritise. Whether intentionally or not, every budget is a declaration of values. Every savings goal is an expression of hope. And every investment is a vote for a future you believe is worth building.

When you spend generously on your children's education but hesitate to buy a third property, you're not just managing risk—you're articulating who you are. When you choose to fund a local non-profit instead of backing a trend-chasing crypto fund, you're not just diversifying—you're signalling belief in social capital. Money, in this way, becomes *moral architecture.* Quiet, yet deeply revealing.

This perspective invites a profound shift: from seeing wealth as personal armour to seeing it as a platform for intergenerational empowerment. Not as a fortress to hide behind, but as a foundation to build from.

The Problem with Vague Goals

Generic aspirations dominate personal finance discourse. "I want to retire early." "I want to be financially free." "I want to leave something behind." These may sound noble, but they're fundamentally hollow unless grounded in specificity.

Consider two investors with identical portfolios. One wants "freedom." The other wants to fund his niece's medical school tuition, relocate his ageing parents to a home near nature, and ensure a decade of support for an environmental advocacy group he admires. The second investor is not just building wealth—he is funding *futures with texture.*

Abstract wealth planning breeds detachment; concrete visions activate discipline. When you know what your money is for, you stop asking "how much is enough?" and start asking "is this aligned?"

Visualising the Future: A Practical Reframe

Psychologists refer to a phenomenon known as *future self-continuity*—the ability to see our future selves as psychologically connected to our present selves. Research shows that people with a stronger sense of continuity are more likely to save, delay gratification, and make sustainable decisions.

This insight holds equally true for *financial future-building*. People save more when they can vividly picture not just their retirement, but the *kind of life* they want to live during it. They give more to charity when they feel emotionally connected to the beneficiaries. They invest more wisely when they perceive the future they're shaping as real, not theoretical.

The implications are immense. Advisors, families, and individuals should stop asking only, "How much do you want to save?" and start asking, *"What life do you want your money to make possible?"*

Try it: Picture your calendar five years from now. Who are you with? What are you doing on a Tuesday afternoon? What do your mornings look like? What activities bring you fulfilment? Now ask: *Is your current financial strategy supporting that picture—or working against it?*

The clearer the vision, the clearer the plan.

The Loved Ones Factor

Too often, financial plans treat dependents as liabilities to be protected, not lives to be nourished. But wealth, rightly conceived, is not a way to merely insulate others from hardship—it's a way to expand their agency.

When we think of our children or future beneficiaries, we often default to funding college or leaving inheritance. Necessary, yes—but limited. What about enabling them to take unpaid internships that shape their values? What about endowing a sabbatical fund, so they can pursue something deeply meaningful mid-career? What about supporting a family member's decision to start a small business, not because it will maximise profit, but because it might maximise dignity?

Money is most powerful when it is not a reward for past behaviour, but a scaffold for future possibility.

A Cause Without Performance

Funding the future is not always about family. For many, the deepest sense of financial purpose lies in contribution to causes they may never directly benefit from: education, clean water, scientific research, justice reform. The tragedy is that many only engage in such giving late in life, or through legacy bequests that feel disconnected from their lived experience.

There is an alternative: *slow philanthropy*. Rather than seeing giving as a tax-planning tool or a performative gesture, we can integrate it as an intentional expression of alignment. You don't need to be wealthy to fund the future. You need to be *awake to the fact that you already are.*

Even modest recurring contributions to causes you believe in—especially if shared transparently with loved ones—can serve as powerful moral anchors. They model generosity without fanfare. They turn values into verbs.

And crucially, they rewire the giver's own identity. When you act in alignment with your deepest commitments, you experience your own wealth differently: *not as something to protect, but as something to deploy.*

A New Metric: Funded Futures

The most transformative shift in personal finance may be this: measuring success not by how much you've accumulated, but by *how many meaningful futures you've helped bring to life.*

Your own. Your partner's. Your child's. Your community's. Your cause's. That metric cannot be captured on a brokerage statement. But it *can* be captured in stories, in choices, and in the clarity with which you answer the question: *"What is this money for?"*

If that question remains unanswered, no amount of accumulation will ever feel like enough. But once it is answered, even modest means can feel abundant.

Because then, and only then, does money become more than security. It becomes *direction.*

The Value Will

Most wills are legal documents. They allocate property, divide assets, and formalise bequests. They are written for solicitors, scrutinised by executors, and typically read only after death. But as vital as these documents are, they are silent on the one thing that most people wish they could leave behind: *the meaning behind the money.*

A standard will answers *what* is passed on. A value will answers *why.*

It offers context, not just content. It communicates the thinking, stories, and principles that animated your financial decisions in life—so that what you leave behind does not feel merely transactional, but *relational, intentional, and human.* Without this layer, inheritance is often experienced as a silent windfall—sometimes appreciated, sometimes resented, rarely understood. With it, legacy becomes *instructional* without being prescriptive, *personal* without being confessional, and *powerful* without being performative.

This is not a sentimental indulgence. It is a strategic act of emotional clarity—one that can reduce conflict, deepen connection, and ensure that the values that built your wealth are not severed from those who receive it.

The Wisdom Gap in Traditional Estate Planning

Conventional estate planning operates on legal efficiency and financial optimisation. And understandably so—tax mitigation, asset protection, probate clarity. But in its fixation on the tangible, it often ignores the *intangible dimensions of wealth*: character, reasoning, generosity, resilience, judgment.

Many people die without ever sharing the philosophies that shaped their financial lives: Why they chose to invest a certain way. Why they declined certain luxuries. Why they funded causes quietly, or taught their children to value self-sufficiency over indulgence. These lessons vanish if not documented. And their absence is not neutral. It leaves a vacuum.

Research in intergenerational wealth transfers is sobering: within three generations, over 90% of inherited wealth is depleted or lost entirely. Financial mismanagement plays a part. But the deeper issue is not competence—it's *continuity*. Heirs receive assets, but not *anchoring*. They inherit capital, but not conviction.

A value will bridges that gap.

What a Value Will Actually Is

A value will is not a legal instrument. It's a moral and intellectual companion to your financial estate. It need not be long, but it must be honest. It can take many forms—letter, essay, audio, video—but its purpose is singular: *to articulate the beliefs, decisions, and hopes that accompany your wealth.*

Think of it as a letter to your future inheritors, not just instructing them on what to do, but sharing what mattered to you. This is not a document to control from beyond the grave. It is a gift of emotional and intellectual transparency.

Such a will may include reflections on:

The hardest financial decision you ever made, and what you learned

The reason behind how you split your estate—not just the split itself

How you defined "enough" in your life, and when you knew you had it

What money allowed you to do that was truly meaningful

What you hope your children or beneficiaries *do not assume* about you or your intentions

The causes you chose to support—and the ones you didn't, and why

The values you attempted to live out through your budgeting, giving, investing, or working

In essence, it's an invitation: to engage not just with your wealth, but with *your thoughtfulness.*

Real-World Applications: Lessons from the Quietly Wise

Consider the case of a woman in her late 70s who had built a modest fortune through decades of frugal entrepreneurship. In her legal will, she split her estate evenly among her three adult children. But in her value will, she explained *why* she had declined to give more to her eldest son, who had sacrificed a high-earning career to care for her in her later years. "He gave me years, not dollars," she wrote. "I wanted to honour that outside the financial structure, in our shared time and memories." That one paragraph—simple, direct, deeply personal—prevented what might otherwise have been years of silent resentment or suspicion among siblings.

Or take a retired engineer who had never spoken much about money with his children. In his value will, he described how his financial habits—always buying used cars, never carrying debt—were shaped by growing up with an immigrant single mother who rationed food. "My frugality wasn't stinginess," he wrote. "It was reverence for what money cost my mother." His children later said it was the most important letter he ever wrote them.

A few pages of clarity can do more than decades of accumulation.

Intergenerational Empathy, Not Just Instruction

A value will is not about moralising from a podium. It is about *narrating from the ground floor* of your own life—sharing vulnerabilities, not just victories. It gives your children or heirs a chance to *meet you as a whole person*, not just a benefactor.

This kind of transmission builds intergenerational empathy. It allows recipients to see that wealth, in your life, was not inevitable or effortless—but *constructed, protected, wrestled with.* That emotional realism has a regulatory effect. It often inspires not entitlement, but *gratitude and stewardship.*

It also humanises risk. Many inheritors assume their parents or grandparents were simply lucky or shrewd. But a value will can demystify the role of setbacks: the failed businesses, the job losses, the investments that didn't work. When framed thoughtfully, these become not shameful episodes but *case studies in resilience*—ones that equip the next generation to face financial reality with poise rather than panic.

When to Write One—and How to Start

There is no perfect moment to write a value will. But there is a perfect motivation: when you realise that your net worth is not your whole worth. That your wealth story is not just *what you earned*, but *why it mattered.*

Start small. Set aside two uninterrupted hours. Imagine your adult child, godchild, niece, or friend reading your words five years from now. Ask yourself:

"What do I most want them to understand about how I handled money?"

"What silent assumptions am I leaving behind that I need to clarify?"

"What values shaped my choices—and what values do I hope to see carried forward?"

You do not need to be perfect. You do not need to be wealthy by others' standards. You need only to be *clear and honest.*

For those inclined, consider pairing your value will with short prompts for your heirs: "What does wealth mean to you?" "What are you afraid to ask about this inheritance?" "What part of my letter surprised you?" In doing so, you open a *two-way moral conversation*—across time.

Legacy Without Lecture

There is a difference between inheritance and legacy. Inheritance is *what* you leave. Legacy is *what endures.* And legacy cannot be deposited. It must be *deliberately written into memory, perspective, and reflection.*

A value will is not a substitute for love, presence, or conversation—but it is a bridge. One that your heirs will walk long after the legal formalities are done. It is not about avoiding disputes. It is about *deepening understanding.*

At its best, a value will is not a letter from the past, but a guidepost for the future—clear-eyed, warm, unpretentious, and enduring. It says: "Here is what I learned. Here is what I tried. Take what is useful. And remember, this was never just about the money."

Teaching Through Your Life

How your financial behaviour becomes your true legacy, regardless of size.

There is a pervasive assumption that legacy begins when life ends—that it is defined by documents, donations, or dramatic bequests. But legacy, in its most enduring form, is neither formal nor final. It is behavioural. It is *demonstrated quietly, repeatedly, and often unconsciously.* What you do with your money while you're alive teaches more than any letter left behind. The question is not whether you are teaching others through your financial behaviour—it is *what* you are teaching, and whether you are aware of it.

Children observe long before they comprehend. Friends notice patterns before they understand motivations. Colleagues and communities take cues not from what you say about money, but how you *interact with it.* And unlike lectures or inheritance, this form of teaching is not optional. *Your financial behaviour is your curriculum.* And everyone around you is enrolled.

The Unspoken Curriculum of Everyday Finance

We tend to treat personal finance as a private domain, reserved for tax returns and spreadsheets. Yet every choice made with money broadcasts a message about values—whether intended or not. Consider the following behaviours:

Avoiding all conversations about money, even with partners or children.

Spending impulsively but hiding purchases behind rationalisations.

Tithing quietly to causes while obsessing privately over status symbols.

Dismissing luxuries publicly, but indulging them privately.

Each of these patterns teaches a version of financial reality: that money is taboo, that wealth is for display, that giving should be secretive, or that frugality is performative. *Behaviour always communicates, even in silence.* The people around you—especially the younger ones—learn what is normal, acceptable, or admirable not by what you claim, but by what you *model.*

The sociologist Annette Lareau observed in her seminal work on parenting and class that middle-class families often explicitly coach their children on how to interact with institutions and navigate systems, whereas working-class families may adopt a more hands-off approach, assuming children will adapt. The parallel in financial upbringing is stark: some families actively educate through example, while others abdicate entirely—often unintentionally reinforcing fear, avoidance, or dysfunction.

It is not only your income bracket that shapes your financial legacy. It is your *consciousness* about the ripple effects of your choices.

Legacy Is Built in the Margins, Not the Milestones

Too often, we treat financial legacy as a function of scale: who left behind the largest estate, the biggest endowment, the flashiest philanthropic footprint. But the most transformative legacies are often intimate, not institutional. They are built in the margins—through habits repeated in kitchens, conversations overheard in cars, routines witnessed in supermarkets or school holidays.

A single phrase repeated over decades—"we don't buy things we can't pay for twice," or "generosity matters more than gadgets"—may do more to shape financial ethics than a library's worth of financial literacy textbooks.

One powerful example comes from a client who, in his thirties, described how his grandfather paid for groceries in cash every week, kept receipts in a worn envelope, and compared them line-by-line at the kitchen table. "He never explained what he was doing," the man said, "but the routine imprinted itself in me. When I got my first job, I found myself doing the same thing, because it felt like *what responsible people do.*"

This is *incidental teaching*—unstructured, unscripted, yet deeply effective. And it raises a key principle: *consistency is more influential than charisma.* You do not need to be eloquent or expert. You only need to be *congruent.*

The Ethical Mirror of Your Choices

Whether you spend freely or frugally, donate regularly or never at all, invest for growth or sleep—you are teaching others about risk, reward, values, and control. And crucially, you are teaching yourself. Money is a mirror. It reflects what you prioritise, avoid, and protect. Over time, that mirror becomes a moral compass—not just for you, but for those watching.

Here lies the quiet power of lived financial example: it transmits *an ethic*, not just a technique. It says: "This is how I relate to power, to scarcity, to security." And unlike traditional instruction, it cannot be faked for long. Children, especially, are expert at detecting hypocrisy. They remember the tension in a household more than the budgeting software used within it.

This insight should not provoke shame, but responsibility. If your behaviour is flawed—and everyone's is—it becomes an opportunity, not a condemnation. *Admitting financial missteps out loud* may be one of the most powerful educational acts you can perform. It teaches accountability, humility, and the critical skill of course-correction.

Imagine the difference between a parent who hides credit card debt and one who says: "I made decisions based on short-term emotions instead of long-term planning. Here's what I've learned." That single act transforms a wound into wisdom.

Modelling Over Mentoring: Why Behaviour Outranks Advice

Conventional wisdom suggests that if you want your children, mentees, or peers to manage money wisely, you should *talk* to them about it—teach them about interest rates, compound returns, asset allocation. But cognitive psychology suggests a more enduring truth: *people adopt what they observe, not what they're told.*

Consider Albert Bandura's foundational research on social learning theory. When children watched adults behave violently towards a toy doll, they imitated that aggression—even without direct instruction. Similarly, when people see financial anxiety expressed as compulsive frugality or avoidant behaviour, they internalise the stress pattern, not the facts. Conversely, when they witness calm budgeting, deliberate giving, or thoughtful restraint, they encode financial self-regulation into their own repertoire.

This dynamic holds true across all ages. Adults mirror peer behaviours more than they follow expert advice. If everyone in your social circle treats money as a tool for status projection, you are likely to absorb that logic, even if you rationally reject it. Conversely, if your life visibly reflects *value-driven finance*—living below your means, investing in experiences, not indulgences—you become a countercultural signal.

And signals matter. They recalibrate norms.

The Politics of Visibility: Should You Make Your Behaviour Known?

A reasonable concern emerges here: if modelling matters, should we be *more visible* about our financial practices? Should we talk openly about our giving, our budgeting, our priorities?

The answer is nuanced. Visibility should never be performative. But it can be *intentional.* Silence, while dignified, often defaults to ambiguity. It allows others to fill in the gaps with projection. "She must be rich because she drives that car." "He must be struggling because he never travels." These interpretations are often inaccurate—and more importantly, unhelpful.

Selective transparency can be a powerful corrective. A simple, sincere explanation—"we prioritise saving because it gives us freedom later," or "we support local charities instead of posting about it"—signals values *without self-aggrandisement.* The goal is not to teach by spotlight, but to *live in alignment*—and to occasionally let others glimpse that alignment on purpose.

Especially with children, clarity matters. If they never hear why a decision is made—why a holiday is skipped, why a gift is modest, why a donation is chosen—they may internalise the outcome without appreciating the ethics behind it. *Narrate the why, not just the what.*

Scaling Legacy Without Scaling Wealth

One of the most toxic myths in modern finance is that only the wealthy leave legacies. In reality, the size of your estate is irrelevant to the scope of your influence. You do not need seven figures to model generosity. You do not need a trust fund to teach integrity. You do not need property portfolios to cultivate resilience.

A nurse who shares how she saves £50 a month for future security is modelling delayed gratification. A teacher who avoids lifestyle creep despite promotions is signalling values-based restraint. A retiree who volunteers time instead of maximising returns is redefining the use of capital.

These examples are not lesser than—they are *often more powerful*, because they are accessible. They say: "You can do this too." And that, ultimately, is the most democratic legacy of all.

You are always teaching. Every purchase, delay, donation, or indulgence sends a signal. Whether you mean to or not, you are constructing a curriculum of financial ethics for the people around you.

The good news? You don't have to be perfect. You have to be *aware*. You have to be willing to reflect, to explain, and sometimes to revise. Teaching through your life means *living with coherence*, not with spectacle. It means embodying what matters more than declaring it.

And in a world saturated with financial noise, where advice is commoditised and posturing is pandemic, that kind of quiet congruence is not only rare—it's *radical*.

Let your life do the teaching. Then let your words confirm what your actions have already made clear.

The Everyday Heirloom

Encourages documenting stories, rituals, and practices that carry wealth beyond numbers.

We often conflate inheritance with items of high market value—real estate, jewellery, art collections. These are the legacy assets that change hands via lawyers and probate courts. But across cultures and histories, the most enduring inheritances have rarely been material. *They have been remembered.* A worn recipe card. A phrase repeated over decades. The precise way a holiday was celebrated, or how tea was poured in the afternoon. These are not keepsakes of economic value. They are *containers of meaning*. They are everyday heirlooms—transmissions of identity, encoded through ritual, routine, and remembrance.

This chapter is not about creating sentimental clutter. It is about recognising the *non-monetary wealth* embedded in the way we live, and understanding how to document and transmit that wealth *deliberately*—not as nostalgia, but as a living system of values.

What Is Inherited When Numbers Are Absent

When money is scarce—or even when it is present but tightly controlled—families still pass things down. A worldview. A resilience strategy. A style of speaking. A distrust of banks. A reverence for education. These intangible inheritances are often more formative than financial bequests because they *shape how wealth is interpreted* when it does arrive.

Consider the difference between two siblings who inherit the same modest sum. One squanders it on status goods, the other invests it methodically, citing their father's habit of reading stock pages at the kitchen table. The money is equal. The outcome is not. What varied was not the asset but the *framework*—the embedded financial literacy, the emotional fluency, the value system inherited invisibly.

These invisible transmissions are often unacknowledged because they are not named, recorded, or discussed. But they are *no less real* than a portfolio or pension.

To ignore these inheritances is to underutilise one of the most scalable forms of family wealth: cultural continuity.

Everyday Objects, Extraordinary Memory

An everyday heirloom does not need to be crafted or curated. It may already be in circulation. A battered rolling pin that has touched three generations of dough. A song sung to calm infants. A phrase your mother whispered when facing decisions. A particular Sunday rhythm. These details are often overlooked precisely because they are so familiar.

Yet these small artefacts and practices encode the larger story of who we are: our preferences, temperaments, aspirations. They demonstrate what we considered "enough," how we responded to uncertainty, how we chose to celebrate or mourn. *They reveal the lived logic of a household,* more than any ledger can.

Take the case of a retired teacher in Bristol who, instead of writing a memoir, created a 12-page illustrated booklet for her grandchildren titled *Things We Do Without Realising Why*. It explained why the family never threw away Christmas cards (a wartime habit), why lemon slices were added to tea (a Russian ancestry), and why loose change was always placed in a dish by the front door (a folk belief in welcoming abundance). No bank account changed hands. But the legacy transmitted was rich: a framework of attention, origin, and quiet intentionality.

Rituals as Cultural Architecture

Rituals, unlike routines, carry symbolic weight. They are not merely repeated; they are remembered, even re-enacted. And they offer a durable vessel for emotional and ethical inheritance.

In many traditional societies, rituals preserved oral history in the absence of written records. They served as insurance policies against amnesia. In modern households, however, rituals are often displaced by productivity. The Friday meal becomes another rushed takeaway. The yearly letter becomes a quick text. The archive of meaning slowly erodes—not because of malice, but neglect.

To preserve everyday heirlooms requires re-inserting intentional ritual into life's rhythm. This does not demand ceremony or cost. It demands *recognition*—that what is repeated with love becomes identity.

This is not about restoring tradition for tradition's sake. It is about using ritual as a delivery mechanism for values. If your family values community, what recurring act affirms it? If generosity, how is it practised consistently? If resourcefulness, where is it visible?

Heirlooms are not just things we pass on. They are the evidence of what we lived for.

Why Documentation Matters—Even for the Modest

One of the quiet tragedies of modern wealth is that most families do not document what made their life meaningful—only what made it legible to tax authorities. We write wills, but not wisdom. We store insurance policies, but not insights.

A voice memo explaining why you made a career choice can mean more to a grandchild than your title. A scanned page of a favourite poem with your marginal notes may become a totem of your way of seeing. These documents are not declarations. They are *co-constructed identity kits*—designed to inform, not impress.

And unlike traditional heirlooms, they do not require possession to transmit. A digital library of recorded stories. A calendar of meaningful dates with explanations. A short letter attached to the family recipe describing *why* it mattered. These artefacts are scalable, searchable, replicable. And they create a new form of permanence in a transient world.

Consider the family in Bangalore who, after the death of their matriarch, compiled a "living e-book" of her sayings, practices, and quirks—crowdsourced from siblings and cousins. It contained everything from her bedtime tea ritual to the way she arranged kitchen spices. That artefact—readable by generations not yet born—now sits alongside her will. Not as an afterthought, but as *a parallel document of value.*

Reframing Wealth Beyond Currency

Part of the resistance to non-financial legacy stems from the idea that if something isn't expensive, it isn't worth passing on. This is a fallacy rooted in consumer culture, not human history.

Throughout most of civilisation, wealth was measured in relationships, knowledge, land, and story—not just liquidity. Oral traditions carried family maps. Proverbs encoded investment strategies. Songs transmitted law. There is precedent—ancient and modern—for understanding wealth as *what outlives us in meaning, not just money.*

If we are to reclaim that broader definition of wealth, we must *curate it actively*—not in a museum sense, but in the sense of conscious transmission.

Ask:

What do I do regularly that reflects what I value?

What object or habit in my life might one day hold meaning for others?

What am I unconsciously teaching through what I prioritise or dismiss?

These questions are not nostalgic. They are forward-looking. They imply that what you touch today can *carry the DNA of your values* into generations you may never meet.

The Case for Creating a Values Portfolio

Just as financial portfolios are diversified for resilience, so too can heirlooms be diversified for continuity. A family that only leaves behind money leaves its heirs vulnerable to confusion, conflict, and consumption. But a family that also transmits context, story, and shared purpose offers *a compass, not just a currency.*

Consider building what some advisors call a "values portfolio"—a structured but flexible collection of artefacts, stories, sayings, decisions, and documented rituals that form a coherent picture of your worldview. This portfolio need not be thick. It must be *clear.* It must reflect lived truth, not aspirational branding. It can be updated. It can be passed forward without hierarchy.

And most importantly, it reminds your heirs that they are part of a lineage—of thought, not just bloodline. Of meaning, not just money.

Wealth is always passed down. But what kind of wealth—*and how* it is passed—is a choice. The everyday heirloom invites us to see beyond spreadsheets. It invites us to honour the daily, the domestic, the deliberate—because that is where our real inheritance lives.

If you are thoughtful with your capital but careless with your culture, your wealth will be misunderstood. But if you nurture both—financial and familial—you offer something rarer: *a legacy that does not just enrich, but orients.*

The most valuable inheritance is not found in the vault. It is found in the *vividness* of how you lived—and your courage to make that vividness *available.*

Conclusion
The Wealth You Can't See

What if the most lasting forms of wealth are precisely those that refuse to show up on a balance sheet?

We're taught—sometimes subtly, sometimes not—to measure only what's measurable. Net worth. Income streams. Portfolio performance. Yet when people pause long enough to consider what a life well-lived truly entails, their language changes. They speak less of numbers and more of qualities—confidence, stillness, sovereignty, grace under pressure. These are not things you can tally. They are not quantifiable, but they are unmistakably felt.

The truest wealth rarely shouts. It shows up quietly—in the way you respond rather than react, in how you honour your time, in the power to decline what misaligns. It lives in your relationship with choice. In the legacy of presence, not possessions. In the texture of an ordinary Tuesday morning that feels—without fanfare—entirely your own.

This final chapter is not a neat bow to tie the book together. It isn't a recap or a list of takeaways. Instead, think of it as a turning of the lens—from accumulation to attention. If what preceded was concerned with financial skill and emotional fluency, this is about recognising the foundation beneath it all: the invisible architecture that supports not just your wealth, but your way of living.

It offers no formulas. No finish lines. Just a quiet, resolute invitation—not to squeeze more from your life, but to see it more clearly. Not to own more, but to notice what's already yours.

Wealth, Reimagined from the Inside Out

Most financial discourse stops at the quantifiable. But this book has argued, implicitly and explicitly, that *wealth is a behavioural system*, not just a financial outcome. It is made visible not through your possessions, but through your patterns. How you think. How you plan. How you pay attention.

The most significant financial decisions you will make are not about asset allocation or tax efficiency, though those matter. They are about *who you trust*, *what you fear*, *how you define enough*, and *why you believe what you believe*. These choices often happen subtly, without fanfare—at the dinner table, during periods of uncertainty, or in moments where you choose restraint over reaction.

And yet, these are the decisions that define your financial character. Not the ones that show up in your annual report, but the ones that repeat silently over decades. That is the wealth you can't see: *your patterns of mind*, and the values they encode.

The Hidden Drivers of Financial Behaviour

Behavioural economics has long taught us that humans are not rational actors; we are driven by a complex tangle of incentives, social norms, memories, and biases. But what gets less attention is that *awareness of those patterns is itself a form of wealth*. The person who knows they are susceptible to urgency is better prepared than the person who simply reads another book on index funds.

This is why two people with the same income and assets can experience entirely different levels of financial stress. The numbers are identical. The perception—and the narrative they live inside—is not. One feels scarcity, the other feels spaciousness. One hoards, the other shares. One fears judgement, the other acts from quiet conviction.

This chapter encourages you to examine those underlying narratives—not to deconstruct them in a psychological vacuum, but to *see them as the soft architecture of your financial life*. Change them, and you change how wealth feels, long before you change how much you have.

Legacy Without Theatre

One of the quieter insights from this book is that *performative wealth erodes the real thing*. When you perform wealth to impress others—through consumption, status, or narrative—you build not stability but volatility. The external becomes a substitute for the internal. But the strongest legacies are often invisible to the casual observer: ethical clarity, intergenerational trust, family rituals, community stewardship.

The family who holds regular financial conversations with their children—even in modest households—may pass on more meaningful financial fluency than a wealthy estate that hides everything behind closed doors. The individual who lives in alignment with their values—not their algorithmic feed—may leave a deeper impression on their community than someone who donates millions, but does so performatively.

The visible is easy to count. The invisible is harder to fake. And harder still to transfer unless made deliberate.

This is why your real financial legacy starts not with the will you sign in your seventies, but with the repeated behaviours that define who you are in your forties, fifties, or sixties. This chapter will help you see that legacy not as a distant point, but as a *daily practice.*

The Architecture of Internal Wealth

What does it mean to feel wealthy, not just be wealthy?

Research in psychology shows that subjective well-being—your lived, internal experience of life—is influenced far more by *a sense of agency, coherence, and social connection* than by absolute income past a modest threshold. And yet, most financial planning never addresses these dimensions. It sells formulas, not foundations.

But the foundations matter: *the belief that you are capable, that your future is navigable, and that your values are not for sale.* This is internal wealth. It is not a replacement for external resources—it is what gives those resources meaning.

This book has introduced dozens of concepts to help you build financial systems that serve your life. Now it invites you to ask: *How do those systems feel?* Not just "Are they efficient?" but "Do they honour who I am becoming?"

Because ultimately, the purpose of wealth is not to win a game. It is to support a life. And not just any life—but a coherent, values-aligned, emotionally sustainable one.

When Enough Is Not a Number

In the traditional script, wealth accumulation is a race toward a finish line—retirement, financial independence, a round number. But what if the finish line is not the point? What if the deeper victory lies in recognising that "enough" was never an amount, but a state of *presence*, *security*, and *confidence*?

The obsession with more is often a placeholder for *a lack of clarity*. A person who knows what matters to them can stop. They can say no. They can orient around sufficiency, rather than scarcity disguised as ambition. But a person unclear on their values will keep accumulating, and never arrive.

This chapter closes by helping you name your definition of wealth—*not in terms of net worth, but net meaning*. What do you want to fund, protect, encourage, and model—starting now, not someday?

It's a question of deep intentionality. And one that requires you to shift from *financial maximisation* to *human alignment*.

What This Chapter Will Help You Do

This final section offers no formulas. It offers a lens. It will challenge you to revisit:

What internal beliefs about money govern your decisions?

Which values do your financial habits reflect—and which do they contradict?

How does your financial life feel, and is that feeling intentional or inherited?

What are you unconsciously teaching those around you about wealth?

Where are you performing success, and where are you quietly embodying it?

In answering these questions, you won't just close a book. You will open a conversation—with yourself, your community, and your future.

Because *real wealth is not what you hold.* It's what you *understand, preserve, and pass on*—in words, in rituals, in behaviours, and in the clarity of your own example.

That's the wealth you can't see. And from this point forward, you are its custodian.

Wealth Is Practised, Not Performed

At the end of a financial life well-lived, no one asks about your portfolio's standard deviation. They ask whether you slept well at night. Whether you were generous without fear. Whether you could sit across from someone you loved and be fully present—not calculating, not compensating, not performing. *That is the invisible quality of financial peace. And it is the real metric of wealth.*

Wealth is not what you declare. It is what you practise. Not once, but repeatedly—in small decisions, quiet sacrifices, uncelebrated habits. It's in the impulse you resist, the values you uphold, the boundaries you protect. No statement of net worth can fully reflect these truths, but your life can.

The purpose of this final reflection is not to tie a neat bow. It is to ask you, directly and honestly: *What are you really building?* Not the façade of success, not the externally validated ideal—but the lived texture of your financial life. What does it *feel* like? What does it say about you when no one is watching?

If this book has been a blueprint, this reflection is the architectural mirror.

Real Wealth Leaves No Receipts

Consider this: some of the wealthiest people in history have left behind very little that was materially remarkable. But they left behaviours. Stories. A pattern of presence that altered the shape of the people around them. Often, they did this without fanfare.

Why? Because financial wisdom, once internalised, becomes nearly invisible. The investor who ignores noise and buys with patience doesn't need applause. The parent who teaches their child how to delay gratification may never make headlines—but will leave behind a self-sustaining legacy. The couple who discusses money with openness rather than ego may not trend, but they will *last.*

Real wealth does not seek attention because it does not need to. This is the paradox at the heart of everything you've learned: *the quieter your financial life becomes, the stronger it usually is.*

This is not a rejection of ambition. It is a redefinition of its expression.

The Practice of Enough

It's tempting to see financial peace as an end state—something you arrive at after enough years, enough returns, enough discipline. But peace is not an endpoint. *It is a recurring practice of alignment.*

You feel peace when your spending matches your values. When your goals match your timeline, not someone else's. When your weekends are not consumed by anxiety about Mondays. These are not dramatic outcomes. They are quiet patterns. They are also reversible. Lose your clarity, compromise your integrity, overreach your comfort—and peace erodes, silently and swiftly.

So the true question isn't "What is your number?" It's "What are your non-negotiables?" Which behaviours, constraints, and boundaries preserve your clarity? Which ones degrade it?

This is not soft advice. It is foundational strategy. A well-diversified portfolio means nothing if your emotional life is leveraged to the hilt.

Financial Character Over Financial Knowledge

If you took nothing else from this book, remember this: *wealth building is a character discipline.* The market rewards patience, not cleverness. Habits beat hacks. Restraint outperforms brilliance over decades. And yet, most people chase novelty instead of cultivating identity.

What is your identity as an investor? As an earner? As a steward of resources?

Are you the person who makes thoughtful decisions even when markets are irrational? The person who can say no to opportunity when it threatens your clarity? The person who listens more than they speak, who learns more than they posture?

If your financial decisions were recorded—not just in statements, but in story—what would they say about you? Were they consistent? Grounded? Generous?

Your financial life is not a résumé. It's a memoir in progress.

Metrics That Don't Show Up on Statements

Here's a quiet truth: the most powerful financial metrics can't be graphed.

The ability to walk away from a toxic job because your expenses are low.

The calm you feel during volatility because your plan already accounted for it.

The dignity of not needing to impress.

The space to be present with your child without resentment.

The confidence of knowing you won't become a burden.

These are qualitative outcomes. And yet, they're the very outcomes most people are chasing *through* quantitative means. What if, instead, you built your financial life *around* them?

What if your investment strategy served your peace of mind, not the reverse? What if your career was structured not just to optimise income, but to protect time, relationships, health?

What if you stopped trying to impress people who are too distracted to care?

You'd be living rich—even if your bank account looked ordinary.

The Behavioural Audit

As you close this book, consider conducting a behavioural audit—not of your income, but of your integrity. Ask:

Do I spend in alignment with what I say I value?

Do I make money decisions from a place of clarity or compulsion?

Do I have the discipline to delay gratification without resenting it?

Can I talk about money with the people I love, without shame or performance?

Am I using money to express my values or to compensate for insecurity?

These are difficult questions. They are also liberating ones. Because once you know the answers, you no longer need to chase validation from outside. You can build something far stronger: *a coherent financial life.* One in which your actions, values, and identity reinforce each other.

That is what financial maturity feels like. Not arrival. *Congruence.*

Closing the Book, Continuing the Practice

This is not the kind of book you "finish." It is the kind that you live.

You will return to these ideas not as doctrines, but as touchstones. They are not meant to dictate, but to *orient.* As your life changes—new responsibilities, opportunities, risks—so too will your relationship with money. That is not a failure of planning. It is the evolution of maturity.

You will have seasons of expansion and seasons of caution. Times when you lead and times when you pause. The only question that matters is: *Will you do so with intention—or inertia?*

Because ultimately, wealth is not what you have. It's how you live. How you show up. How you sleep at night. How you speak to those around you. How you treat yourself when no one else is watching.

You don't have to be visible to be free. And you don't have to be rich to be whole.

About the Author

Zayn Elric is a behavioural finance researcher, wealth philosophy strategist, and advocate for the silent strength of salaried professionals. With a background in economic psychology and over a decade of experience advising professionals across industries, he bridges the gap between sound investing and soulful living. His work draws on Eastern simplicity, Stoic clarity, and modern financial frameworks to help everyday earners build lasting wealth without losing peace of mind. A frequent speaker and mentor, Zayn is passionate about transforming how working professionals perceive money—not as a chase, but as a craft.

www.ingramcontent.com/pod-product-compliance
Lightning Source LLC
Chambersburg PA
CBHW031339230926
51848CB00002B/302

* 9 7 8 9 3 7 1 3 4 6 3 4 4 *